THE STORYTELLERS

FROM MEL ALLEN TO BOB COSTAS:
SIXTY YEARS OF BASEBALL TALES
FROM THE
BROADCAST BOOTH

CURT SMITH

MACMILLAN • USA

MACMILLAN
A Simon & Schuster Macmillan Company
15 Columbus Circle
New York, NY 10023

MACMILLAN is a registered trademark of Macmillan, Inc.

Library of Congress Cataloging-in-Publication Data available
ISBN: 0-02-860411-3

10 9 8 7 6 5 4 3 2 1

Printed in the United States of America

For Sarah

OTHER BOOKS BY CURT SMITH

America's Dizzy Dean

Long Time Gone

Voices of The Game

The Red Sox Fan's Little Book of Wisdom

ACKNOWLEDGMENTS

Save Treasure Island, *no book is an island. Many people helped write* The Storytellers. *They were generous with their time and memories—and I cannot help but be generous in my gratitude toward them.*

The announcers, of course, supplied its flesh and blood. For details, see "The Announcers" chapter: I am indebted to each. A number of writers were most helpful—especially Rob Rains of Baseball Weekly *and the staff of* Baseball America. *As always, the Baseball Hall of Fame in Cooperstown—and library researcher Dan Bennett—provided nonpareil aid. All nurtured this book from conception to birth.*

I want to thank Rick Wolff, who suggested The Storytellers. *I am grateful to his father, Bob, for its title. Traci Cothran edited the manuscript with great insight and care. Stacey Bauer transcribed hundreds of hours of tape. My wife, Sarah, and literary agent, Bobbe Siegel, shone from the first pitch to final out. Finally, let me thank the reader—for grasping what baseball once was—now, often isn't—but perhaps with luck evermore can be.*

CONTENTS

PREFACE

Shakespeare wrote in *Love's Labour's Lost* of "the heavenly rhetoric of thine eye." For three-quarters of a century, the rhetoric of baseball's Voices of The Game has been heavenly, horrific, funny, risqué, humane, and more often human—turning us to the summer game like a heliotrope turns toward the sun.

Baseball on the air debuted August 5, 1921, over KDKA, America's first radio station, from Forbes Field in suburban Pittsburgh. From faraway places—Comiskey Park, Crosley Field, Yankee Stadium, the Polo Grounds—the new medium soon ferried a galloping world of big-league vibration. The cathode fun house was not a household core, and radio chatted as around a pot-bellied stove.

From its start the baseball broadcaster became a Rubik's Cube of actor, writer, director, producer, cameraman, and salesman. At best, he etched the pastime's theatre of the mind. Think of Mel Allen—The Voice. Jon Miller—sport's Rich Little of the airwaves. Harry Caray—mocking the laws of probability, longevity, and cirrhosis of the liver. They rode work like Secretariat, hit boredom like Louis vs. Schmeling, and used irony like Jascha Heifetz did a violin.

To Emerson, language was "the archives of poetry. Language is fossil poetry." Baseball Latinists include Vin Scully and the late Red Barber, Bill O'Donnell, and Bob Prince. They and other big-league bards have fossilized language, not themselves.

In 1963, a writer asked, "What's your wife's name and what's she like?" Mets' catcher Clarence "Choo-Choo" Coleman treated the question like a knuckleball in the dirt. "Her name is Mrs. Coleman," he huffed, "and she likes *me*, bub."

Another catcher was once accosted at a party. "You look pretty cool tonight," a woman told Lawrence Peter Berra. "Thanks, ma'am," replied Yogi. "You don't look so hot yourself."

It was Casey Stengel who said of the 1969 Miracle Mets, "They did it *slow*, but fast." Yankees' pitcher Lefty Gomez, who defined his secret of success: "It's easy—clean living and a fast outfield." Dizzy Dean, "commentating" how a batter "swang" and runner "slud" and slugger stood "*confidentially* at the plate." Baseball is America's oldest and greatest talking game. "Other sports permit only play-by-play," observes Al Michaels. "Baseball's pace lets you show your personality and humanity." Each links the happening and its public: If the Voice towers, so often has the event. Today, many liken football and baseball. To Voices, the differences more intrigue. Football is weekly, an event—baseball daily, a fact of life. Football is a greyhound you thrill to. Baseball is a cocker spaniel who steals your loyalty and love. One is show-biz—TV's Bundys. The other is the Waltons—religion passed from one generation to the next.

Phillies' manager Danny Ozark once sniffed of a losing streak, "No problem. Even Napoleon had his *Watergate*." As a child no problem kept me from the "only game," Bill Veeck said, "where you don't have to be seven feet high or seven feet wide." Baseball is the most democratic (also, republican) of sports, which is why it's the most American. Consider the pages that engrave this book—baseball as oral history.

Here are stories, by broadcasters still alive, from seven big-league decades. Read of Ernie Harwell fighting Leo Durocher, Chuck Thompson blurring bar and bedroom, and Bob Costas telling his beloved cheesecake tale. Also, Bob Starr nude in a hotel hallway, Charlie Jones inventing a twin brother, Bob Uecker shagging fly balls with a tuba, and Jerry Coleman crying, "They throw Winfield out at second, and he's safe!"

However vague and selective recall may be, there is no trick in trying to recapture growing up in the 1950s and early '60s to note that I was extraordinarily lucky through accident of birth. *The Storytellers* says the same of years before and since. On television—which, like a centerfold, left little to the imagination—and radio, leaving all, like Sally Rand enticing the glands—they drew baseball not in black and white, even when the picture was, but with muted tints and bold pastels—a panoply of color.

From the 1920s to '90s, radio/TV men have linked the Church of Baseball with America's labyrinth of life. Memory and, I think it fair to say, simple fact salute them as keepers of the big-league flame. The journalist Lincoln Steffens once visited the Soviet Union and predicted an absurdity. "I have seen the future, and it works." Baseball's future is yet to be written. Its past rises like a Ryan fastball jeweled against the sky.

THE ANNOUNCERS

*If a baseball Voice is good enough, lasts long enough, and has an easy famil-
iarity, he becomes an extended member of the family. Following are the kin
whose stories grace* The Storytellers. *These tales stem from talks by phone, tape,
journal, or in person, over the last decade. Most were told specifically for this
book, and to benefit the Baseball Assistance Team, which will receive a portion
of the proceeds.*

*For that generosity, I wish to thank these men—and for retrieving bits and
pieces of their past. I hope you will find, as I did, that their stories are possessed
of an honest identity and surpassing ability to relate.*

*Complaints abound that today baseball reeks of phony grass, sorry domes,
greedy players, swinish owners, litigation, and prima donnas. It does: Stereotype
is born of truth. By contrast, view the past 75 years as a kind of splendid arca-
dia. Neighbor, grab a 'Gansett, pull up a chair, smoke a White Owl, fling your
fish net, salute a malapropism, and shout "Hey-hey!" to baseball as it once
was—and pray can be again.*

*Think of Curt, Vin, Mel, Harry, Jerry, and Jack, respectively, and their fel-
low beckoners of a thousand afternoons. They show why at age 10, oblivious to
Thomas Wolfe, I would have grasped why he said of baseball, "Almost everything I know of spring is in it."*

MEL ALLEN. As 1939-64 Voice of the Yankees, he became an institution—and made "How About That!" a household term. Some prayed that laryngitis would silence Mel forever; most thought him more compelling than being at the park. Allen called more World Series (20) and All-Star Games (24) than anyone. *Variety* called his among "the world's 25 most recognizable voices." Later, hosting TV's "This Week In Baseball," he made a new generation swear that a florist decorated his voice. Sportscasting's *The Natural* is "the best there ever was." (Hall of Fame, inducted, 1978.)

JOE ANGEL has brought wit to the Giants, A's, Twins, Yankees, Orioles and since 1993, south Florida—Joe's current stop on the big-league trace. Like Desi Arnaz, Angel uses English and Spanish to 'splain a baseball thin' or two to Miami's bilingual public. Joe played quarterback for a Bay Area high school and was O. J. Simpson's teammate. More recently, he has aired USF hoops and Stanford football play-by-play, and enjoyed son Jonathan as a cast member of NBC's "Saved By the Bell." Think of Angel's rolling voice as baseball's answer to "Babalu."

RICHIE ASHBURN is a Valiant to whom Philadelphia gave its 1948-59 heart. No. 1 played 12 of his 15 big-league years in Pennsylvania's largest city. Ashburn led the 1950 Whiz Kids to a pennant, won the 1955 and '59 batting titles, and three times led the National League in hits. A paladin in the field, he caught more fly balls than all but four outfielders in history. In 1963, Richie traded jockstrap for jockocracy. "Those first years behind the mike," Ashburn said, "I had a lot to learn." Learning, he remains among the most popular all-time Phillies.

BUD BLATTNER was world doubles table tennis champion at 16, a big-league infielder in his 20s, and, later, part of network TV's first sports series, CBS' monumental "Game of the Week." Never did ego become his ball and chain. Bud was a pioneering athlete-turned-announcer. He started with the Browns, then Mutual and Liberty Broadcasting Systems, then as sidekick to as Falstaffian a legend who ever lived. From 1955-59, Bud and Dizzy Dean  evolved into a phenomenon, as did their twice-weekly CBS series. Blattner later did the Cardinals, Angels, and Royals, retiring in 1976.

MARTY BRENNAMAN. The author of "This one belongs to the Reds" has belonged to Cincinnati since 1974. It was then that the North Carolina alumnus arrived from Virginia, where he was Sportscaster of the Year three times in a row. Succeeding Al Michaels, Brennaman became a magical property in Louisville and Zanesville and Muncie and Marietta, binding the Reds' family over a huge radio network originating from WLW Cincinnati. What a '70s couplet: the Big  Red Machine playing and Marty Brennaman speaking. It stirs Rhineland memory even now.

JACK BRICKHOUSE'S calling card was "Hey-Hey!" A big man with a larger voice, he buoyed both sides of the Second City. Even as a young man, Jack played in his home town, Peoria. Then, in 1942, Bob Elson entered the navy, and Brickhouse inherited his niche as Voice of the Cubs and White Sox. In 1948, Jack became baseball's first daily TV mikeman— soon, airing the Wrigleys' entire home schedule. Later, his act turned national over Mutual Radio and NBC-  TV. Brickhouse did three World Series before retiring in 1981. Hey-Hey! Sadly, none involved the Cubs. (Hall of Fame, inducted, 1983.)

JACK BUCK is cause and mirror of the Cardinals' vast appeal. Wounded in World War II, Jack spent V-E Day in a Paris hospital. Returning home, he went to Ohio State University. In 1954, Buck trekked to Busch Stadium, joined Harry Caray on spiring KMOX, and found out why St. Louis may be the best baseball city in the world. When Caray was fired in 1969, Jack—replacing him—rode Mid-America's redbird waves of loyalty. Buck's credits include network baseball, football, and basketball. In an age of broadcast vanilla, this stylist never scents of bland. (Hall of Fame, inducted, 1987.)

HARRY CARAY is a balladeer mixing sarcasm, jarring cadence, and evident love of The Game. It might be! Baseball's Jackie Gleason. It could be! A half-century as Voice of the Cardinals, A's, White Sox, and Cubs. It is! Harry selling beer, sacking pomp, and seeming deliciously truant across the land. From 1945-69, he used St. Louis' KMOX Radio to become a red-hot mikeman. More recently, he evolved into a patch of folklore on SuperStation WGN-TV. Bud man, or Cub fan—Holy Cow! God broke the mold *before* He made Harry Christopher Carabina. (Hall of Fame, inducted, 1989.)

SKIP CARAY is Harry's oldest son, who "grew up with and around baseball," majored in journalism at the University of Missouri, and at 23 began calling games for the International League's Atlanta Crackers. Two years later, he subbed for Mel Allen on the broadcast of a 1965 big-league game out of Houston. In 1976, Caray *fils* became a full-time Braves' announcer, spurring interest by using sass and insight on SuperStation WTBS. Megapopular, Skip made 1991 history: Three generations of Carays—he, son Chip, and father Harry—aired a game from Wrigley Field. *Photo © 1993 Turner Sports, Inc.*

HERB CARNEAL seems to *be* the slogan of Twins' radio flagship WCCO: "The Good Neighbor to the Northwest." Carneal worked five years in Baltimore before moving to Minnesota. Since 1962, he has been regaling Bismarck and Boise and Fargo with names like Kaat and Killebrew and Puckett and Carew. Herb has called two world titles, brought a family feeling to a network of more than 60 stations in six states, and rendered respectability, good manners, and pluck. "If Herb had broadcast in New York," an admirer said, "they'd have built a monument to him by now."

JOE CASTIGLIONE grew up in Red Sox' country—Hamden, CT—learning early how Fenway Park is New England's Canaan, Medina, and Jerusalem. In 1979, Castiglione hit the bigs as TV Voice of the Indians, then did 1981-82 Brewers' and Tribe cable before retrieving the turf of John Winthrop, William Bradford, Tip O'Neill, and Willie Tasby. Since 1983, Castiglione has anchored Red Sox radio—and also taught a broadcast journalism course at Northeastern University. "Why not?" he says. "In New England, the Sox are required study."

TOM CHEEK embraced the Toronto Blue Jays as naturally as a smile—the first and still-Voice of Canada's parish team. It wasn't easy. The Jays finished last their first five seasons (1977-81). Then came high deeds in lieu of lowest comedy. In 1992, Toronto became the first non-U.S. team to win the World Series. A year later, Joe Carter wrote *déja vu* with a Classic-ending blow felt from the Yukon to Grand Pré'. For Canada, a new pastime, and for Cheek, a new "home and native land." In '92, the Florida native and ex-U.S. Air Forceman became a Canadian citizen.

JERRY COLEMAN excelled as a 1949-57 Yankee and World War II and Korea marine. Enter Al Jolson: He "ain't [showed] nothin' yet." Coleman called the 1963-69 Yankees, then took his ingenuity to San Diego for the 1972– Padres. "Hi, folks," he said, "this is Jerry Gross." Jesus Alou was "in the on-deck circus." "There's a long shot up the alley—and it's foul." Since 1976, Coleman has also buoyed CBS Radio, his rhetoric telling a clean, lively story-line. "I used to worry about Colemanisms," says this baseball artist. "Now I figure they add to my sex appeal."

KEN COLEMAN was born in suburban Boston, majored in Oratory at Curry College, and took his first broadcast job in Vermont's Old Northern Baseball League. In 1954, he became TV Voice of the Cleveland Indians and Browns. Twelve years later, Ken returned to the Athens of America, and the oft-scarred, ill-starred Red Sox. In 1967, he etched Boston's spurning of ghosts, deflations, and pratfalls of the past to win the pennant—aka "The Impossible Dream." Coleman still dubs The Year of The Yaz "the greatest thrill of my life."

BOB COSTAS. For years a Mickey Mantle playing card graced his wallet. "You should carry a religious artifact at all times," he said. Perhaps the Deity led Bob from Long Island to Syracuse University to KMOX. In 1982, Costas joined "Game of the Week" and flaunted humor out of George Burns by way of Johnny Carson. Bob has done four World Series, anchored Super Bowls and Summer Olympiads, and hosted the late-night "Later. . .With Bob Costas." Today, the five-time Emmy Award recipient blends journalism and superb banter as Voice of NBC baseball.

DAN DANIELS began broadcasting at Red Barber's alma mater, the University of Florida. From there he moved to stations in Jacksonville, Orlando, Birmingham, and Washington, D.C. Daniels filibustered for 1961-65 Senators' teams whose salvation was excuses and whose perpetuity befit last place. Not once did his Nats near .500. Bravely, Dan endured bad players and empty seats and sought to warm the Potomac chill. "People kindly say I was a good broadcaster," Daniels says of his years at WTOP Radio. "I figured with those clubs I had to be."

JERRY DOGGETT shows how patience can be a virtue, dredging the minor leagues until Brooklyn called a year before its '57 Westward-Ho! Jerry had gone to night radio school while working days, aired Liberty's "Game of the Day," and worked 18 seasons in the minors. Now, he began the first of 32 years as Vin Scully's colleague. In California, the Dodgers' Brooklyn heresy met redemption at the gate. Doggett waved nine pennants, did more than 5,000 Dodger interviews, and retired in 1987, breaking up baseball's then-longest-running broadcast team. *Photo © Jon Soohoo*

JIMMY DUDLEY stirred anyone who loved a story told with beauty and panache. From 1948-67, his rhetoric made signal sounds in the Indians' lake-front somnolence. In one eight-year stretch, the Tribe never drew a million people, never missed the pennant by less than 15 games, or hinted that hope might breathe past June. Dudley was interest's life-preserver—"So long and good luck, ya' heah"—his voice bespeaking courtesy, hospitality, and Wait Till Next Year (again). "The longer I was there, the worse they seemed to play," he laughs. "I concede no cause and effect."

GENE ELSTON was the 1962-86 Voice of the Houston Astros (née Colt .45's). His voice carried out into the Gulf and Panhandle, and eastward toward New Orleans, bringing baseball to the lonely towns and booming cities of the larger-than-life Southwest. The Elston roundup climaxed a cattle drive that led from 1941's Ft. Dodge, Iowa, to Class-A Des Moines in 1950, to Wrigley Field and Mutual's 1958-60 "Game of the Day." Today, Gene lifts the CBS Radio Saturday "Game of the Week," saying, as Goethe did, "America, you have it better."

DICK ENBERG worked his way through Central Michigan University, earned graduate degrees at Indiana, and entered broadcasting with the 1960s Angels. In 1971, he went big-time as host of the TV series "Sports Challenge." Joining NBC in 1975, Dr. Dick corkscrewed into a latter-day Curt Gowdy. Its Renaissance Man has called—"Oh, My!"—the World Series, Wimbledon, the Rose and Super Bowls, and the NCAA hoops final. Enberg did balls and strikes in the early 1980s. Losing baseball in 1990, NBC retrieved it in 1994, and Enberg returned as a still-lyric Voice.

LANNY FRATTARE links Erie, Oil City, and Ashtabula as Voice of the Pittsburgh Pirates. Upon a Buccos' triumph, Lanny's KDKA predecessor Bob Prince cried as in a seance, "We had 'em allll the way!" Less rococo, Lanny wags, "There was no doubt about it." Born in Rochester, New York, he graduated from Ithaca College, went on to call the Triple-A Charleston Charlies, and in 1976 rafted to the confluence of the Ohio, Allegheny, and Monongahela rivers. Lanny admits to liking presidential history. As Richard Nixon might say, Frattare's Tri-State popularity is "perfectly clear."

JOE GARAGIOLA is a pastiche of gag, charm, and devotion to the personal—baseball's Bob Hope of the resin bag. As a catcher, Garagiola made a good funny man, hitting .257 and retiring in 1954. The next year, he joined the KMOX broadcast team. In 1960, Joe wrote the best-selling *Baseball Is a Funny Game.* Later, he did NBC's "Today" and "The Tonight Show," won a Peabody Award, and graced the 1973-88 "Game of the Week." Garagiola now aids the Baseball

Assistance Team charity. An ordinary Joe on the field, he has been extraordinary off it. (Hall of Fame, inducted, 1991.)

EARL GILLESPIE. In 1953, the Braves became the first major-league team to change cities in half-a-century. Fleeing Boston for Milwaukee, they found Valhalla in the Midwest. Their Voice was a Chicagoan who floated down a river of handclapping over a radio network linking Wisconsin, Michigan, and parts of Minnesota, Illinois, and Iowa. Warm and emotional, Gillespie used a fish net to corral foul balls, rejoiced as the Braves won two pennants, and

watched County Stadium sell out night after night. He resigned in 1963, before the Braves became Atlanta's.

CURT GOWDY. What could the Wyoming Cowboy possibly have left to do? The 1951-65 Voice of the Boston Red Sox, Gowdy became network TV sports' paradigm for a later generation: 15 All-Star Games, 12 World Series, seven Olympics, and two decades of "The American Sportsman," winning four Emmy Awards. From 1966-75, Curt called virtually every network baseball game. In 1970, he became the first sportscaster to win the George Foster Peabody Award

for broadcast excellence. "Nobody did what he did," NBC's Carl Lindemann said of the Rocky Mountaineer, "and nobody ever will." (Hall of Fame, inducted, 1984.)

HANK GREENWALD mixes bite and light as baseball's Liegeman on the Bay. The Syracuse graduate moved from Orange football to University of San Francisco and Golden State hoops, and then, in 1979, to Pacific Coast League baseball, bringing to San Francisco a sturdy set of credentials. Through 1986, he helped the Giants brush against the elements, then traded one wind (Candlestick Park) for another (George Steinbrenner). Hank returned west in 1989, and still hails the Giants over KNBR. Many find listening to him warmer than trooping to the park. *Photo © 1993 San Francisco Giants*

MILO HAMILTON was only 25 when he joined the Browns for their final year. "I'm not sure I was ready for the majors," he said of 1953. "'Course, neither was my team." His tumbleweed of turns then led to the Cardinals, Cubs, and White Sox. In 1966, the Braves moved to Atlanta, and Hamilton became their Voice. "For a decade, I talked to a whole region," he says. "My time in the South made me." Let go in 1975, Milo roamed to Pittsburgh, Wrigley Field, and in 1985, Houston. He endures as a broadcast warrior—bright, studious, and, oh, so smooth. (Hall of Fame, inducted, 1992.)

MERLE HARMON beamed his voice through the window of mid-America. The Illinoisan began balls and strikes at 1949 Class-C Topeka. He made the bigs as Voice of the 1955-63 Athletics. Fleeing Charlie Finley, Merle changed Twilight Zones to join the marching-to-Georgia 1964-65 Milwaukee Braves. Next came his selection as Voice of baseball's first truly national TV series, ABC's '65 "Game of the Week." Later, Harmon stopped at Minnesota, Texas, and the 1970-79 Brewers—embossing coverage more with the tangible than quaint.

KEN HARRELSON has less beat his own drum than followed his own drummer. As a player, he earned the name "Hawk," brought the batting glove to baseball, and owned Boston in 1968—35 homers and 109 RBI in The Year of The Pitcher. A year later Ken was dealt to Cleveland as picketers stormed Fenway Park. He retired in 1971, played pro golf, turned 1975-81 Red Sox' mikeman, and became White Sox' TV Voice in 1982. After moving to New York, Ken U-turned in 1990 to Comiskey Park. Today, his charm, trademark "Yes!" and humor staple viewers to WGN-TV.

ERNIE HARWELL began play-by-play with the 1946 Atlanta Crackers. He soon leapt to Brooklyn, the Polo Grounds, and Baltimore; and, in 1960, the steep-walled rectangle at the corner of Michigan and Trumbull. As Tigers' Voice through 1993, Ernie became the most popular man in the state of Michigan. Said Joe Falls. "He could probably be elected mayor of Detroit, if not governor." Instead, Harwell starred as poet and essayist, author, lay preacher, and family man. Today, he says grace around baseball's dinner table on the CBS Radio "Game of the Week." (Hall of Fame, inducted, 1981.)

MARK HOLTZ is like the Lone Star State—a composite of proud parts. He has aired college football and basketball, the NBA Mavericks, and baseball's pride of Texas. In 1982, Holtz began Rangers' radio play-by-play. A decade later, he segued to KTVT and its five-state TV network. Holtz was elected to the Texas Hall of Fame in 1990. Next came a '94 trek to the grass, angles, scarce foul terrain, close-up box seats, and Home Run Porch of The Ballpark in Arlington. "Parks are like broadcasting," Mark says. "Both express the heart and soul of the game."

ERNIE JOHNSON rode 1980s cable to become baseball's TV *paterfamilias.* It seemed a natural evolution for the son of Swedes who emigrated at the turn of the century. He fought in World War II, was 40-23 as a 1950s reliever and spot starter, and joined the Braves as a 1962 color man. In 1976, Ernie was named their Voice. Later, he helped make Atlanta "America's Team" over WTBS. The soft-spoken Vermonter is respected for his modesty and lack of sham. Listening, you swear he would be a grandfather to the entire population if he could. *Photo © 1992 SportSouth*

CHARLIE JONES is among sportscasting's most recognized and recognizable Voices, for 35 years airing NFL football (30 on NBC-TV) as well as the Summer Olympics, golf, boxing, soccer, Wimbledon tennis, track and field, and nine different college bowl games. Among Jones's historic firsts: the initial Super Bowl, AFL title game, NBC "SportsWorld," World Cup gymnastics, Senior "Skins" golf, and a multination athletic event in China. He has also called baseball's backup "Game of the Week" as well as the Reds, Angels, and the 1993– Colorado Rockies.

JIM KAAT has used an accordion string of tickets on his tour of the major leagues. From 1959-83, he was a 283-237 pitcher, three times topped 20 victories, won 16 Gold Gloves, and appeared in 898 games—fifth all-time high. Next, he became a pitching coach, then a Voice of the Yankees, Braves, Twins, and CBS- and ESPN-TV. Growing up in Zeeland, Michigan, Kaat wanted to play big-league ball. He now describes it via Madison Square Garden Network play-by-play. This Kitty depends less on claws than on an encyclopedic knowledge of the game.

HARRY KALAS. His face belongs in the Vienna Boys Choir. Deep and voluble, his voice rivals a wrecker demolishing cars. Kalas advanced from the University of Iowa to Hawaii Islanders to 1965-70 Houston Astros. For the past quarter century, the Phillies' Voice has done Notre Dame football, Big Five basketball, and voiceover for NFL Films. Pennsylvania's top sportscaster's home run call—  "It's outa' here!"—spreads like jam across the Delaware Valley. Harry is a minister's son, but it's baseball fans who give thanks.

GEORGE KELL studied baseball as a kid, smashed pitches as a player, and since 1959 has graced Tigers' radio and TV. He lives in the town where he was born—Swifton, Arkansas—which he left to become the American League's best 1940s and '50s third base-  man. Nine times, Kell hit more than .300. In 1949, he led the league at .3429, beating Ted Williams by two-thousandths of a point. Retiring, the Tiger who became a Red Sox and then an Oriole debuted on CBS' 1958 "Game of the Week." The next year, he returned to Briggs Stadium, switching to TV-only in 1965. (Hall of Fame, inducted as player, 1983.)

RALPH KINER hit 369 career homers, won seven home run titles, and was cosmic in Pittsburgh's 1946-53 concourse. In 1961, Kiner entered broadcasting at Comiskey Park. A year later he moved to the Polo Grounds, mixing story, scene, and vernacular speech  as 1962– radio/TV Voice of the New York Mets. Once, Ralph identified Howard Johnson as Walter Johnson, Marv Throneberry as Marv Strawberry, Gary Carter as Gary Cooper, and Milt May as Mel Ott. His popu- larity makes TV's "Kiner's Korner" post-game show a Big Apple institution. (Hall of Fame, inducted as player, 1975.)

VINCE LLOYD linked the Friendly Confines and millions of midwesterners for whom, fanatically and even mystically, the Cubs were the sports center of the globe. Lloyd took the WGN Radio job when Jack Quinlan died in a 1965 car accident. Quickly, his appeal rivaled the North Siders' munchkin of a team. Vince did play-by-play through 1982, then switched to color before retiring in 1986. In April 1961, he became the first announcer to interview a U.S. president at a baseball game: John Kennedy, prior to the White Sox' opener at Griffith Stadium.

TIM McCARVER played big-league ball from 1959-80—one of seven in our modern day to span four decades. He then turned to analyzing it, wiling listeners with wit, wisdom, and, above all, work. In 1983, McCarver was named a Mets' announcer. Next followed a holiday of plums. Tim graced ABC 1984-89 baseball, worked the bigs and Winter Olympics at CBS, and returned to Camp Arledge in 1994. Dry and trenchant, he appeals to both eggheads and blue collars. *Sports Illustrated* was right in 1986, and now: "Tim McCarver is the very *best* at what he does."

SEAN McDONOUGH has already stomped upon the limits of possibility. In 1988, he became Red Sox' TV mikeman at age 26. In 1992, Sean added CBS baseball to his *vitae*. As its Voice he peaked in the 1993 Fall Classic, breezing, "The Phillies have taken the lead by a field goal, 10-7." Losing baseball, CBS shifted Sean in 1994 to college basketball and the Winter Olympics. Today, McDonough does ESPN and Bosox' baseball. "I intend to be here," he says, "when the Sox finally win the Series." Longevity has its place.

NED MARTIN. Raised 18 miles from Center City, Ned was fated *not* to be in Philadelphia. Instead, he became a bard who, quoting Hamlet, said of Red Sox' ineptitude, "When sorrows come they come not [as] single spies, but in battalions." In 1961, Martin arrived at Fenway Park after taking his theatre of expression to advertising, publishing, and Triple-A radio. His signet—"Mercy!"—built a Jacob's Ladder of popularity. Fans hailed radio's 1974-78 duo of  Martin and Jim Woods before Ned turned to '79-92 TV. Mercy! What a void the Pennsylvanian leaves.

DENNY MATTHEWS rolled "7" from the start for the Kansas City Royals. In 1976, he replaced Bud Blattner as radio *duce*. Whether cause or effect, the Royals won a first of three straight divisions. They took the 1980 pennant and beat St. Louis in the '85 Series, their first world title in franchise year 17. Holding sway was the Voice who has stroked college hoops, football, and CBS baseball playoff coverage. The Royals' network is the American League's largest: 115 stations in 11 states from Florida to New Mexico.

AL MICHAELS. A man stuck in the mud with his car was asked by a wayfarer whether he was really stuck. "You *could* say I was stuck," he said, "if I was going anywhere." Al has gone places since his boyhood, spent a block from Ebbets Field. In 1958, he moved from Flatbush to Los Angeles, later graduating from Arizona State to do Reds and Giants' play-by-play. Michaels joined ABC in 1976, becoming its baseball/NFL Voice and three-time Sportscaster of  the Year. His defining line—"Do you believe in miracles? Yes!" at the 1980 Winter Olympics—is remembered to this day.

JON MILLER grew up in California, played Stratomatic while friends were surfing, and now sets a standard for play-by-play. At 22, he began his blue-chip consortium in Oakland, then moved to Texas and Fenway Park. In 1983, he became Voice of the Orioles and built a cult over their seven-state network. Since 1990, Jon has also been ESPN's Comstock Lode, miming Vin Scully, spawning humor, and bringing elegance to his craft. "Baseball entertains you," he says, "and you care about it. What I like is the company of baseball." It is *Miller's* company that fans enjoy.

MONTE MOORE is a native Sooner who reached the big leagues via outlets in Oklahoma, Kansas, and Missouri. He broadcast the 1962-67 Kansas City Athletics, rode the Finleys' '68 Wagon Train to Oakland, and aired the A's from Campaneris through Jackson past Canseco to Henderson *redux*. Highlights: Monte's 1962-77 iron streak (2,801 straight games), three straight world titles (1972-74), and kudos for 1980s NBC and USA Cable play-by-play. Walt Whitman said, "I hear America singing." For a quarter-century, Moore helped baseball sing beside the Bay.

BOB MURPHY. The Greek poet Sophocles wrote, "One must wait until the evening to see how splendid the day has been." Already, Murphy's day is sunlit. It began with the marines, University of Tulsa, and Oklahoma Class-A radio. In 1954, Bob went to Fenway Park; in 1960, to Memorial Stadium; and in 1962, to the expansion New York Mets. He used "marvelous" before Billy Crystal, has called three Mets' flags, and made his "The Happy Recap" enduring in the ephemera capital of the world. "All I've done," he says, "is try to bring friendliness to the game." (Hall of Fame, inducted, 1994.)

LINDSEY NELSON. In 1962, the Mets endured their first spring training. Finally, manager Casey Stengel said, "Can't anybody *play* this here game?" He never asked whether their Voice could broadcast it. Over four decades, Lindsey did events from Notre Dame football to the NBA "Game of the Week" to the Amazins' first 17 seasons. His rythmic country gabble and glaring sports coats—in time, he owned nearly 350—made him a national prize. Nelson has been a professional and a *professor* of announcing, teaching America the definition of class. (Hall of Fame, inducted, 1988.) *Photo courtesy of the National Baseball Library, Cooperstown, N.Y.*

DAVID NIEHAUS. For nearly two decades, his "My, oh, my" and "It will fly away" have fashioned baseball's Northwest Opening. Dave reached Seattle by way of Indiana University, Armed Forces Radio/TV, Madison Square Garden, Chavez Ravine, and eight years at the Big A. He aired the Mariners' regular-season baptism—an April 6, 1977, 7-0 loss to California—and went on to navigate a voyage of Gaylord Perry, Ken Griffey, Jr., and only two plus-.500 logs in Seattle's first 18 years. No. 1 on *this* Dave's List: Keeping interest alive even when the M's weren't.

MEL PROCTOR treats play-by-play as sport, not Armageddon. Fortuitous: He calls each Orioles' game on cable/free TV. In 1978, the Coloradan left the Hawaii Islanders to come to Washington for Bullets basketball. Later, Mel added the 1980-81 Texas Rangers and 1984- Orioles. Other satellites in his orb include acting (Proctor was a recurring character in NBC-TV's "Homicide"); network broadcasting for Mutual, TBS, NBC, and CBS; and writing. Mel's first book, issued in 1995, recalled the TV series "The Fugitive."

JAY RANDOLPH is the son of a politician—U.S. Senator William Jennings Randolph—who tramped to America's *other* pastime. Jay began sportscasting in Clarksburg, West Virginia, in 1958. Fast-forward to the Dallas Cowboys, SMU football, and NBC's pro and college football, men and women's golf, NCAA hoops, and three Olympic Games. For 18 years, Randolph did Cardinals' television—also, the Reds, Braves, and 1993– expansion Marlins. Today, the three-time local Emmy recipient brings grace and intellection to southern Florida's baseball life.

RONALD REAGAN re-created 1930s Cubs' games over WHO, Des Moines. His stronghold of enthusiasm brought a springtime of possibility to fans hundreds of miles from Chicago's North Side. Born and educated on the steppeland of Illinois, the Dutchman later wrote a biography, *An American Life.* In Depression Iowa, he was already an American Original. Yearning for Wrigley Field, Reagan settled for the Oval Office. "In re-creations and politics, you had to be an actor," said the fortieth president. "How can I not love baseball? It made me what I am today."

PEE WEE REESE. From 1940-42 and 1946-57, the captain of the Brooklyn franchise of the National League led with bat and glove—and more with his heart than with either. Retiring in 1959, the Dodgers' shortstop chanced face on a medium he barely knew, becoming Dizzy Dean's partner—to Ol' Diz, "pod-nuh"—on CBS' 1960-64 "Game of the Week." Each Saturday and Sunday, the two ex-players made Middle America close down. "To this day," Reese says, "folks come up and say, 'Baseball hasn't been the same since you and Diz left.'" (Hall of Fame, inducted as player, 1984.)

PHIL RIZZUTO has thrived on and off the field. Born in Brooklyn, he helped win nine World Series as a 1941-42 and '46-56 Yankees' shortstop. In 1957, the "Scooter" became a broadcaster, evolving into more playactor than play-by-playman. Tune in, say, before the seventh inning (to beat traffic, he often leaves early) and hear talk of allergies, birthdays, and veal Parmesan. Unorthodoxy makes bucks for the Yanks—and fans for The Game. Some forget Phil was small as a player. Maybe it's because his persona is so larger-than-life. (Hall of Fame, inducted as player, 1994.)

TED ROBINSON had already aired the A's and Twins upon joining CBS Radio's original 1985 "Game of the Week." There he helped forge baseball's greatest wireless feat since Mutual's 1950s coverage. "Game" ferried baseball past backyards and general stores and gentle small towns. Ted rode its sounds to a roundup of other stops: college football and basketball, back to the (1987–92) Twins, and 1993– TV Voice of the Giants. Each was theatre—like calling "Game of the Week" over 325 affiliates to nearly seven million listeners. *Photo © 1993 San Francisco Giants*

JOHN ROONEY began his career in 1981 with the Triple-A Oklahoma City 89ers, quickly shed a minor-league moniker, and joined CBS Radio in 1985. He became its MVP as utility infielder, doing "Game of the Week" and the playoffs, World Series, and All-Star Game. In 1988, John added White Sox video, moving to WMAQ Radio a year later. Today, he does TV/wireless of the Pale Hose, Cotton Bowl, Big Ten and NCAA Finals basketball, and CBS regular- and post-season baseball—tying sites a light-year distant from the nearest big-league park.

BYRUM SAAM's history was Philadelphia's baseball history. He was styled "The Man of a Zillion Words," and listeners felt a peculiar bond. "Would you please talk a little louder?" wrote a woman from New Jersey. "My radio battery is getting weak." From 1938-75, Saam called more losing baseball games than any man in history. Nineteen times, his A's and Phillies finished last. His specialty was malapropisms. Saam's first big-league words were "Hello, Byrum Saam, this is everybody speaking." It was a hint, as they say, of boffo things to come. (Hall of Fame, inducted, 1990.)

BILLY SAMPLE graduated from James Madison University, played eight years with Texas and the Yankees and Braves, then leaped from the field to radio/TV. In 1988, Sample moved to Atlanta; in 1990, to the Mets and ESPN; and in 1992, to Seattle and CBS Radio. In '93, he began the first of two years at Anaheim Stadium. Direct and anecdotal, Sample is a past host of cable Sports Channel's "The Art of Baseball."

RAY SCOTT. "When [he] intoned, slowly, profoundly, simply, 'First down, Green Bay,'" *TV Guide* wrote of pro football's best-ever mikeman, "a million spines would quiver." From 1960-74, the Johnstown, Pennsylvania heir flooded network TV with four Super Bowls and nine NFL title games. Few recall that Scott shone on balls and strikes. The Voice of the Packers also worked for the Pirates, Senators, and Brewers. Earlier, he exteriorized Northland ball as 1961-66 Voice of the Twins—a cross between Alexander Scourby and Billy Graham.

VIN SCULLY has exalted baseball since before the Grand Army of the Potomac staged its last reunion. At 22, Scully went to Ebbets Field under Red Barber, Vin's "most influential person in my life." In 1958, he moved to California with the Dodgers. Ultimately, fans voted him the "most memorable personality" in franchise history. The 1980s brought a broadcast Peabody Award and a sustaining niche on NBC's "Game of the Week." Once, Vin said, "It was so hot  today the moon got sunburned." The sports' Laurence Olivier daily links its sun, moon, and stars. (Hall of Fame, inducted, 1982.) *Photo © 1993 Los Angeles Dodgers, Inc.*

LON SIMMONS pitched in the Phillies' organization, hurt his back, became a carpenter, and decided that to make the major leagues he needed a different kind of resumé. His solution: radio at Fresno, California, and as 1957 sports director of San Francisco's KSFO. A year later, Simmons and Russ Hodges began Year One of the California Giants. Soon one visitor dubbed San Francisco "The City of the Deaf." Everyone seemed to walk around with a  hearing aid—in reality, a transistor radio. Lon did the Giants through 1978 and, since 1981, has chattered for the cross-bay A's.

KEN SINGLETON grew up in Mount Vernon, New York, idolized Willie Mays and Willie McCovey, entered Hofstra University, and was drafted by the Mets in 1967. Traded, he thrived for 1972-74 Montreal and the 1975-84 Orioles, wafting 246 home runs and making two World Series. In 1986, Singleton rejoined the Expos as a TSN (The Sports Network) analyst. Three years later, he added free TV, and radio in 1991. Today, the Baltimore resident does  Expos' color and play-by-play—above the field, as on it, a switch-hitting star.

DEWAYNE STAATS went to Southern Illinois University, started broadcasting in St. Louis, and called the 1977-84 Astros. In 1985, he replaced Houston-bound Milo Hamilton as radio Voice of the Cubs. Through 1989, Staats ballooned their cult of listeners, distant fans, and rooters for the underdog, then traded Wrigley Field's vines, wind off Lake Michigan, and animal-cracker size for Yankee Stadium. Dewayne did 1990-94 baseball for the Madison Square Garden Network. Like the Cubs, his Yankees missed the World Series, too.

BOB STARR is nearing his fifth decade of broadcasting. Possessed of a *basso* voice, the Oklahoman has spanned both coasts and major leagues. Starr did eight years of 1970s Cardinals' baseball, was '80s Voice of the Angels, and spent 1990-92 at Fenway Park before returning to Anaheim—also stargazing for the NFL Rams and Cardinals and college football and basketball. Napoleon said, "Ability, yes, but give me generals who have luck." Bob's *sans* pennant teams have been *luckless*. His *ability* is clearer than a cloudless Pacific sky.

CHUCK THOMPSON first learned baseball in a boarding home owned by his grandmother, which had Connie Mack as a tenant. "She relayed to me a love of baseball," said Chuck. "She helped to set the stage." Since 1946, Thompson has crossed it as Voice of the Phillies, A's, Senators, and, above all, 1962–Orioles. Fans treasure Chuck's decency, knowledge, and war cries: "Ain't the beer cold!" and "Go to war, Miss Agnes!" From Virginia to the Catoctin Mountains to Baltimore's "Little Italy," his voice is still as magic as a day behind the rain. (Hall of Fame, inducted, 1993.)

BOB UECKER. "Ah, those fans," chants Mr. Baseball, "I love 'em." In turn, they love the ex-player who is his own best material: cult figure, stand-up comic, movie/TV actor, and 1972– Brewers' Voice. As a 1962-67 backup backstop, Uke foresaw an afterlife beyond the playing field. Reaching it, he became a Joe Garagiola with hair. From "Mr. Belvedere" to "Major League II" to Lite Beer for Miller ads, Bob has been an Archetype of Everyman—a full course of humor

and aside. Was J. D. Salinger a baseball fan? Check the front rooow for this *Catcher in the Wry.*

DAVE VAN HORNE lives and (mostly) dies Montreal baseball, the first- and still-Voice of the Expos since their first game in 1969. He began on radio, added TV in 1971, and annexed cable's The Sports Network in 1990. Born in Easton, Pennsylvania, Dave has done *Les Expos* from Coco Laboy through Gary Carter to Larry Walker in Jarry Park and, later, Olympic Stadium—the horrid Big O, as in zero. Win or lose, Oshawa, Ontario, and

Brandon, Manitoba, and Saskatoon, Saskatchewan, have been forgiving toward the Expos, devoted to Van Horne.

KEN WILSON's career rivals a AAA Triptik. Born in Detroit, he entered baseball with the Hawaii Islanders. Segue to the 1977-82 expansion Mariners, 1983-85 Reds, 1986-90 Cardinals, and 1991– Angels. Wilson has ministered Gaylord Perry's 300th victory, the Redbirds' 1987 pennant, and Charlie Hustle's September 11, 1985, Ty-breaker—career hit no. 4,192. "For Pete Rose, his crowning achievement," Ken said. "This city mobs their native son." A devotee

of the shiny game, Ken has moonlighted as Voice of the hockey Blackhawks and 1985– Blues.

BOB WOLFF laughed and barbed his way through 1947-60 Washington Senators' teams whose God-awfulness rivaled that of the 1962 New York Mets. Not once in his administration did the Nats flee the second division. The Duke graduate deserved better and got it on Mutual Radio (calling Don Larsen's 1956 perfect game), NBC-TV's 1962-64 "Major League Baseball" (his partner, Joe Garagiola), and the 1954-89 Madison Square Garden Network. Today, Wolff's award-winning cable work recalls the skill that kept the Senators from becoming the Atlantis of the American League. (Hall of Fame, inducted, 1995.)

CHAPTER ONE

THAT OLD FEELING

THE ART OF RE-CREATION

*T*ools were primitive for radio's Voices of the 1920s: a scorebook, a box seat as press box, a converted telephone turned microphone. Most play-by-play men did home games live. Yet line telephone charges voided live away coverage. The solution: baseball's off-Broadway of re-creations. A Western Union reporter at a game, say, in Pittsburgh, sent Morse Code signals to an operator in Boston, who gave the paper to an announcer, who embellished action he had never seen.

By the 1930s, baseball was more wed to re-creations than Bogart and Bacall. In Cleveland, Jack Graney told stories in the showroom of an auto dealer. At Navin Field, Ty Tyson called Hank Greenberg "Hankus Pancus" and Lynwood (Schoolboy) Rowe "Schoolhouse" or "Schoolie" or "the fella' playing hooky." To the east and south, Arch McDonald played to a studio crowd three blocks from the White House. The "Rembrandt of the Re-creation" smashed a gong to hail a rare Senators' feat—for example, four times for a home run.

Before fiber optics, downlinking, and satellite telegraphy, you felt close enough to the action to reach out and touch the field.

Return to a time before Ike was President and America loved Lucy. Radio was in its Heaven, and ad-libbing stilled the sky.

*I*n the 1930s a team didn't have its own announcers, and five or six of us did the same game. We kinda' competed for the audience. What made it tough is that some of our competitors were doing games live at Wrigley Field while I was in Des Moines, hundreds of miles away.

I was doing the games by telegraphic report. Well, just picture that the fellow sat on the other side of a window with a little slit underneath, the headphones on, getting the Morse Code from the ball park, and he typed out the play. And the paper would come through to me saying something like, "S1C." That means strike one on the corner. But you're not going to sell Wheaties yelling "S1C!" So I would say, "So-and-so comes out of the windup, here comes the pitch . . . and it's a called strike breaking over the outside corner to a batter that likes the ball a little higher."

One day I saw him start to type, so I started another ball toward the plate. Then I saw him shaking his head, and I thought it was a miraculous play. But when the slip came through it said, "The wire's gone dead." Well, with those other five or six fellows out there doing the same game, I knew that if I said, "We will pause for a brief interlude of transcribed music until they get the wire fixed," everybody'd switch to other stations.

Then, I remembered the one thing that doesn't get in the scorebook—a foul ball—and knew I was on my own. I looked at Curly on the other side of the window, and he was helpless. It was the Cardinals and Cubs, and Dizzy Dean was pitching. I made Dean use the resin bag and shake off a couple signs to take up time. Then he threw another one, and another. Billy Jurges was at bat, and, when he hit a foul, I described kids in a fight over it. Then he fouled one to the left that just missed being a home run.

About six minutes and 45 seconds later, I'd set a world record for someone standing at the plate—except that no one keeps such records. I was beginning to sweat, when Curly sat up straight and started typing. When he handed me the slip, I started to giggle, and I could hardly get it out. It said, "Jurges popped out on the first ball pitched." But maybe I shouldn't tell this story. Politicians have enough problems with credibility as it is.

—*Ronald Reagan*

Today too many guys come into the booth with no background and make mistakes in the light of the big leagues. It's too bad they don't have our training ground of re-creations. In the '40s you'd sit in a studio with paper that said "S1F" (strike one, fastball) or "B3I" (ball three inside) and had to imagine what was occurring wherever your team was. Re-creations taught me early that dreams don't always immediately come true.

One night my minor-league Atlanta Crackers were playing Mobile. I was in a radio station in Atlanta. The sponsor, Wheaties, sent a man from Minneapolis to monitor the broadcast. Wheaties then sponsored nearly a hundred different baseball broadcasts all over America, and, once a season, their representative flew to each city to check up on the announcer.

Obviously, that night, I wanted to be at my peak. "If I do well," I told myself, "maybe he'll go back to headquarters and give me a good report. Then maybe Wheaties will hire me for one of their big-league broadcasts." I did my best—and did it solo. I called each play, commercial, and station break—didn't leave the mike. The game lasted 21 innings and ended in a tie. And all that time, I just knew that the Wheaties man was in the studio lobby listening, just waiting with my big chance.

After midnight, I finally stumbled into the lobby. My back was sore, and my throat was sorer, but it was all worth it, right? Surely, the Wheaties man was all atwitter. Then I saw him. He'd been asleep for hours.

—*Ernie Harwell*

The first club I broadcast was Longview of the East Texas League. Living there in the 1930s and '40s, I viewed Dallas of the Texas League as the ultimate. I made friends with the man who owned both teams, and he offered me the Dallas job. I wind up doing 16 years of games there for WRR, doing wire reports by teletype. You'd make up a bunch of lies and make like you were at the park.

Toward the late 1940s, WRR lost broadcast rights to Dallas station KLIF, and it seemed I'd be out of business because Gordon McLendon, who owned the station, was going to hire Dizzy Dean. But at the last minute, talks fell through, and Gordon offered me the job. And, as things happened, it was a great break because in time I became his right-hand man of an amazing project: the Liberty Broadcasting System, with KLIF its flagship.

McLendon founded Liberty in 1949—its lynchpin, "Game of the Day." [For $27.50, KLIF got a complete game of Western Union play-by-play—in turn, sending a re-creation from Comiskey Park or Ebbets Field to LBS affiliates who covered line charges, sold ads, and paid McLendon $10 per contest. "Back then, big-league localcasts existed only from Boston to St. Louis," said Lindsey Nelson. "So it was only time before someone realized: 'Gee, whoever brings radio baseball to the rest of America—people panting for major-league games—will strike it rich.'" Suddenly, outlanders confined to All-Star and World Series games heard Voices like Nelson and McLendon—"The Old Scotchman"—air 200 regular-seasoncasts over as many as 431 affiliates. "It made for yearly exposure like nothing before or since," Lindsey said. "Day in and out, enormous interest."]

As Gordon's sports director, we did games each day. In 1951, the Giants and Dodgers went down to the wire, and, on the final Sunday of the season, Gordon did the Giants live from Boston while I stayed in Dallas to re-create the Dodgers-Phillies. His game ended first. Mine went extra innings and was won on a homer by Jackie Robinson after he saved the game with a leaping catch. I still grieve that Liberty went bankrupt. [Baseball ensured exclusivity by banning McLendon in 1952 from big-league parks.] So do other people. The series was on four decades ago, for exactly three years, yet people still remember.

—*Jerry Doggett*

I grew up in Zeeland, in southwest Michigan, and I'd hear Bert Wilson and Jack Brickhouse of the Cubs, the Tigers' Harry Heilmann, and later Earl Gillespie when the Braves came to Wisconsin [1953]. But I remember Bob Elson of the White Sox. I can't tell you how many Sunday afternoons I spent listening to [World War II navy veteran] The Commander do double-headers—many re-creations. Elson was a sharpie, owned a lot of stock in Magnavox. When I became a player, we'd talk about the old days, and he took a liking. "Kid," he said, "when you're paid as lousy as we are, you gotta' try the market." So I invested in Magnavox, and made enough money to buy a Mustang when it came out in the '60s. Yes, in effect Bob Elson bought me one of the classic cars of all time! Whenever I see a TV ad, I think of The Old Commander, probably still buying and selling in the sky.

—*Jim Kaat*

My first season was in the Class C Western Association, 1949. One night Topeka plays Ft. Smith behind a pitcher named Jimmy Price. In the fourth inning, the circuit breaks. Arnie, the Western Union operator, looks at me and gives the stretch sign that something's wrong. Quickly, I start delaying. "There's the wind-up by Jimmy Price. The pitch. Oh, wait a minute, something happened to his arm. Jimmy's grabbing his left shoulder. Here come the catcher and manager to the mound."

I'm hoping the circuit is soon OK, but five minutes later, no resumption. Reality says they'd already have taken Jimmy out, but who am I to complain? So I had him throw practice pitches, look in for the sign, he steps off the mound, and the arm's hurting him. Here come the catcher and manager again—all this 'til Arnie gave a sign that all had been restored. Next day, I read in the Topeka newspaper how Price hurt his arm but recovered after a long delay to pitch a complete game. I thought, boy, that's incredible. I must be psychic.

A few days later, we come home. The paper's sports editor, Stan Emerson, asks if I'll drive him to the park. We start talking. "That was quite a trip," he began. I said, "Yeah, and what's amazing is that I started making up stuff and then found it happened!" Stan asked, "What?" "Well," I said, "we lost our circuit, so I invented things about Price hurting and them working on him." Suddenly, Stan went silent. We got to the park, and he didn't say a word. For days he didn't speak to me. Finally, I said, "What's wrong? I talk, and you ignore me." He exploded: "*Ignore* ya'? Why wouldn't I?" I said, "What do you mean?" He explained, "I knew you radio guys were alike. I listened to that game and wrote my story based on what you said, 'cause I trusted you. Now I find that nothing happened at all."

For a long time Stan snubbed me. I learned that when you re-create, tell the truth. From then on, I put a disclaimer before and after the game that it's re-created. Soon I added sound effects like crowd noise and a wood block that had a crack in it. Hit it with a pencil: foul tip. Hit another area: sounds like a guy belted one. If we lost a circuit, I said, "We'll be back when it's restored." Today, nobody does re-creations. It's less expensive to travel and do games live off satellite than use Western Union. Too bad. They were often better than the real thing.

—Merle Harmon

In 1950, my first broadcast year, I did Liberty's "Game of the Day" from the St. Louis studio. As we usually did, this day we carry two games by ticker, and in the eighth inning of Game Two the Yankees led the Tigers, 12-8. Pat Mullin then hit a grand-slam homer for Detroit to make it 12-12, and after three and a half hours the game went extra innings. In the 10th inning, totally exhausted, I turned the play-by-play over to my partner but still checked the tape to make sure there were no mistakes. In the tenth inning, Mullin came to bat again, and I wrote on the tape above his name, "The bastard." My partner grinned and began calling Mullin's turn at bat. I guess impressions don't fade, because he said of the next hitter, "And now to Chuck the bastard, I mean batter." That shook up the network a bit and made mine a shorter day than I thought.

—Bud Blattner

I'd never seen a minor-league game until I did the Hawaii Islanders of the Pacific Coast League in April 1970. For the next three years, I did road games via re-creation. What an acting job—strictly make-believe, and so many close calls trying to broadcast in a studio in downtown Honolulu. A Cuban refugee ran the studio board, whom we'd hand-signal to raise or lower crowd noise, or whack wood with something as though to say, "Boy, that ball is hit!" Above all, you prayed for a phone call from somebody in the press box wherever the Islanders were playing on the mainland.

One day the call didn't come, and, at the end of three innings, we've got no information. We're waiting, and my partner Al Michaels finally says, "Well, that's it. Now Ken Wilson with the fourth inning." And I had absolutely nothing true to say about the Islanders at Tucson. Al got up, and away I went: The manager comes out, weather turns bad, a big wind came up and blew dust around the ball park. I was very young and struggling to death, and Michaels is down on the floor laughing his head off. Don't sell me on the nostalgia of re-creations.

—Ken Wilson

Henry Aaron's 715th home run wrote history April 8th, 1974, in Atlanta Stadium. But as George Plimpton said, chronicling the homer that broke Babe Ruth's record, "Maybe I'd been rehearsing and didn't even know it." In the old days, I re-created a basketball playoff game in Davenport, Iowa, and a Three-I League baseball twin-bill. The basketball was in the afternoon, so we delayed baseball and re-created it at night. As I began the double-header, I learned there'd been 37 walks. Holy Toledo! How'd you like *that* finale to a day?

Later I broadcast the Cubs and White Sox, and I'd re-create a game for their network when the team wasn't scheduled. That put you at the transmitter's mercy. You'd do the Senators-A's—both near the cellar—and one team scored nine to lead, the other rallied, and you're jazzing up a game that otherwise wouldn't matter. Then you get a correction on the ticker: "They only scored one run in that last inning." Gee, what a stinker. That leads to Roger Maris' home run on the last day of 1961. The White Sox and Orioles closed the season Saturday so the Colts could have Memorial Stadium Sunday. The next day we were obligated to re-create a game for our Sox' network. We pick Yankees-Red Sox, and Maris smacks No. 61 to break Ruth's mark.

OK. Let's go to 1974. Henry had tied Babe's record of 714 on Opening Day in Cincinnati. Then trouble. [Commissioner] Bowie Kuhn's worried Atlanta would bench Aaron to save 715 for our Monday home opener, so he orders him to appear in prior games. That Sunday in Ohio, Aaron didn't homer. So the stage was set for April 8 against L.A. and a roaring Atlanta crowd. Aaron walks in the second and scores on an error by Bill Buckner— that name will appear again. In the fourth, a Bill Russell error puts Darrell Evans on, and up comes Aaron. He hits a drive to left, and Buckner climbed the old wire fence in Atlanta-Fulton County Stadium and almost caught the ball before it reached the bull pen and the waiting glove of Tommy House.

All winter, Plimpton had tried to get me to say what I'd do when Aaron homered. I told him, "No, gotta' be spontaneous." I wanted to say that Aaron and Ruth were the same age, both hit No. 714 as Braves, and so on. Fortunately, I waited 'till the ceremony at home plate with the fireworks before I included that. [The call: "He's sitting on 714. Here's the pitch by (Al) Downing . . . swinging . . . There's a drive into left-center field! That ball is gonna' be . . . outa' here! It's gone! It's 715! There's a new home-run champion of all time! And it's Henry Aaron! Henry Aaron's coming around third! His teammates are at home plate! Listen to this crowd!"]

What odds would you give that the guy who called Maris' 61st would describe Aaron's toppling of the Babe? I'm telling ya'. The greatest stories in baseball are the most bizarre.

—*Milo Hamilton*

I started doing baseball in 1965 for the Dallas-Ft. Worth Spurs in the Double-A Texas League. We were on this 50,000-watt clear channel station and got mail from 39 states and all the ships at sea. One lady in Birmingham, Alabama, kept moving her huge old-fashioned Zenith radio around the living room—pushing it from one place to another—till she picked up the broadcast. Or how about our player from San Anselmo, California, in the Bay Area? Each night, his parents drove up to the top of a mountain, left the car radio running, and ate a picnic dinner.

Now, this was near the end of an era where minor league announcers did re-creations from the studio when the club went on the road. We had a great audio engineer who didn't miss a thing. To please our beer sponsor, he'd tape a vendor actually saying, "Get your Falstaff here!" Near the El Paso park was a mission. So for an 8 o'clock game, he rang the mission bells and taped 'em, but only seven, to accommodate a time-zone change between Dallas and El Paso. Oh, yeah, the airport. Let's say a flight from Dallas to El Paso was due to land at 8:05 P.M., El Paso time. Our guy called to see if the plane was on time. If it was late, he'd wait till it landed, then put his airplane-noise tape on at precisely the right time.

I loved making most of the stuff up. Start a story, and you got time to finish because you'd invent an equipment change or have somebody go to the dugout. All sorts of things, and the fans never knew! That first season went smoothly until the second month. Then, one night, the Spurs play the Braves in Austin, Texas, and the ticker dies. First thing I do, have the batter foul off five straight pitches. Then I get creative and from our Dallas studio saw in Austin a *snake* meandering into the screen behind the catcher. The fans start screaming as our engineer plays war whoops, chairs moving around, the umpire calling time. We have players from both dugouts form a semicircle around home plate. They're watching to see what it was; nobody wanted to fool with a snake. The groundskeepers cowered because it might be, it looked like, hey, it could be a water moccasin, and they can kill! Ain't show biz grand.

By now we're rollin'. I say the umps have phoned the Humane Society. That, of course, took time. Had to get a number, call, and, on the air, you could hear in the distance the siren from the Humane Society van as it neared the park. We had men get out with ladders and long wooden sticks with pinchers on the end to try to catch the snake. Every time it bobbed his head, he'd weave through more of the screen. People are transfixed! For 20 minutes we tell the snake story, and then the ticker goes back on. So we immediately have the Humane Society grab the snake, get it down, put it in a box, close the box, put the box into the vehicle, slam the door of the vehicle, and away they went.

I went back to the game, which wasn't nearly as good.

—*Charlie Jones*

For six years, I did the Hawaii Islanders, whose three-week road trips made it too costly to do live. It was all re-creation—when guys forgot to call from location, you had to dream up things to buy time—and in the '70s that included streaking. We'd describe a young man jumping out of the stands and running naked across the field, and how security people chased and finally caught and cuffed him. Anything until we got the hi sign from our assistant that the phone call had come through.

But, hey, we went beyond that. We had people fall out of the stands and receive medical attention. Third base came uprooted, and the grounds crew had to fix it. Rain was a great way to stall even if it's sunny. Which leads to 1978. I did a talk show from a local bar and restaurant called the Columbia Inn, and my wife-to-be, Julie, and I decided that we'd get married there because it's where we spent so much of our time. The wedding was set for 9 at night, and our baseball started at 7:30. So, to get married on time, I staged maybe the fastest game ever played.

"Here's Jones into his windup, the pitch, high fly ball to left field—one out. Next batter can't wait to hit, sprints to home plate, here's the pitch, ground ball, throw to first—two outs"—fast-forward. The re-creation lasts maybe an hour, I rush to the Columbia Inn, and the rest is history. Or should I reserve that term for my last game in the minors, 1978, having accepted a job as Voice of the NBA Bullets. For my final re-creation, I install every sound effect conceived by man.

We got people screaming, fire engines, police sirens, thunder, canons booming—don't ask how we got 'em in the game. The third inning, a plane flies overhead and drops bombs, and we crack up, then try to explain our way out. A lion's roaring in the jungle, must be the bull pen. Any other time, and I'd be fired. But I'm leaving, so they let me have my fun.

—*Mel Proctor*

CHAPTER TWO

JUST LIKE YESTERDAY

EARLY MEMORIES

*P*erspective is all," a teacher once said. In my youth, a Waite Hoyt, Ned
Martin, or two Jacks—Buck and Brickhouse—made baseball dominance,
not diversion. Hitting fungoes, citing batting averages, or trading Red Sox' play-
ing cards for a dog-eared Mickey Mantle, my friends and I thought of little else.

The upstate New York town where I grew up divided the lowland of Lake
Ontario and rolling scenery to the south. Winter ended with pepper, catch, and
Little League. Summer brought pickup games in a field adjacent to a cemetery.
Rites linked grass stains, broken windows, and our Holy Grail a long drive, an
automatic homer—clanging off a stone.

In Caledonia—pop. 2,188, one bar, six churches, no traffic lights, and 300
miles from the nearest big-league park—each player aped a universe. I chose the
Yankees' bantam second baseman, Bobby Richardson—to my father, "a fine
family man and Christian gentleman." Germane to me was Bobby's smooth
sailing at the double play. Then, back home for radio/TV plots and stories and
comedy that rounded out scenes.

Later, we learned how "Baseball is like church," as Wes Westrum said.
"Many attend, but few understand." At the time, I knew it as umbilical cord—a
small boy's link with the outside—and was not alone. Few forget ingress to
baseball, or the craft that becomes a career.

I was born [on Valentine's Day, 1913] in Johns, Alabama, and graduated
from grammar school and high school a little before the usual age [11 and
15, respectively]. It wasn't that I was a genius, just that Johns was so tiny that

we had outhouses. I was four or five, and, whenever I had to go to the bathroom, I'd take a Sears or Montgomery Ward's catalogue and look at pictures of baseball gloves and bats. When I was done, I'd go inside and have Dad or Mom [Julius and Anna Israel, both natives of Russia] read me what was under this or that picture. I learned baseball that way, and to read before I got to kindergarten—skipping three or four classes in elementary school. Today we have an education crisis. Maybe outhouses would help; you might even call them "johns."

—*Mel Allen*

Looking back, certain objects stick in memory. I grew up listening to Graham McNamee do boxing. Our radio was a rectangular box called an Arbiphone, the strangest-looking thing you've ever seen. To hear more than a jumble, you had to adjust—exactly—three different dials. The speaker itself rested on top of the box. The box looked like a big question mark. Worse, it *sounded* like one. But it made me aware that there was such a *thing* as broadcasting.

From then on radio owned me. Years later I went to the University of Tennessee. Our football games were aired from the second deck of a wooden shack on top of the stadium's left stands. And the only way to reach it was by climbing a wooden stepladder that swayed in the wind. Once there, you were stuck, because coming down was even more terrifying than going up.

One day in November 1939, I was spotting for Jack Harris, who did play-by-play of Tennessee games over WSM ["The Station of the Grand Ole' Opry"]. Keep in mind that swerving stepladder, and that there were no restrooms inside the broadcast shack. At half-time I climbed down to get the statistics from the Tennessee athletic department, which I'd then take back to the booth. I get there, and see Harris staring at me with a pained expression. "Here are the stats," I said. "*You* do 'em," he said.

Jack had drunk a second cup of coffee at brunch that morning, and I guess the extra cup was too much for him. So as he rushes off to find a restroom, I'm reading the stats. My broadcast career had begun! If Jack Harris had been content with a single cup of coffee, my life might have turned out differently. There but for the grace of Maxwell House go I.

—*Lindsey Nelson*

My career's been hit or miss. The hits were my grandmother, a high school classmate, and a balky elevator—all of which led to baseball.

I grew up in a Massachusetts boarding house owned by my grandmother. A tenant was Cornelius McGillicuddy—to the public, Connie Mack—and he stayed there as a semipro. The stories he relayed to my grandmother she later told to me. I left high school with no special talent. Knowing I loved music, a girl in my class dared me to take an audition as a dance band singer at the local radio station [WRAW, Reading, PA]. I took it, and they hired me as a sportscaster. Singing didn't lose a Sinatra.

The elevator helped me a few years later. I was working at WIBG in Philadelphia, and one day in 1946 they had radio appreciation day at Shibe Park. The ceremonies on the field were being handled by By Saam and Claude Haring, who got delayed in the elevator, and the game began with no one behind the mike.

I was alone in the booth and took over until they arrived. Les Quailey was an executive with the N.W. Ayer ad agency, and when they got there he said, "Chuck's doing OK. Let's keep him on an inning." That inning's lasted 50 years.

—Chuck Thompson

My father and mother were dead before I was five. I don't remember either one. I lived with friends of theirs, and then with an aunt married to the brother of my mother. One day the brother of my mother disappeared, and yet I lived with my aunt during my high school years. She's as close to a mother as I ever had.

Knowing that I'm part Italian—my father's name was Carabina—people'd say, "Oh, are you from the Hill in St. Louis?" I'd say, "Hell, the Hill in St. Louis is like Beverly Hills compared to where I came from at 1909 LaSalle Street." Each day, I made 37 to 40 cents by selling papers. A leasing and lending library was right on the corner. I'd go in and get a book for only 3 cents—lots of 'em on baseball. I'd go to the soda fountain. It cost me 10 cents for a chocolate marshallow sundae. Before I finished, I was halfway through the book. When I came back the next day, I returned the book and got a new one. Looking back, that may have been the start of my career.

—Harry Caray

I was four when my parents moved our family to Columbia, Tennessee, 40 miles from Nashville. From then on, I was smitten by radio. That was especially true during the World Series, when our entire town became a festival. The games were in the afternoon, and we got to go into the auditorium during recess or a non-class period to hear the Series. Not the kind of privilege—nor event—you're soon likely to forget!

One October, I had a history class in a room near the auditorium. We had no air conditioning, and it was still hot outside. So the windows were open, and I found that by paying attention I could hear the broadcast as I sat in class. One day our teacher was talking about Julius Caesar. I was more intent on hearing Lou Gehrig double. Spying my inattention, the teacher, referring to Caesar, asked, "Lindsey, who was that?" I immediately exclaimed, "Gehrig—doubled to right!"

Many years have passed since then. I am pleased that my priorities were correct at such a precocious age.

—*Lindsey Nelson*

A s a kid I sold pop, popcorn, and papers in Ponce de Leon Park, home of the Southern Association Crackers, and was a visiting team bat boy. I began reading *The Sporting News* and thought their coverage of my Crackers was, shall we say, inadequate. I had no experience as a baseball writer, but I knew that *The Sporting News* then had no Atlanta correspondent. So I sat down and applied in a letter to the editor, Edgar G. Brands. I signed it "W. Earnest Harwell"—anything to seem older. I got a letter back asking me to "shoot some stuff along." Mr. Brands didn't know I was 15 years old.

His letter was dated August 7, 1934, and my first article appeared a week later. I kept writing but didn't have the courage to contact Cracker head Earl Mann. "Who *is* this guy, W. Earnest Harwell?" Mann kept asking. Nobody knew. Finally, I showed up to write a feature about him, and we became friends; Earl hired me for my first play-by-play. After World War II, I came back from overseas to work for him in 1946. That team won a pennant.

One of the '46 Crackers who went on to the big leagues was Lloyd Gearhart, who had a lasting impact on the Harwell family. My first son was three when his mother told him, "Bill, the Lord's going to bring us a baby." One day, Lloyd rang our doorbell. My wife, Lulu, was busy, and I was in the back yard. Bill answered the ring and came running to his mother. "Mama," he shouted, "the Lord is here and he doesn't have our baby."

—*Ernie Harwell*

Being raised near Chicago in the little town of Naperville—not so little now, but it was then—the first game I saw was at Comiskey Park. My dad took me to see the White Sox play Washington—a rainy day, field covered, not much of a crowd. So we were able to obtain seats behind the Senators' dugout.

I'm an 8-year-old kid wide-eyed at my first major league game, just praying that the rain subsides so I can see a game. Because of the weather there was no batting practice—nothing for the players to do. Maybe that's why Mickey Vernon, who now, incidentally, is a neighbor of mine in Wallingford, Pennsylvania, popped his head out of the dugout and saw this excited kid. He picked me up, took me in the dugout, introduced me around, and gave me a ball. Thus began my love of baseball—and of the Washington Senators until they moved to Minnesota [in 1961].

From then on my life-long goal was to become a big-league announcer. As a kid I didn't know what kind of voice I'd have, but I knew my limitations as a player. It's a good thing I could talk better than I hit the curve.

—Harry Kalas

I grew up in the San Francisco area. It's fair to say I was strange as a child. Friends would say, "Let's go surfing in Half Moon Bay." I'd answer, "Hey, I got a big series [on the baseball board game, Stratomatic]. I got the Dodgers and Cardinals for four, and then the Giants and Dodgers finally meet at Dodger Stadium—first place up for grabs. If there is any way I can get away I'd be with you—but, hey." We never met.

There I was wasting away my youth. Every day I'd roll dice—that's how you play the game—and became the whole park rolled into one. I was the public address announcer. [Echoing the Yankees' Bob Sheppard]: "The right fielder, Number 9, Roger Maris—Roger Maris—Number 9." And the organist. That was, "Dunt, dunt, dunt, dunt"—sometimes in key. Then I was Russ Hodges doing play-by-play—"The 1-1 pitch to Maris—base hit" [crowd sound effect]. Very weird.

It was a pretty odd sight for someone to walk in on me [again, crowd sound effect]. They'd say, "Mrs. Miller, who *is* this?" My mother would always deny that she knew who the hell I was. "I've never seen him before. It sounds, though, like he has a little bronchial condition."

—Jon Miller

I've done golf and basketball and Winter and Summer Olympics to women's field hockey, but baseball has a special place in my heart. My dad was a U.S. senator, so we lived in Washington, and as a kid I'd sit in the dugout with Connie Mack and get a fascinating view of this man with a high starched collar and great dignity. A family friend, Herbert Dubois, kinda' baby-sat me because Dad and Mom were busy in the whirl of the D.C. social set. Among his friends were people like Mr. Griffith [Senators' owner Clark] and Al Schacht, the clown prince of baseball.

The game's changed a lot since then, and the big money is a big reason why. Technology, stadia, Astroturf are all different. But the game itself is still The American Game. Baseball can go along so slowly and rather dully for eight innings, and then in the ninth a crescendo rises with the tying run at first, the bases loaded, three and two, two out—uncanny. It has a way of developing like no other sport—plus, peerless memories. One of my all-time was doing the first-ever game of the Florida Marlins in April '93—seeing Charlie Hough get the win and Bryan Harvey the save, a sellout crowd, Joe DiMaggio throwing out the first pitch—to be a part of baseball coming to Florida.

Best of all, the Marlins beat the Dodgers!

—*Jay Randolph*

In 1957, the Dodgers and Giants were winding up in New York, and my father took me to the Polo Grounds and Ebbets Field. I remember the stunning smells and cheering and emerald green of the diamond. Baseball to me had been radio, or gray images on TV; like most people, we had black and white. Suddenly I walked into Ebbets Field at night and saw this vision, like *The Wizard of Oz* when they land in Oz and change from black and white to Technicolor. I don't even remember the game.

The first game I remember was at Yankee Stadium. I was seven, and it was the next-to-last day of 1959, a year the Yankees *didn't* win the pennant [missing only twice in 1949-64]. My dad took me and my cousin, we sat in the bleachers, and I was sure a ball'd be hit there—457 feet to the left-center field barrier. My cousin and I had our gloves and each inning kept moving down a row to the field. You know—490 feet away, no chance, but at 457 we're a cinch to catch a homer. The Yankees lost, 7-2. Then what I remember happened. In those days, you could leave by way of the field. Fans could walk by the dugout, on the warning track, and exit by way of gates they opened in center field or bullpens in left- and right-center that opened into the street and elevated subway behind Yankee Stadium.

The Yankees didn't have Roger Maris yet. So I stand in front of the 344 sign in right field, and pretend I'm Hank Bauer jumping up and robbing somebody of a homer. We go to right-center, and now starts my loss of innocence. Out there is the pristine "407" that looked so clean on TV, and it was full of graffiti. People had written "Joe loves Sally" and things like that. I hated Joe and Sally because I didn't care what the hell they did on their own time, but I couldn't grasp why they'd desecrate a shrine. We got to center field where the flag pole and monuments were [to Babe Ruth, Lou Gehrig, and Miller Huggins], 461 feet from home plate. Since they remodeled the Stadium, they've been moved behind the fence in left-center, but then they were on the playing field. I stand there reverently and start crying, and my father asks what's wrong. I told him I was sure this was the sacred Yankee burial ground where Ruth, Huggins, and Gehrig were laid to rest—and that when Joe Dimaggio went and Mickey Mantle followed him, they'd be buried right next to them.

The solemnity of the situation was just too much for me. I broke down. My father tried to reassure me: "They're dead, but they're buried someplace else." I was having none of it, so we walked to the street hand-in-hand and left my real first game.

—*Bob Costas*

B aseball in Brooklyn was another planet. The first game that I attended was in 1949. My father took me to Ebbets Field, which was within walking distance of our apartment on Ocean Avenue. Jackie Robinson played for them. Duke Snider, Carl Furillo, and Pee Wee Reese—all the boys of summer. Add Red Barber, a young Vin Scully, and a great announcer by the name of Connie Desmond who got lost in the shuffle—nothing like it before, or since.

Even in the late 1940s and early '50s, New York had an education crisis. Our school had a lack of funds, so I went only a half-day. Thank God it was 8 to 12! That let me go to Ebbets Field for games that started at 1:30. I had what we called a GO card—I think it stood for General Organization— which for 25 cents got you into the left-field grandstand. On weekends my dad took me, and we'd have better seats above the broadcast booth. My first remembrance in life is Ebbets Field, looking down into the booth at the back of Red Barber's head and saying, "What a job—can you imagine, seeing every game for free." It's where I learned to love baseball—and what got me into broadcasting.

—*Al Michaels*

My first broadcast was in the early 1940s between schools too small to play regular football—Pine Bluff and St. Mary's in Cheyenne, Wyoming—so they played a six-man game four blocks from my home. Sub-zero weather. About 15 fans, and 14 relatives of players, on hand. My mother drove me down to the field on a cold November afternoon, and there were no yard lines, no sidelines, no goal posts. I stood on a soapbox and broadcast for a tiny station. The players went on the field—no numbers—kicked off, and I made up the whole game. Still the best broadcast I ever did.

—*Curt Gowdy*

We only did a few games in the early days of television. Even then I'd be on radio most innings—it being the prime outlet—and climb down a little ladder to do a couple innings on TV. We had just one staff—as opposed to today's three for cable, [free] TV, and radio—and starting in 1949 we had a simulcast. That meant you did your regular radio over one microphone—and on a secondary mike talked to people watching on TV.

You can imagine the problems of using the same words over different vehicles. Some guys said, "Don't talk too much for TV because people can see what is happening." The only trouble is that TV wasn't yet saturating homes. So you had to use some of your radio style to accommodate listeners, while at the same time pulling back so not to overwhelm viewers. Good luck! Talk too little, and you offended people who need you to describe things. Too much, and you get letters about TV.

I remember the 1958 World Series—not a simulcast, but it proves my point. A wire reached me in Game Two. It read, "Allen, you Yankee-lover, shut up." The message was sent two hours before the game *began*. In the end, you just do the best you can. People think what they're gonna' think.

—*Mel Allen*

I played baseball at Duke University, then the springboard college for play-ers hoping for the majors, but by the end of World War II my aim was broadcasting. The supply corps had stationed me in Washington, so I called on radio stations there for work. The best offer was from WINX, owned by *The Washington Post*. Working for its station boosted my career, but they didn't have rights to Senators' games. I yearned to do their play-by-play, and it came about through this magic box, television, that I'd heard added pictures to words.

I called on an enterprising gentlemen, Les Arries, Sr., who was getting set to put Washington's first TV station, WTTG, on the air. The only other station in the country was WABD in New York. In retrospect, it's amazing how few people had faith in this new invention. Radio was so firmly entrenched that it took years before TV schedules were even printed in papers. Broadcast columns were devoted entirely to radio in TV's early years.

These early television models were small, sold as part of big cabinets, with flickering pictures, and programming limited to sports events and a few studio shows. In those days, appliance stores, trying to lure customers and sell TV sets, showed the picture in the window while piping sound into the street. What helped was that my early baseball-playing days helped get me close to the players; I'd work out in uniform and gain insight. In spring training, I was a great morale booster for young rookies. I'd take batting practice with the irregulars and keep spirits high. "If that guy's a big-league player," I could fancy them saying, "I've got a real chance to make the club, too."

A lot more kidding went on then. Ballplaying seemed more like fun, not business. The lobby was always the social gathering place. Players hung out there by the hours, spinning tales, talking strategy, discussing inside baseball. They roomed together, stars and rookies. Baseball was the talk, not contracts, agents, free agency, or all the business, legal, and police blotter entanglements we see today. Larger salaries have resulted in less enjoyment—to my mind, not much of a trade.

—Bob Wolff

B y 1955, I'd been working minor-league baseball for more than 15 years when I got a call from the Dodgers that they were looking for an announcer. Lindsey Nelson and I had worked together at Liberty, and now he was at NBC. Curt Gowdy had been a friend in the Texas League and was now in Boston. I lived in Dallas and was talking to Baltimore when the offer came from Brooklyn, just when I'd abandoned hope that my chance would ever come.

I'm told to report to spring training in February 1956.

One of the Brooklyn announcers was Connie Desmond, who had a drinking problem and missed a lot of games at the end of '55. Well, about February 1st comes a call from New York saying that Mr. [owner Walter] O'Malley had decided to give Connie another chance. He got a reprieve after I'd given up all my jobs: public relations, two sports shows, basketball and hockey. I somehow retrieved them, including play-by-play for the Dallas club in the Texas League. Amazing. It was affiliated with the Giants, and here I was negotiating with the Dodgers!

In mid-August I got another call. Connie was gone again, and they asked if I'd finish the '56 season and work next year. I say, "OK," quit my jobs again, and fly to New York. Arrived early in September, got off the plane, looked at the big city, and figure I'm out of my league. But I stayed, and my first broadcast was at the Polo Grounds—a double-header between the Giants and the Dodgers—not a bad way to start! A couple weeks later I called Sal Maglie's no-hitter for the Dodgers. Brooklyn won the pennant, and I went to the clubhouse to interview the players. I've been gone four weeks from Texas, and here I'm talking to guys from Duke Snider to Jackie Robinson. It pays not to give up.

—Jerry Doggett

I was a Dodger coach when Dizzy Dean asked me in early '60 to join him on "Game of the Week"—I said yes, but was terrified! [Dean's first partner, Bud Blattner, resigned in October 1959.] I'd never done anything on the air. That first spring in Arizona I'd be in the stands taping play-by-play—not for broadcast, just practice—and *still* I had problems. Then I'd see Diz come over. "Having a little trouble, pod-nuh?" I say, "Boy, no kidding." He starts singing "The Wabash Cannon Ball"—that's all he had to do—and the whole *crowd* starts applauding. The season starts and I sputter. I settle down, then one week I have breakfast with [producer] Gene Kirby. I'm expecting Dean as Kirby says, "Oh, by the way, Diz is on vacation this week. You're doing play-by-play." I try to act unconcerned. He says, "You OK?" I say sure. He asks, "So how come you're pouring coffee on your pancakes?"

I loved Diz. Just being around him relaxed me. He knew when I was uneasy. He'd come in, "Poh-nuh, why don't I take over?" Or, "Pod-nuh, little problem here—here's what you do." And I'd just laugh. Sometimes I did a commercial. Diz'd come on the air: "Pod-nuh, let me pick this up, you just lost some sales." We'd get through a game, and then Diz had to call his wife. We had our ritual. "How'd it go?" I said when he got off the phone. Diz'd answer, "Pat said *I* was terrific." Wouldn't say another word, and we'd roar.

When I think how remote Diz could have been, and instead how he helped me. Well, I go to card shows. People come up and don't talk about the great Brooklyn clubs I played on. Instead, it's, "We loved you and Ol' Diz. Baseball was never better than when you two were on." My years with Diz were the happiest of my life.

—Pee Wee Reese

In the Minnesota Twins' first year, 1961, the club trained in Orlando and I was congratulating myself on my first opportunity to do major league baseball. It was a weekday—no broadcasts till the weekend—so I was sitting in the bleachers. Needless to say, I had a cold one in one hand and a hot dog in the other, and just by coincidence sat next to a Twins' scout.

We were watching the type of young left-handed pitcher that kills a manager. On the one hand, a great fastball—on the other, no control. A pitching coach would rave, "So what if he can't find the plate? We can teach him that—and breaking balls. But what a fastball!" He starts out with ball one high and outside, ball two high and outside, and so on. Finally, the scout looks at me and says, "Scotty, if they ever move the strike zone to high and outside we're seeing a future Hall of Famer."

I'll never forget that day—nor the pitcher, Ralph Lumenti.

—Ray Scott

Fans don't realize that most players don't know baseball rules beyond their own position. I was a Yankee infielder, and knew what happened at second base—but most stuff you don't pay attention to. Then you become a broadcaster, and you'd better know the rules because it's the only sport where some official doesn't jump up and say "traveling" or "15 yards for unnecessary roughness." My first play-by-play as a broadcaster was 1963 spring training at Ft. Lauderdale. "Oh, God, make this one easy," I kept hoping, "'cause I don't know what's going on."

My first day it hits me—I'm ignorant of everything on the field. I'm pleading for a quick inning—get me out of here!—three up and down. Instead, the first inning I do 12 guys came to the plate—passed balls, wild pitches, errors, and I can't review things for our audience 'cause I can't even keep score. The half inning mercifully ends, and I'm supposed to do the bottom. Mel Allen looks at me and says, "Jerry, I think you've had enough for today." I said, "You're right"—went over to the corridor and got into a fetal position and curled up.

—Jerry Coleman

Baseball's tie does bind. Edwin Martin, Jr., was first to instill in me a love of the game. When I grew up in Wayne, Pennsylvania, my dad was a semi-pro pitcher and a life-long fan of the A's. He took me to my first game at Shibe Park in 1932 when Foxx and Grove and Cochrane and all those guys were playing. I was an Athletics' fan until the [1955] time they left Philly.

I'll never forget working on the Pennsylvania Turnpike and listening to the Yankees sweep the Whiz Kids in the 1950 World Series. Those Phillies were an Impossible Dream team long before my '67 Red Sox. What a wonderful time their pennant brought to Philadelphia—Robin Roberts and Curt Simmons, Del Ennis and Andy Seminick, Jim Konstanty. My dad and I saw a bunch of games together. But it was a long time before the Phillies gave him much to cheer for again. In '64, the Red Sox weren't going anywhere—but for a long time it seemed the Phillies were going to the World Series. They had a 6 and a half game lead with 12 games left to play—then ran out of gas and blew it.

That fall, the Red Sox left on a road trip and I stopped by to see my dad in Wayne. He'd had several heart attacks already that year. He was thin, seemed tired, but looking forward to going with his cronies when hunting season came. I was worried, but said good-bye and off I went. A few days later I was to call a Yale football game. That morning my wife, Barbara, called and said, "Your dad has died." I called my mother. She said, "Finish the road trip, there's nothing you can do." That night I got to Detroit to join the Sox, and my dad's death hit me as I went to bed. We came home as the Phillies were losing 10 straight games and the pennant. A letter was waiting for me from my dad. After I'd left Wayne, he predicted the Phillies' collapse. "I don't see how they can win," he'd written. "They're still ahead but they keep pitching Jim Bunning and Chris Short and nobody else. I'm afraid they're going to fold."

He went on to say how much he enjoyed seeing me and how he loved the kids. By now, I completely broke down. It was my father who started me with baseball. I was glad that I had made the major leagues because I knew it made him proud. The fall of 1964 could have been wonderful. But the Phillies' collapse and Dad's death really brought a resounding nothing to its end.

—*Ned Martin*

My first three Yankee partners were Mel Allen, Red Barber, and Phil Rizzuto. Red was a great teacher—Mel, the pro. Scooter and I were kids who had a wonderful time but maybe not as professional as you'd like. When you first get off the ground as a broadcaster, you're so insecure and want to impress people that you need someone to pat you on the back—tell you you're doing a great job. Kids ask, "How long does it take to be a broadcaster?" I say, "Well, in 10 years you may know what you're doing." My first year in New York I had a lot of things happen to me that weren't so great. The worst was somebody sending me a record—one of those old 33 RPM discs. The title of it was "Famous Jungle Sounds" and on the bottom it said, "Listen to yourself." Not exactly the best way to build confidence.

—*Jerry Coleman*

I played football and basketball at Illinois Wesleyan. After college, I figure there's nothing left to do but major league baseball. The [1969] American League expansion teams were Seattle and Kansas City. I wrote the Cardinals asking if I could bring a recorder, find a spare booth and do a game. They agreed—so I loaded the recorder and reel-to-reel tapes in my car and headed to St. Louis. Later, applying for the Kansas City job, I sent the three half-innings that sounded best.

This was early '69—the Royals were looking for a second banana, having hired Buddy Blattner as Number One. A friend told me: "Look, a lot of people'll apply. Make yours unique. It's not enough that they like your tape. They gotta' *remember* you." Schlitz beer was the Royals' primary sponsor—that's why a Milwaukee agency had the account. So I go to a local Schlitz distributor and pick up menus they gave bars and restaurants. On the outside was a Schlitz ad—inside, blank, for the local place to print its menu. They also had serving trays with a Schlitz logo. I printed my resume on the menu pages, put my tape in the round serving tray, and sent 'em off.

That was my packaging—that, and a letter I'm ashamed of. I wrote, "I hope you don't think I'm a bush-leaguer [August Busch leaguer?] for having done a Cardinal game, but here is my final pitch for the Royals' job." Ambition can be brutal—after all, the Cardinals gave me my chance. A couple months later I met Buddy Blattner, was one of 130 applicants cut to 3 finalists, and got the job. Who says corn's passé?

—*Denny Matthews*

By 1974, Charlie Finley'd owned the A's for 13 years and had more broadcasters than managers—and he had more managers than any team. Harry Caray was in Oakland for a year [1970]. Boom, he's gone. Then Bob Elson—Bob's in the Hall of Fame. Boom, Finley fires him. Then Jim Woods, one of the best broadcasters ever. Boom, he fired Woods. Jim went to the Red Sox. Best thing ever happened to Jim was Finley waving good-bye.

In '74, I sent Charlie a tape without any hope of getting a job. I had no baseball experience, but lucked out. Charlie had the tapes shipped to his announcer, Monte Moore, and this great guy listened as a matter of principle. He said, "If you take time to send a tape, I've got to listen." He liked the tape, played it for Charlie, and they hired me. I was 22, which I didn't list on my resume. I had little hair even then—already combing it forward. Guys wrote my biography after I was hired, and said how old are you? Better put 26, I said, on the biographies. What's truth in advertising when you've got baseball on your mind?

—*Jon Miller*

Baseball grabs you early or not at all. I grew up a Cubs' fan in Wood River, Illinois, who found that at night I could pull in the Cardinals, Cubs, Pirates, Reds. I was nine when the National League expanded in '62, and for some reason the new Houston Colt .45's caught my fancy. Imagine, a team in Texas! I'd listen over WWL, New Orleans, and WOAI, San Antonio, to Gene Elston, the Houston announcer, and it seemed magical. So I got this idea that if I jotted him a note, he'd respond. He does, and we start to correspond. Later, we met and discussed the game.

After college, I spent a couple years doing baseball in Oklahoma City. Dick King ran the club and gave me $100 a game to do everything at the park; the game itself seemed like recess. By '76, through Gene and Art Elliott, director of broadcasting, I did an Astros' audition one day at Wrigley Field.

I'm 23, and Gene's partner is *another* guy I'd heard as a kid. The previous fall the Pirates had fired Bob Prince, and he'd come to Houston, where common knowledge said he didn't like it. I'm going over notes in the press room, and Prince came up (he knew what's what, this kid may be replacing him), yet put his arm around me and said in that gravelly voice, "Don't worry, kid, we'll fuck it up together."

That fall Prince went back to Pittsburgh to do the hockey Penguins. I'm named to join Gene, who taught me that preparation is 90 percent of the job. Before I got there, he was also the club's official statistician, and, to this day, there are facts and situations I'll note because of him. Not to be allegorical, but baseball is Every Man's Game, and for the son of a farmer and steelworker to realize the dream I had as a kid sort of personifies what baseball's supposed to be.

—*Dewayne Staats*

In 1981, I was coming off the Dallas Mavericks' NBA season and went to Detroit to broadcast my first Rangers' game. Walking into the dugout and then looking at a pasture [Tiger Stadium] that [Ty] Cobb was on: unbelievable. The director said, "Go get Danny Darwin"—the starting pitcher—"and we'll intersperse his interview in the game." I was full of myself back then, walked into the Ranger clubhouse and said to the trainer, "Is Danny Darwin here? I'm Mark Holtz"—you know, a big deal. He said, "Last I saw, he was sitting in the dugout." I go down, and at the end of the bench on this cold night is a man in a jacket and ear muffs.

I say, "I'm Mark Holtz, just done the Mavericks," and go through my litany. "I'd like to ask a few questions." He said, "I'll be glad to do it, except there's one thing you should know." I said, "What?" Charlie Hough said, "I'm not Danny Darwin." Charlie was the last pitcher to make the team in '81—and only because general manager Eddie Robinson got him from the Dodgers and was too embarrassed to release him. Great. Where's Danny Darwin to impress Texas in my first game? Here's my problem: I'm running out of time. So I said, "How 'bout us doing an interview?" He said, "I'll be glad to, but I haven't had much success." His ERA was about 12. My director asks me who I got to pre-tape the interview. "Charlie Hough." He goes, "Charlie Hough?" I said, "Let's just do this." My face was red.

My first question is, "After those years with the Dodgers, what's the American League like?" Charlie says, "I don't know. I've only pitched in two games." I ask, "How do you like the parks here?" He says, "Don't know. I've only pitched at home." I ask, "How do you like Detroit? I hear the ball carries here." He says, "Again, don't know. I've never pitched in Detroit." We go on—finally talk about his knuckleball—but I hadn't found Darwin and figure I still don't have an interview. If Darwin goes nine innings, we won't have a word.

Now the miracle. Darwin pulled his muscle in the third inning. No one's warmed up, and our manager, Don Zimmer, is in a muddle. He didn't want to wreck his rotation early in the season, so in comes Hough—unknown, so far atrocious—and suddenly I marvel at my luck. He got out of the inning, then threw about 10 pitches in the fourth—all knuckleballs swung on and missed. We go to the seventh, and Charlie's pitched a perfect game since Darwin left! I'm doing cartwheels. By now, the same director riding me in the first couple of innings for getting Hough had changed his tune. He asks me to say (and I do), "I think it's time to use my Charlie Hough interview to tell the fans what this man is like." In the eighth inning, we use the interview, and everyone back in Texas applauds my genius.

Charlie went on to become the all-time winningest Ranger pitcher, but he never had more luck than I did that day.

—*Mark Holtz*

The first major league game I ever did was at Riverfront Stadium. I was calling Triple-A ball in Louisville—the Cardinals' top farm club—and we'd just clinched our division and drawn a millionth fan for the first time in the minor leagues. So I'm already up when I get a chance to sub for the late Dan Kelly on Cardinal radio the next day, because Dan was going through Canada doing interviews for his hockey broadcasts to begin that fall.

My father and I used to go out, sit in the car, turn the radio on outside of Kansas City, and the only station we got the Cardinals on was KMOX, so we'd endure the scratchy reception to hear Harry Caray and Jack Buck. It'd always been my dream to do big-league baseball, and this is it, and I'm working with Mike Shannon and—I pinch myself—Buck. The booth in Cincinnati is up the first-base line, so it's hard to see when a left-handed batter drags a bunt. And wouldn't you know it: The first inning a guy bunts a ball, the throw hits him, but he's called out. I see the runner went into fair territory, and that's why he was out. Jack says the ball came up and hit the hitter leaving the batter's box, and *that's* why he's out.

I said on the air, "No, Jack, I think the throw hit him while he was in fair territory," and Buck looked at me like, *"What?* Don't correct me, son." He then asks Dick Wagner, the Reds' general manager next door, "Did that hit him?" And Wagner goes, "Yeah, in fair territory." I say, "Thank you very much"—and immediately see my career going up in smoke the first game I ever did with Jack. Still, I'm excited and start doing play-by-play like a machine gun—"Here's the first pitch, taken outside for a ball"—when Buck hits the call switch and goes, "Son, slow down. You're gonna' be on like 190 games a year if you do a team full-time; you'll wear them out by the end of the inning."

The next year, I went to work for KMOX covering some baseball and football Cardinal games, and I never stopped loving being around Buck and learning from the master.

—John Rooney

I was an alternate back-up Voice for NBC-TV's "Game of the Week" for four years, but I'll never forget how my first game turned to dust. I was 28 and ecstatic to have the chance off a recommendation from Bob Costas to work a "Game": Angels-Twins, with Jim Kaat. I'm fired up as the first game of the double-header ends early, and, to fill time until the 4 o'clock second games(Bob and Tony Kubek in Boston, and us in Anaheim), NBC switched to the back-up first game. The trailing team scores a run in the top of the ninth inning—tie score—and NBC's now obligated to stay with it until conclusion.

Well, that game went extra innings and was so long that it didn't end until our *second* games were over. We sat with Rod Carew, who'd recently retired from the Angels, and never got on the air. Thankfully, NBC later said this wasn't a one-shot deal, which was good because I was about ready to shoot myself.

—Ted Robinson

By 1986, I'd already done some minor-league and college games for ESPN-TV. But my debut covering a club was that year's New York Yankees—a frustrating, and learning, experience. It featured George Steinbrenner and Phil Rizzuto; what a 1-2 punch.

When I joined the club, Bill White, the Yankees' announcer, told me, "You're going to get notes from [owner] Mr. Steinbrenner telling you what to say. You have to make a stand." Good advice from a mentor. With Steinbrenner you had to prepare for anything. That was true of the Scooter, too. He was a lot of fun, but you never knew what was going to happen.

In those days, I did only color and only six innings a game. We're in Cleveland one night, and it's freezing. Come the seventh inning, and Rizzuto says, "Kaat, I got to go to the men's room." I say OK, Phil goes, and he never comes back. Our producer, Don Carney, says, "Where's that SOB? I know he went back to the hotel room; he does that all the time."

Phil did me a favor. Leaving me by myself, he forced me into play-by-play. I liked it, as Yankee fans do the Scooter. I'm glad he's finally in the Hall of Fame. Mr. Steinbrenner? He did not renew my contract after 1986; guess I'd stepped on too many toes. This may amaze him, but somehow I've survived.

—*Jim Kaat*

I got interested in broadcasting at three or four when my father [Will McDonough] covered the Red Sox for *The Boston Globe* and each spring training our family went down to Winter Haven. I'd be out of school a month, the teachers gave my mother lesson plans, I did school work before my father took me to the ballpark—and as he went about his business I sat in the booth with Ned Martin and Ken Coleman. They taught me to keep score and I was even on a pre-game show. From that I became a kid with a tape recorder who sat in front of the TV and broadcast games.

One of the great things about baseball broadcasting is how many people say, "You have the job I'd love to have." That's especially true in New England, where baseball's clearly number one. I mean, think of the great announcers they've had like Ken and Curt Gowdy and Dick Stockton—I feel a great responsibility to uphold that tradition. I'm still not sure there was ever a better radio announcing team than [1974-78's] Ned Martin and Jim Woods. I think of them and pinch myself. In my case baseball—unlike youth—wasn't wasted on the young.

—*Sean McDonough*

CHAPTER THREE

YOU WEAR IT WELL

THE VOICES ON ONE ANOTHER

*P*lato said, *"Before we talk, let us first define our terms." Perhaps he knew that baseball broadcasting is chockablock with slant. Pick baseball's most recognizable announcer: Is it Mel Allen, Harry Caray, or Red Barber? Most literate: Bob Wolff, Jimmy Dudley, or Vin Scully? Most volcanic: How 'bout Bob Prince or Dizzy Dean "sludding" into controversy? Most eclectic: Lindsey Nelson, Jack Buck, Dick Enberg, or Curt Gowdy?*

Statistics verify number of World Series called or All-Star Games dotted. They cannot show who makes of baseball existential pleasure, and to whom, and why. Who makes the muses dance? At the other end, who rivals Sominex? Who flaunts what the Pirates' late Rosey Rowswell observed: "It's not just play-by-play that matters. It's what you say between the pitches that counts"?

"Choose any announcer, and compare reaction," said 1942-65 Reds' Voice Waite Hoyt. "A Hades or Canaan? You'd never know you were talking about the same guy." Announcers talk, viewers and listeners respond, and only God has a monopoly on truth.

If you listen to games of the '30s, many sound like someone talking into a megaphone or reading wiretype. Not Red Barber. He was baseball's first prominent announcer [at 1934-38 Cincinnati and 1939-53 Brooklyn], and first to combine reporting skill with a lyric patter. Well-prepared, dotted every *i*, with a melodic way of speaking.

Barber at Brooklyn may have been the best ever. He had a lot more pizzazz than his Yankees' work in the 1950s and '60s. When he went to Yankee

Stadium [1954, joining Mel Allen], he still had the storyteller skills, but was more of a dry reporter, somewhat bitter, and the verve in his voice was gone. Barber on the Yankees wasn't anywhere near as good as Mel, who retained his enthusiasm and the voice so recognizable and those expressions. "Going, going, gone!" "How about that!"

Barber was loved by the press. Mel, like Harry Caray in a different way, embodied the warmth that a fan relates to readily. You can argue all day. Each side has a case. It's interesting that both were southern. [1962-78 Mets' Voice] Lindsey Nelson is from Tennessee. They had that easy way. Red's appeal soared because Brooklynites sensitive about the image as "Dees and dems guys—I'll meet ya' at Toydy-toyd and Second Avenue"—were delighted that this erudite man represented their borough. He'd do the World Series and mention bases being "FOB"—full of Brooklyns—or "rhubarb in the cat-bird seat" or tell a little homily. It put a gentler touch on Brooklyn.

At Ebbets Field, fans literally heard conversations on the field—saw faces of players without binoculars—more human than the most part today. Barber was the voice of that experience. [Talk show host] Larry King told me that you could walk down Brooklyn streets without a radio and never miss a pitch because somebody'd have the window open and Red's voice would loft out. You'd go by a newsstand; someone had the radio on. A cab stopped, and you'd hear the Redhead. He was everywhere.

Brooklyn was really a separate city within New York. Consider, too, the sociology of Jackie Robinson and then Roy Campanella breaking the color line and that post-World War II television hadn't taken hold—radio was still king. Add that the Dodgers were good enough to always contend for the World Series, but star-crossed enough to break your heart. Total it, and there'll never be a team that means as much to its city as the Brooklyn Dodgers. Or a Voice who meant more to his listeners than Red.

—Bob Costas

Walter Lanier Barber was radio's first poet, the beloved Voice of the Dodgers for 15 years, and a baseball announcer for 33. Except for my mother, he was also the most influential person in my life. My father died when I was young, and Red became like a father to me in every way.

I first heard Red when I was a kid in New York City. My family had one of those four-legged radio monsters that sat so high off the floor I could put a pillow under it and crawl up under it—actually, *under* it. I'd lie there for hours with a box of saltines and a carton of milk and listen to guys like Ted Husing do college football. I shouldn't have cared about games like

Alabama-Tennessee, but I was mesmerized. I'd get goose bumps hearing the roar of the crowd wash over me.

In school, the good nuns asked what we wanted to be when we grew up. Everybody else said doctor, nurse, or lawyer. Not me. I wanted to be a sportscaster. That was especially true when Red was hired by the Dodgers. I liked the irony of his soft voice informing Brooklyn's raucous fans. I sensed his justness. "That Barber," groused a Brooklyn taxi driver, "he's too fair." But what I admired most was how he made broadcasting a conversation with the listener, chatting as around a potbellied stove. He didn't listen to other broadcasters and urged me to do the same. Not that I couldn't learn from them; Red didn't want me to *copy* them.

He didn't want me to lose one precious ingredient that no one else could bring to the booth: *me*, and whatever qualities made me a human being. Anything I have done I owe in large part to Red.

—*Vin Scully*

I worked with Barber in 1948-49 at Ebbets Field and Russ Hodges at the 1950-53 Polo Grounds. Red was the perfectionist. Russ was an Everyman. He didn't have Red's flow of language, but knew the game and had an authenticity to his work. Barber was *better*. Hodges was better to work *with*.

Russ' first words to me were, "Let's have fun. There'll just be two of us working radio and TV. We'll do a good job, but we'll enjoy it." Russ respected Red, but affection ended there. Once they did a football game. "Red did the first quarter," Russ told me. "When he finished, Red introduced me to the audience, saying, 'Now, for the second quarter, here is Russ Hughes.' I said, 'Thank you, Red Baker,' and went into my play-by-play."

Russ loved to laugh. Our booth at the Polo Grounds was tiny, hard to get in and out of, and hung down from the upper deck. For a double-header, we did a between-games show on TV. "I hate this little booth," Russ'd say. "The worst part is there's no toilet." Eventually, we spelled relief by using paper cups. Out of sight, we'd urinate and then put the cups on the floor of the booth. One afternoon, a visitor kicked a cup over. The fluid spilled over the floor and leaked onto people in box seats below. Before long, Barney O'Toole, head usher at the Polo Grounds, appeared in our booth.

"Hey, you guys," he said, "we're getting complaints from people in the box seats. They said to quit spilling beer."

"Barney," I said, "if it's beer, it's used beer. We'll be careful, but don't tell those folks what really hit 'em."

—*Ernie Harwell*

Russ was the most thoughtful man in the booth I've ever seen, always looking out for his partner. I feel like Jim Woods [joining Hodges in 1957 at the Polo Grounds. Years later, Woods dubbed Russ "the greatest human being I knew."]. We called him 'The Fabulous Fat Man'—more fabulous than fat.

One thing I hate is people who knock Russ' call of Bobby Thomson's homer. [On October 3, 1951, Thomson's ninth-inning blast beat Brooklyn, 5-4, won the best-of-three playoff, and gave New York the pennant. Russ chanted, "They're going crazy! They're going crazy!" and five times cried, "The Giants win the pennant!"] It was baseball's greatest-ever call, part of Americana, a chapter in history.

It upset me when [in 1992] Red Barber was quoted that Russ' broadcast was unprofessional. Russ was dramatic, but also gave the essentials: score, meaning, who won and lost. He was nothing if not mature. Russ'd seen guys ruin careers by boozing before or during a game. He was adamant that only after the game was it OK. "Here's what we're gonna' do," he'd tell me. "If we win the game, we'll have a drink because we're happy. If we lose, we're gonna' have a drink because we're sad. The only way we won't go out and have a drink is if there's a tie."

The game goes 16 innings. Hobie Landrith's the catcher and returns the ball to Mike McCormick by throwing it over his head in the bottom of the inning to allow the tying run to score. The game ends by curfew, so it winds up in a tie. Just as Hobie throws the ball over McCormick's head, Russ scribbles a note and hands it to me. It says, "We're just gonna' break a rule."

—*Lon Simmons*

In 1951, five of the Hall of Fame's first six announcers—Mel, Red, Russ Hodges, Vin Scully, and Ernie Harwell—broadcast in New York. Choosing between Mel and Red is like comparing nobility. Either way you get a Sir. Some liked Barber, the professional southerner, who used all the phrases they had down there: "rhubarb," you know, or "catbird seat." Red *worked* at being a personality. Allen didn't, just *was*. Like his knowledge of the game, Mel's sayings were natural. Even "How about that!" was a phrase he grew up with in Alabama.

Mel was the best *ever* to broadcast the game. Which doesn't mean that he didn't have his days. In the 1950s, my boss as NBC sports director was a fellow named Tom Gallery who knew what he believed as to what should and should not be included in sports coverage, especially baseball, which he loved. Specifically, Tom felt that an announcer obsessed with statistics could numb the average fan. Which brings me back to Mel.

In one game of the 1958 World Series, Tom decided Mel had used enough statistics about how it compared numerically with the rest of Classic history. So he said, "*Enough* damned statistics. Just do the game." The trouble is that Mel had become America's premier sportscaster doing it *his* way, which explains why he now grabbed a book and started reading it beneath the table. It was *The Little Red Book,* a statistical volume. When Gallery saw what Mel was doing, his face got even redder.

I won't soon forget Tom looking for *anything* to whack Mel over the head with. Finally, he found a headset. It did the trick. "Didn't I tell you to leave statistics alone?" he roared. We had fewer the rest of that World Series.

—*Lindsey Nelson*

In 1954, I came to Kansas City to broadcast for the Blues, then a Yankees' Triple-A farm club. The next year the Philadelphia A's arrived, and I was asked to stay. There were then only 16 major league teams; the odds of getting a broadcast job seemed prohibitive. But the ad agency that purchased the A's rights decided they wanted local announcers—right place, right time.

I'll never forget my first trip to New York. I'd never been there, and Yankee Stadium overwhelmed me. I was preparing for my first game, doing my scorebook, when I stood up and saw this fellow walking toward me. I was shaking in my boots because it was the most famous broadcaster in America. He said, "Merle, I'm Mel Allen"—as if I didn't know—"Welcome to Yankee Stadium. If there's anything we can do to help you, why, we have a lot of statisticians . . . ," and I was stunned. This was a man that I had long admired, and here he was befriending me.

Broadcasting can be a jungle. You don't often see that type of kindness. I was really bewildered coming into that ball park. I'll never forget being put at ease by someone who I thought, and think today, was the greatest ever to do baseball.

—*Merle Harmon*

I was a journeyman announcer whose biggest break was to spend 32 years with [the 1950– Dodgers'] Vin Scully. I grew up in Iowa, and out of high school went to Chicago and lived with my mother for awhile. I'd always wanted to be associated with sports, preferably as a writer, but I didn't have enough ability, so I decided to try and talk my way through instead. I joined the Dodgers in 1956, and all of a sudden it was '87, time to get to know my family. So I retired and don't look back too often, but, when I do, my association with Vin is the highlight of my life. Vinnie used to say, "We haven't got married yet. We're gonna' have to pick out the silver and get ready." It was kind of a standing joke, and rare that two announcers get along as well. I can honestly say I worked with the best broadcaster to ever come down the road.

—Jerry Doggett

Bob Elson was a great announcer who perhaps lasted too long. We used to kid that Elson *had* to be on the take. I've never heard *anybody* do as much shilling when he was on the air. Bob'd mosey along and say, "There's ball two, and speaking of ball, did we have one last night at Rosa Mesa's Restaurant," or something like, "Al Lopez is making a pitching change now, and I know you'll like the change at" whatever restaurant he favored.

Now, it is true that baseball and commercials have always fused. Mel Allen would mix spots for White Owl and Ballantine with play-by-play, but they were regular Yankee sponsors. With Elson, the White Sox never got a penny for Bob's shilling. That's why announcers used to think Bob had to be getting a commission for these restaurants, bars, and the like. They get free publicity; he had to be getting bucks in return.

Say what you will about The Old Commander. If shilling was an art, Bob raised it to a new plateau.

—Lindsey Nelson

Waite Hoyt was a great announcer and, before that, pitched well enough to enter the Hall of Fame [winning 237 games in 1918-38]. He once confirmed for me a story. Anyone who played when the Dodgers were in Brooklyn knows about Brooklynese. They have a tendency to refer to someone by the name of Earl as "oil." But if they want a quart of oil in the car, they say, "Give me a quarter of earl." Once, Waite was sliding into second. And he twisted his ankle. Instead of getting up, he lay there, and a deep hush fell over the ball park. And then a Brooklyn voice was heard above all that silence. It said, "Gee, Hurt is hoyt."

—Ronald Reagan

Flipping the dial. Curt Gowdy was long-time Voice of the Boston Red Sox and really the Voice of NBC Sports in the '60s and '70s. Super Bowls, Final Fours, World Series, did "The American Sportsman" for ABC while at

NBC. One of the most versatile guys ever and good to all of his partners. Tony Kubek calls Curt his favorite partner to work with. I've tried not to take offense.

Gabby Street was baseball's first humorist on '40s radio. Today, you got the [John] Maddens and Dick Vitales. But the first to use humor to become a national figure on network TV was Joe Garagiola. Joe combined baseball's humanity with an expert's eye, transcended sport as long-time host of "Today," did game shows, parades, hosted "The Tonight Show." [In 1995, he called USA Network's coverage of the Westminster Kennel Club Dog Show.] Exempt Howard Cosell. Joe was the most recognizable person you'd call a sports announcer. Maybe it was the hair.

—Bob Costas

It was early in my broadcast career [1955] when I joined Dizzy Dean on CBS' "Game of the Week," a program which let millions of baseball-starved fans view big-league action for the first time. Diz didn't *provide* the program. He *was* the program. He created the audience before we ever said a word. It was going to be Dizzy Dean with me, or like he said, with "pod-nuh."

Working with Dizzy taught me a lot—among other things, the need to focus and prepare to fill in his gaps. Diz brought a very powerful and popular personality, utterly unpredictable, didn't worry about convention, did it his way. [Once, Dean refused to do a beer ad, because the date was Mother's Day.] He didn't know many players, keep a scorecard, or care about baseball's inner workings. "Score some runs," he'd say. Man, Diz was down to the basics. If he wanted to sing, he did—usually, "The Wabash Cannon Ball"—or go to the restroom and not reappear for an inning. One time, he left in the eighth inning—just walked out, never to be seen again.

Diz lacked a formal education but wasn't dumb. If ya' answer to "Dizzy," you're not supposed to be a Phi Beta Kappa, so he rarely got out of character. One day, on Mutual's "Game of the Day," he actually did a half-inning of polished play-by-play. Then, between innings he told me, "That's enough a' that poop. Now Ol' Diz is gonna' make some money," and proceeded to butcher the next half inning absolutely beyond repair. He winked 'cause, boy, he knew people loved it—guys returning to their "respectable" positions—everything he later made famous on CBS.

And, all the while, I was giving the score, trying to inject sanity, just marveling at Ol' Diz.

—Bud Blattner

Diz and I laughed about mistakes as only two ex-players could. [In 1960, Pee Wee Reese succeeded Blattner as Dean's "pod-nuh."] You know, if I butchered a name, he'd wreck it worse. Diz didn't take stuff seriously. If he wanted a steak, he'd leave me in the booth, and they'd get a picture of him eating. In Philadelphia, we had a steel ladder leading to the booth, and the shot showed Diz [at 300-plus pounds] overwhelming it. You couldn't help but laugh.

One day, Diz does four innings of play-by-play and I ask, "What would you say he's throwing out there?" Diz says, "Well, Pee Wee, I *have* been watching him four innings, and I believe that's a baseball." I'd do balls and strikes, and Diz'd fall asleep. I got a shot, nudged Diz, and said, "Pod-nuh, am I keeping you awake?" Same thing off-air. We're in the New York airport, and I'm walking ahead of Diz. He's got the Stetson, the western boots on. Everybody's shouting, "Hi, Diz. How ya' doing?" Diz shouts to me, "Hey, Pee Wee." I say, "Yeah." "How come you played here for 18 years and nobody knows you? Everybody knows Ol' Diz." I said, "Hell, if I had that hat on, everybody'd know me, too."

Once we were in his hotel room, and I said, "Dizzy Dean. High, hard fastball. I wish I could have the chance to hit your shit." Diz was in pajamas, like he always was, and started bringing his arm up in the air, like he was going to pitch. "You might have hit it, pod-nuh, but you'd be on your ass."

—*Pee Wee Reese*

In the '50s with the Milwaukee Braves I met my favorite broadcasters—Russ Hodges, the Dodgers' Vin Scully, the Cubs' Harry Caray. Raised in Chicago and later living in Green Bay, I also loved Bert Wilson of the Cubs—many thought we sounded almost identical in our delivery. As a consequence, Bert once knocked on the window that separated our booths in County Stadium and whispered that he had to go to the bathroom and couldn't hold it. "People think we sound alike," he said, putting our mikes together, "so don't pull for the Braves, just do play-by-play until I get back and nobody'll know the difference." Nobody said anything, so I guess nobody did. What a guy, Bert Wilson—died far too young [November 1955, at 44, of a heart attack]. I'll bet he's still doing his trademark chant, "I don't care *who* wins as long as it's the Cubs."

—*Earl Gillespie*

My relationship with Phil Rizzuto precedes his joining the Yankee broadcast staff. I'd covered him since the early 1940s—and though by the mid-'50s he was a backup shortstop the Yankees kept him 'cause he'd been central to their dynasty. In August 1956, the Yankees were in a tough fight for the pennant, and they needed a left-hand hitter when up pops an available player who'd been around quite a while.

The Yankees called Phil in and asked what he thought about the Cardinals' Enos Slaughter. He said, "Boy, gettin' him would sure help." What Phil didn't know is that Slaughter would replace him on the roster. The Yankees trade for Enos, release Phil, then say, "If we win the pennant and get in the Series, we'll give you a full share." Over the winter, the club goes further. They make Phil a member of the announcing team.

I could tell lots of stories about the Scooter and broadcasting. Early on, the Yankees were leading the Tigers, 4 to 2, in the ninth inning when the Tigers score twice and we go to extra innings. At this time, Phil only did two of nine innings. I said, "And now to take you into the tenth inning, here is . . ." And I look around, and no Phil! At that moment he was listening to this halfway across the George Washington Bridge going home. A true story. He thought he didn't have to tell anybody he was going to leave early.

Phil was great and is, but he got into a habit. Instead of doing the game, he had long lists of birthdays and he'd read them off even with the bases loaded. Bill White, a great first baseman who became president of the National League, was then a Yankee broadcaster. Bill is sitting there listening to a recital of all these birthdays. Suddenly, he interrupts and says, "Hey, Phil, don't you have a name on there that doesn't end in a vowel?" That's the Scooter—one of a kind.

—*Mel Allen*

One day in Kansas City, Phil Rizzuto and I were doing Yankees' radio and TV. It was so hot that we took off our pants and are dancing back and forth in shorts—boxer, I hope. About the fifth inning, somebody walks in, puts his arm on my shoulder, and says, "Put on your pants." In Kansas City, you could see into our booth from the catwalks, and some lady had seen us and complained. I thought, "Hm, that's stupid," that in the middle of the game—here I was, hot and miserable—I had to put my pants back on. Not that I took them off that often, anyway.

—*Jerry Coleman*

In 1957, the Phillies were about to begin a night game when their announcer, Gene Kelly, was informed that Joe McCarthy had died. Moments later Gene went on the air with a lyric tribute to the long-time manager. He recalled how Marse Joe never played in the major leagues, led the Cubs to a [1929] pennant, switched to the Yankees and forged a dynasty, and managed the Red Sox his final three seasons [1948-50] only to lose two pennants on the final day. In all, a five-minute poetic eulogy before Kelly took a commercial break. The phone in the booth rang. "Gene," said a voice from the studio. "That was a great tribute. But you had the wrong McCarthy. The one who died was Senator Joe McCarthy."

—*Ernie Harwell*

The first 11 years [1962-72] that I did Minnesota Twins' baseball one of my broadcast partners was Halsey Hall. Halsey was a legend in the Upper Midwest. He'd been a sports official, writer, and broadcaster, and his dream came true in late 1960 when Minneapolis-St. Paul acquired the Washington Senators. Talk about Cloud Nine. Major league baseball was coming here, and Halsey was hired as a color commentator. A great guy, kind-hearted, we had a lot of fun. A person that things happened to that wouldn't to anyone else. Halsey had a reputation of being frugal. One day the Twins were playing the Brewers in Milwaukee. My play-by-play partner was Ray Christensen, who mentioned on the air a talk he'd had with a player coming over on the team bus to the park. When Ray said that, I saw Halsey squirm, and, when we went to commercial, Halsey reached over, grabbed Ray by the arm, and said, "For Pete's sake, don't say anything about us riding a team bus. The station thinks I take a cab."

—*Herb Carneal*

Halsey was my 1961-66 partner with the Twins, a fantastic memory, though we accused him of telling stories from before we were born so that we couldn't dispute what he said. Halsey never met a foul-smelling cigar he didn't like, carried onions in his pocket if a restaurant didn't have them, and usually had a flask for something of an alcoholic nature. On road trips, he had a store in Chicago and Washington where he knew to the penny what his favorite beverages cost. He'd carry a small bag for clothing and a larger one for booze.

In Boston, we get on the bus after a game, and Halsey's already had a few belts in the press room. He's one of the last ones to board and can't find a seat, so he holds onto the strap, smoking a cigar, face glowing. A rookie finally said to him, "Mr. Hall." Halsey got the young man in focus and said, "Yes." The rookie said, "Everywhere there are bars. Why do you carry booze?" To which Halsey gave one of the classic answers of all time. He took the cigar out of his mouth and said, "Young man, one never knows when one will run into a local election."

—Ray Scott

A s a kid, I heard an announcer send a woman to a foreign land. Chuck Thompson had a voice made for radio—authoritative, yet gentle. When the Orioles did something good, he'd say, "Go to war, Miss Agnes!" I had no idea what he was talking about, but it sounded OK to me.

Chuck was a guy I picked up when I was 10, 11 years old and would fiddle with the car radio in the driveway on Long Island. This was before ESPN or CNN, so you turned to radio to follow baseball. On a clear night, you'd get seven or eight broadcasts from around the major leagues. You only vaguely knew what the ball park looked like, what the weather was, or anything until the announcer *spoke*. This romantic figure sitting in a booth somewhere. Baseball was nothing till he said it.

This wasn't TV, adding captions to picture, but a blank canvas. The announcer's art was style—the strokes and shadings; very personal—now mostly gone as the Thompsons and Jack Bucks and Ernie Harwells disappear and Bob Princes and Mel Allens and Red Barbers are dead or retired. For the most part, their sensibility of how to call a game isn't around any more. That's why Jon Miller is such a treasure. I listen to him, just like Chuck in the early and mid-'60s. In 1964, his Orioles were in a pennant race with my Yankees, so if the Yankees played by day, at night I'd listen to the Orioles playing Kansas City—and I'd root—actually try to *will* the Orioles to lose.

If they turned a double play or something to kill a rally, Chuck'd punctuate it with, "Mmm, ain't the beer cold!" It summed baseball up so perfectly, a guy sitting at home, sipping a beer on his back porch, listening to the game. What's any better?

—Bob Costas

When I was a kid in the 1960s, only NFL teams' road games were sent by CBS back to your city. In San Francisco, we'd get the 49ers. Other weeks we'd get a game of the week, and often it was the Baltimore Colts or Green Bay Packers. The Packers' Voice, Ray Scott, sounded like he was covering the Persian Gulf. "Starr. Dowler. Touchdown." What excitement! Then there'd be a Colts' game with Chuck [Thompson]. [Turning mimic]—"Well, Lenny Moore got about five yards of real estate." Listening to Chuck on CBS, I didn't even know he did baseball. The first time I learned better was my first ['74] trip into Baltimore with the A's. We come in at night; I get to my room and flip on the radio 'cause on the road I'm a pretty exciting guy. Turn to the O's game, and here's Chuck! What a voice! Recognized him instantly. For me it doesn't matter what he says—as long as he says it.

One of my favorites is [the Dodgers'] Vin Scully. Now, I just say, "Here's the pitch. A curve ball outside, 2 and 1." I speak English. Vinnie's great, but much more elegant. Ever notice *his* 1-1 pitch? [Miming Scully] "It's on the way, currrve loowww." Or, "Two and one to Dusty Baker, and it's interesting to note as Molière once said in 17th-century Paris. . ." Whoever heard of Dusty Baker or even baseball in the 17th Century? Yet people go bonkers about Vinnie quoting Molière!

The amazing thing is that Vinnie's so great that young broadcasters emulate him. I hear them around the country, and it's unmistakable: "The 1-1 pitch, loowww." Even abroad, you can't escape him. One reason I went to Japan in 1993 was one of the great voices of the game, the Yomiuri Giants' Jenshiro Assami. I'd heard *of* Assami-san but never *heard* him, so I can't wait to see this legendary announcer. I turn the TV on and can't believe it; *he's* doing Scully. "Watashi-wa Korakuen Stadium Ne-oremus. Hajime-mashite dozo yorushku loowww."

The topper came when I went to Venezuela on the Orioles' winter cruise and had the chance to hear the top broadcaster down there, and he was doing *Chuck.* It was astounding. You know, Ripken socks a foul. "Dos y dos. Ripken tiene vente siete y ain't the cervesa fria!"

Ain't the beer cold! True story.

—*Jon Miller*

From 1962 through '64, I worked with Joe Garagiola on NBC's "Major League Baseball." Every week, games on Saturday and Sunday afternoon. When two people work side by side, you've got to be a team. Some announcers won't do that—play games, want to overshadow. But if I looked out to the bull pen and couldn't tell who the right- or left-hander was, instead of saying, "That's Smith, the right-hander" on the air or "That's Joe, he's a left-hander," Joe would write me a note: "Smith to the left, Jones to the right." He'd bypass a little edge so that I'd look good.

Joe didn't have a formal education but developed a superb vocabulary with all sorts of descriptive words. He wouldn't say, "The fielder tagged the base runner," rather, "The guy stapled him to the bag." Joe worked at being a humorist, went to nightclubs, studied timing. We'd travel together to and from the game. Afterward, he'd go over each pitch, recall every word. "Bob, first inning, count 3 and 2." Let's say Mickey Vernon was at the plate. "The next ball was a foul to the right. You said this and I said that and if you'd said this I'd have come back with that." By next game, my "this" jibed with his "that."

—*Bob Wolff*

You never forget your first major-league game. I'm calling the 1966 Dallas-Ft. Worth Spurs in the Double-A Texas League when NBC called. By now, I had been with the network several years and done AFL football. But not baseball. And this was when NBC was *the* baseball network and the Saturday "Game of the Week" a truly big event. Each week, there was the major game and a back-up—"B"—game in case "A" had a rain delay. My call told me to do the back-up game that Saturday with Tony Kubek.

I flew into Pittsburgh on Friday. Tony, whom I'd never met, couldn't get in till late. So I go to the park and am in the men's room when [1948-75 Pirates' broadcaster] Bob Prince introduced himself. He knew my football work and asked if I'd ever done big-league baseball. I said no—I was excited but nervous—and with that the man called the Gunner took me under his wing. "Kid, come with me," he says, and has me take notes in the booth. Does a complete outline—it's still amazing—a mini-bio, guys' strengths and weaknesses, anecdotes to use on each player. The game ends, and he says, "C'mon, kid" and drove downtown for drinks and goes over the next day's starting pitchers. I'll never forget how comfortable Bob Prince made my major-league debut. Over the years, I've tried to do the same thing for young broadcasters. Kinda' a payback for what he did.

The next day was gorgeous, in Pittsburgh. Not so the primary game; by 11 A.M., it's called by rain. At breakfast, I'd met Tony. Now we learn we have the "A" game; the whole network is ours. I'm really thrilled. Not Tony, then an NBC rookie. He says, "I'll be back in a moment," and leaves. Time goes by, and I'm putting game notes, statistics together, but I don't see Tony, can't find Tony. It's 30 minutes before air time. No Tony. Finally, 10 minutes before we go on camera, he walks in the booth, and Tony's pale white. I said, "Where you been?" He said, "To tell the truth, throwing up. I'm not ready to go national." Of course, he was. And became one of the great analysts of all time. I'll always remember when he didn't think he was up for the job—only to show how big-league he was.

—*Charlie Jones*

Tony Kubek was my partner at NBC from 1969 through '75. We used to have a gag. We'd get into these TV meetings, and producers would go on forever, like Cecil B. De Mille. Finally, I put my hand up, and they said, "Yes, Gowdy," and I said, "What about the ball game?" "Oh, hell with the ball game," they said, "we got to have the opening and the close." "Yeah," I said, "but fellas, we're here because of the game." Tony'd be cheering as I stuck the needle in. Pure baseball—nobody did it better.

—*Curt Gowdy*

I've never understood why guys don't want the best for their partners. To me, there's no "Number one" or "two" broadcaster. If the guy you work with is good, the whole broadcast is better. Look at Howard Cosell. I don't see why he ripped guys. I used to tell him, "You've never *played* the game, Howard. You'll never know what it feels like to have your chin shaved by a 90-mile fastball. You can *assume* what it's like, but never know."

I think Howard liked me [on ABC 1976-80s baseball], but he took it personally if you challenged him. Merle Harmon, on the other hand, helped me from the start. I'd never done baseball when I joined him in the ['71 Brewers'] booth, not unless you count my play-by-play into beer cups in the bull pen. Beer cups don't criticize. Listeners do, and at first there was a lot to criticize. My problem was ad-libbing; I'd repeat the count like a crutch. But Merle and [partner] Tom Collins let me do color, then play-by-play, and saved me if I screwed up.

Then one day, Merle and Tom got together before the game and decided to test me. Comes the fifth inning—I'm supposed to do a half inning—and they get up and leave. I was terrified, but being alone made me grow up. Actually, I don't want to give the wrong impression about Cosell. One time he told me on the air that since I was a former player I couldn't possibly know the meaning of the word *truculent*. I said, "Sure I do, Howie. If you had a truck and I borrowed it, that would be a truck-you-lent." I'm almost as proud of that as I am of my playing.

—*Bob Uecker*

I've worked baseball with Blaine Walsh, Leo Durocher, and Jackie Robinson—none better than my 1970s partner. When Bob Uecker was released as a player [1968], he came back to his home town, Milwaukee. He filled in on some of my cross assignments, then was hired full-time and became like a brother. At first, I don't think Bob realized his talent. It took him a while to get going, but he worked and did a balancing act. Funny stories, yes, but always as a humorist, not clown.

Bob so did his homework that players came to him and asked, "I think I got a hitch in my swing. Will you watch me from behind the plate?" All the wonderful monkey business that he comes up conceals his great depth as a person. Brewer fans would tell me, "Golly, I want bad weather. I want to hear you guys tell stories in the rain delay." That's Bob, and he hasn't even scratched the surface. Mr. Baseball—what an apt name.

—*Merle Harmon*

In 1974, I was named Voice of the Reds after doing three years of Triple-A ball with the Tidewater, Virginia, Tides. Nirvana! The irony is that this was the only time I've doubted my ability. The reason is that everywhere I went I heard people say, "Boy, you sure got big shoes to fill by replacing Al Michaels."

Al was enormously popular as the Reds' [1971-73] Voice. Come '74, and he goes to the Giants—later to become one of the greats. But at the time, I didn't know much about him, only that in Cincinnati I kept meeting his ghost. I'd been a big fish in a small Virginia pond. A month after arriving in Ohio, we go to spring training, and like a puppy dog I follow [partner] Joe [Nuxhall] around. As we get closer to the first spring training broadcast, I know I have to put my act on display. People are going to find whether Marty Brennaman can cut the mustard.

Our first broadcast was in Bradenton, Florida, against the Pirates. Reflecting later, I felt the broadcast went well. After a month of hearing about Al, I'd gotten through the first game with a minimum of problem. The ghost was gone! Next day, the Reds opened their home schedule at Tampa's Al Lopez Field against the White Sox, and, as nervous as I'd been a day before, I look forward to the second broadcast because I'm not nearly as uptight. Air time drew near, and the engineer gave us the cue. Without a care in the world, I open, "Good afternoon, everyone, from Al Michaels Field in Tampa, welcome to Reds' baseball."

This wasn't a mistake which you don't realize. I knew what I'd said, and was mortified. Clearly, the ghost hadn't disappeared. In commercial break, Joe almost fell off the bench. "I can't believe it," he said. "We haven't played a regular-season game, and I've already got material for next fall's banquet circuit." People don't believe the story when they hear it, but it's as vivid in my memory as in 1974. I might add that Al Michaels got a big charge out of it, too.

—*Marty Brennaman*

In 1971, Don Drysdale worked Expo television with me. The next year, he went to Texas, and Pee Wee Reese did a majority of our TV games. A couple times another ex-Brooklyn player, Jackie Robinson, filled in for him. Remember, Montreal had once been the Dodgers' top farm club. This was late in Jackie's life, diabetes had wracked him, and he was almost blind. The first night that I worked with him in the booth, Jackie pointed to the monitor and said, "Dave, I'll be able to discuss the game, but just point to the ball so I'll know where it is when I'm talking about replays." Kind of hard to forget a moment like that.

—*Dave Van Horne*

When I was a kid, my dad listened to Red Barber and his easygoing style on radio. I'd get a rush, like later hearing Bob Murphy, Ralph Kiner, and Lindsey [Nelson] with the Mets. I learned the importance of how to *present* the game. When I joined TSN [Canada's TV The Sports Network] in 1986, Tony Kubek was a mentor. Then, on to radio. I remember Jack Buck coming up and saying, "Well, you're gonna' be with us every day." It makes a difference. Dave [Van Horne]'s been *my* difference. With the Expos since the start. You can count his games missed on both hands. He's an encyclopedia. And like all the best tries to leave footprints where the game is—and where it's come from.

—*Ken Singleton*

After winning the [American League] Western Division title in 1970, the Twins struggled on the field and at the gate. Following 1973, they decided to hire a young announcer named Larry Carlton who'd done Triple-A ball, filled in a few games for the Cardinals, and had an exuberant manner. In his application, he vowed that if the Twins didn't draw at least a million fans in 1974, he'd give back half his salary.

Larry's pledge became common knowledge. We come to the last game of the season, and I'm in the press box talking to some writers. The broadcast booth was separated from the press box by a glass partition. Pat Rickey, then of the St. Paul *Pioneer Press*, saw Larry enter the booth and turned to me. "Well," he said, "it looks like your broadcast partner might be in a little financial trouble if the Twins don't draw 345,000 today."

The Twins drew only 662,000 for the season, the worst attendance in team history. I still don't know whether Larry gave back half of his salary.

—*Herb Carneal*

Baseball broadcasters have different backgrounds and styles. Today, Houston's Larry Dierker is a baseball historian and literary figure who had to survive working out as a kid with those wild Colt .45's clubs of the early '60s, especially Dick Farrell, their ringleader. Larry'd come inside from that awful Houston humidity and no matter how parched he was wouldn't go for a Coke across the locker room. The reason was that to get there he had to pass Farrell's locker. Or think of Loel Passe, Gene Elston's first partner. He had a briefcase with everything there including the kitchen sink. In April, somebody put a hot dog in his case, and in September Loel finally found it.

In Illinois, I grew up in the shadow of Harry Caray and Jack Buck. In 1984, Milo Hamilton was let go by the Cubs and joined the Astros. Bet ya' he was glad to leave; Milo didn't get along with Harry who by then was with the Cubs. Well, that same off-season, I left Houston to join Harry at Wrigley Field. Sort of a trade, Milo for me! I'd grown up hearing Lou Boudreau over WGN. Vince Lloyd, too; nobody ever delivered spot ads as well. And Caray, where would you find a copy? A year earlier, in the Houston press room, I'd got a sense of what Harry was all about. It's one thing hearing him on the air—bombastic, critical, thespiatic. Talking, you get a different idea just of the *passion*. Gees, Harry wakes up, and every day is special.

Say today is August 7. Bingo, that means something, just like April 10 or October 25. Whatever, he's off and running. We're talking, and he says, "Today's the anniversary of a day I was writing an alimony check to my first wife, and I compose, 'Dear [so-and-so], how long must this go on?' A few days later, I received a letter from her—on very expensive stationery, I might add—and she said, 'Dear Harry. Till death to us part.'"

—*Dewayne Staats*

Looking back at the Blue Jays' first five years [1977-81] isn't always easy. [Understandably: Toronto had a .359 winning percentage.] What made it tolerable was my first broadcast partner, Early "Gus" Wynn. As a pitcher, Early'd knock you down. He was just as combative behind the mike, getting perverse joy from tossing live verbal hand-grenades and watching me juggle them.

One night, we're in Texas when a foul pop-up lands behind the Ranger dugout. I could see it was going to land close to a young man with a young lady at his side. He reached out to catch the ball, and it popped in and out of his hands and landed on the field. Needless to say, everybody in the park hooted at him as he sat down. A few pitches later, there's another pop-up, same place, and the same guy jumps up for the ball. But this time, the young lady reaches in front of him and makes a great one-handed catch. I'm amazed: "Can you believe it? *He* boots it, and *she* catches it. How about that?" And Early says, "Well, she probably knows all about his hands."

Another year, Early drove up to Toronto in his motorcoach after the All-Star break. But he didn't make it back for the first game—instead, called and said he was marooned in a place called Coon Hollow, Tennessee. Seems he'd lost a wheel off his motorcoach and was there a few days getting it fixed. When he got back, we talked one night on the air about how Early was driving down a hill and suddenly looked out to the side of the road and saw his front wheel rolling along the shoulder.

"Your life must have flashed before your eyes," I said. "What was going through your mind?"

"Tom, I was recalling the lines of that song," which was popular back then. "'You picked a fine time to leave me, loose wheel.'"

—*Tom Cheek*

The first time I worked with Lindsey Nelson was a Texas Ranger game in Minnesota. He came upstairs to the press box, and I expected to see one of the checkered tablecloth sport coats that made Lindsey famous over the years, something wild that maybe he bought down in St. Petersburg during spring training with the Mets and was wearing 25 years later. Not in this case. He walks in with a blue sport coat on, and I said, "Lindsey, what's the deal? I'm disappointed. The first time I've had a chance to meet ya', you're wearing a blue sport coat." He looked at me and said, "Young fellow, it's a perfect coat for radio." And it was.

—John Rooney

Timmy McCarver gave me great advice as a young broadcaster: Focus on what the average fan cares about, the game between the lines. "When you retire, you're no longer in the fraternity of players," he said. "You're an outsider. Broadcast like one." He told how Mike Schmidt one day hit a ball toward the gap and broke into his trot. But it wasn't gone, and Mike wound up at second. "He should have been on third," Tim says on the air. "Often, power hitters develop a certain feel; they hit one like that and assume it's a homer."

The next day, McCarver sought Schmitty out. Mike says, "I hear you ripped me on the air for not hustling." Timmy explained what he said, then asked if Mike was hustling. Schmidt admitted, "No." "Did I tell the truth?" McCarver said. The answer was "yes." Tell the truth. No one does it better than Timmy.

—Jim Kaat

John Lowenstein joined me in the 1984 Home Team Sports booth after the Orioles released him. I remember his first telecast—spring training, West Palm Beach—when on the air John leaned out the broadcast window and yelled to a vendor, "Hey, give me a ham sandwich, and hold the mustard." I sort of knew then John was a little off-center.

The sandwich was duly delivered, and John duly went on to offend. The Orioles had a little infielder, Lenny Sakata, of Japanese extraction. So John tells viewers, "After the Orioles went to Japan in '83, Lenny got lost in a crowd, and we couldn't find him for two weeks." Another time, in New York, I saw that in the right-field bleachers no one was leaving after the game. John said, "Oh, that area's known as Peso Park. Takes 'em two hours to clear immigration." When Wade Boggs' extramarital affair with Margo Adams became public, Boston played in Baltimore, and fans were hollering at Boggs and singing a song they called "Margoville"—like "Margaritaville." I noted that Wade's wife cooked him chicken before each game—a superstition. John said, "Wonder who cooks his chicken now?" I said, "I don't know who's cooking his chicken, but we know who cooked his goose."

In about 1985, the Orioles had Seat Cushion Night at Memorial Stadium and dropped off cushions they were giving away so we'd show them on the air. That night Rex Barney was, as usual, the Orioles' public address announcer. As he said to the crowd, "OK, hold up your seat cushions," we showed a shot of John holding up his cushion before, for some reason, he let it fly. Out goes John's cushion, befitting an air traffic controller, and it spins through the air toward the field. The fans see it, figure they'll join in, and, suddenly, thousands of cushions are thrown Frisbee-style onto the field. The game is stopped, the grounds crew spent a long time collecting 'em, and it's much longer before we had another Seat Cushion Night. Just another notch in the gun for Brother Lo.

—*Mel Proctor*

In 1986, I worked an NBC "Game of the Week" at Comiskey Park, and my partner was Brother Lowenstein. John is a wonderful guy to be around and, it's fair to say, a character. On this gray, overcast day, he wears sunglasses throughout rehearsal. We're readying for a pre-game show feature when the producer said, "John, you're taking those sunglasses off, aren't ya'?" and John said, "No." The producer said, "Sure you want to wear them?" and John said, "Yeah." The producer told me in my earpiece, "You'd better make some reference," so I make an on-air joke about how on this gray day John can't see the ball without his sunglasses. John comes back, "It's not the ball but the fifth or sixth cocktail from last night that forces me to wear these." We chuckled, but unknown to John was that NBC's pre-game show had just aired a piece on what Don Newcombe was doing to help players with substance problems. I'm not 100 percent sure that this was the reason, but John wasn't asked back after that incident, despite being a fine announcer. Some days, "Oops" says it all.

—*Ted Robinson*

Two unforgettable things involve my dad [Harry] and my son [Chip]. The first was working with Chip the first game he did with the Braves. Talk about overprotective. I wouldn't let him say anything 'cause I was afraid he'd screw up. Once *I* was OK, *Chip* was even better. More memorable was the [1991] time that Chip, Dad, and myself did the same game at Wrigley Field. They had a news conference at Dad's restaurant at noon. We went to the game together in a limo. It was unbelievable. For the first time in my life, I felt what rock and roll stars do, or a David Justice and Greg Maddux. Mob scene. Stupid questions. Microphones in your face. Now I tell players, "If I ever give you guys guff because I don't think you're cooperative, just remind me of that night."

—Skip Caray

One of my favorite people is the Colonel, Jerry Coleman, who I teamed with to do a lot of Saturday '80s CBS games before we started its "Sunday Night Baseball" together. Jerry is known for his Colemanisms, and he's sensitive about them because people write about things Jerry comes up with like, "He slides into second with a stand-up double," or "Dave Winfield goes back, hits his head on the wall, it rolls toward the infield," and things like that. I think the Colemanisms will get Jerry into the [broadcast wing of the] Hall of Fame—that, along with his personality and the way people in baseball simply love him.

I'm working a CBS game with Jerry in Kansas City one time, and he comes on the air saying, "It's such a beautiful day for baseball here in Kansas City, John Rooney, that you can see Missouri." I didn't want to show Jerry up, but I said, "Jerry, we're *in* Missouri. You used to play down the road five miles west of here. Remember the Kansas City Blues days?" He just picked it up and said, "Well, John Rooney, it's a beautiful day anyway. The starting pitchers tonight. . . ," and ran with it after that.

From time to time, you might not see every pitch because you're trying to locate a drop-in, commercial announcement to read, or a note to support a thought. This same game, Jerry was looking for something in his paperwork and he saw the pitch fouled off, said, "Foul ball, grounded on the right side," as the pitch comes back and hits the front of our booth. He hit the call switch and said, "Screwed that one up, didn't I?" The only screw-up will be if he doesn't get into Cooperstown.

—John Rooney

CHAPTER FOUR

OUR HOUSE

GREAT FIELDS, GRAND FANS

*I*n 1988, A. Bartlett Giamatti first saw a model of the Orioles' proposed new park. "When this thing is complete, each team will want one," he said with his teddy bear of a laugh. Born April 6, 1992, its quirks, angles, and peals of intimacy retrieved a déjà vu *not of stadia but of* ball parks *heavy with individuality.*

Camden Yards recalled sites, built on a human scale, that once exalted baseball. The ivy at Wrigley Field. Shibe Park's surf of sounds. The furnace of Sportsman's Park. Forbes Field's stretch of acreage grown heavy with base hits. One did not visit League Park or Braves Field to see mascots or exploding scoreboards, but the baseball *of* grass, knowing fans, odd nooks, and asymmetrical shapes that changed the game played within. A long out to left-center field— "Death Valley"—in Yankee Stadium might be a home run at Griffith Stadium. A pee-wee homer to left-field in the Bronx would have hit Fenway Park's 37-foot-high wall. It made a difference.

At Crosley Field, pokes dented cars parked at an adjacent laundry. In Kansas City, a mule—Charlie O, named for owner Charles O. Finley—grazed beyond right field. Fans knew the real jackass. Someone put pen to a Lifebuoy soap ad on the outfield wall at Baker Bowl: "The Phillies use Lifebuoy and they still stink." Ebbets Field flaunted a Sym-Phony Band and bell-ringing Hilda Chester and goings-on of memory. Xanadus of personality sprung from baseball's Cathedrals of the Outdoors. Still enduring is their Flatbush of the mind.

I 'member the first-ever night game in New York [June 15, 1938] when a lot of us went over from CBS to Brooklyn to see baseball under the lights. And what a bonus, the first guy, the Reds' Johnny Vander Meer, to pitch his *second* straight no-hitter. Or Dave Righetti, at Yankee Stadium, striking out Wade Boggs to end *his* 1983 no-hitter. In 1951, another Yankee, Allie Reynolds, pitched two of them. And the last man he had to get out in the second game was Ted Williams—again, in the Bronx. What's special? Each of these moments I still identify with a particular park.

—*Mel Allen*

E very baseball fan should have had the chance to visit Ebbets Field. It stays with you, just like its P.A. announcer, Tex Rickard. It could be 100 degrees—didn't matter—he'd have a big sweater on. Tex didn't sit in the broadcast booth or press box, but made announcements from right next to the Dodger dugout. He didn't know all the ballplayers. Again, didn't matter. He just said things on the P.A. that made even visitors laugh.

One day Preacher Roe was removed from the game. Suddenly, you heard Tex explain why: "He don't feel good." Another time, fans put some clothes on Ebbets Field's left-field railing. That came out, "Will the people in left field take their clothes off?" If you weren't a star, Tex might inadvertently forget you. He'd look into the Dodger dugout and say, "Quick, what's his first name?" One day it happened to me. I came in to pitch—a middle reliever, no wonder Tex forgot—and he yelled into the dugout. Sometimes, Dodger players intentionally gave him the wrong name. So, as I near the mound, Tex informs the crowd, "Now coming in to pitch for Milwaukee, number 32, Cy Johnson."

I never found whether my new name came from a Dodger releasing a sigh on the bench, or my uncanny likeness to Cy Young. There was no P.A. guy like Tex—or circus like Ebbets Field.

—*Ernie Johnson*

F or two years [1948-49], I broadcast baseball in Brooklyn, and early on tried to explain the Dodger fan to my wife. Lulu had met the players and their families in spring training and at parties. She didn't know much baseball, but was more or less familiar with the fellows on the team. Yet she never really got what I was talking about until she went to Ebbets Field.

Lulu sat down behind a fat fan in a T-shirt. When the Dodgers' Pee Wee Reese led off in the last of the first inning, this man stood up and shouted, "C'mon, you bum. Get a hit."

My wife was appalled, and tapped the fan on his shoulder. "I beg your pardon," she said. "Do you know Mr. Reese?" The fan said, "No, lady, why?"

Lulu said, "If you did, I'm sure you'd find him a very nice gentleman." The fan responded, "OK, lady, I'll lay off him if he's a friend of yours."

Billy Cox was the next batter, and as he got into the batter's box the fan jumped up again. "Do somethin', Cox. You're a bum." Again, Lulu tapped the man. This time, before she could say anything, he whirled around. "Lady, is this bum a friend of yours, too?"

Lulu nodded. "And what about the other bums on this team?" he asked. "I know almost all the players," she said. With that, the fan began to move away. Before he'd taken three steps, he turned and said to Lulu: "Lady, I'm moving. I came out here to root my Bums to a win, and I ain't gonna' let you sit here behind me and spoil my whole afternoon."

—*Ernie Harwell*

Iplayed most of two decades in Brooklyn. Just being there was amazing. It was like walking in a bar and saying, "Hi ya', Curt," or "How things going, Ned?" Friends. And the ball park was so great—the stands right on top of you. Everything was on a first-name basis. You knew fans not as a crowd but as people. There'll never be anything like it. That's why I bet a couple players that we'd stay. They said, "Man, we're moving" [to Los Angeles in 1958]. I said, "Hell, we're drawing over a million people ever' year." Brooklyn would have done anything to keep the Dodgers. They should have got the chance.

—*Pee Wee Reese*

Fenway Park is an intimate night club that seats 35,000. My booth was right above home plate, and I loved being close to the field. Also, the wonderful—Joe Cronin called 'em "lousy"—geometrics. The Green Monster in left, 37 feet high and 315 feet from the plate! Some say 300. It curves away fast, takes a good poke to center field. Big right-field area—380 to the bull pen—which was 420 until after Williams' rookie year [1939]. They put in a pen so Ted could hit more home runs.

Fenway has always been kept like a Japanese garden. You're worshipping at baseball's Holy Grail. Look what Baltimore has done with their new ball park, built like the old. Cleveland, Texas, and Denver doing the same thing. Thank God the new parks springing up aren't like these cavernous domes with no feeling or romance. I hope the Red Sox never leave Fenway. They could probably draw more people. Some of those Yankee-Red Sox games I did could have totaled 100,000 a game. That doesn't matter, only this: Take the team out of Fenway Park, and they're no longer the New England Red Sox.

—*Curt Gowdy*

I spent one afternoon in Fenway that I'll never forget. It was the day [July 20, 1969] Neil Armstrong landed on the moon, and I was working an Orioles-Red Sox' game.

I'm sure that when that announcement was made anywhere, Americans stopped and cheered. At Fenway, Sherm Feller was the P.A. announcer, and, when he reported it, the applause was so overwhelming that it stopped the game. The umpire said, "We've got to wait till this dies down." Brooks Robinson, the due batter, couldn't hear what Feller said and started for the plate. When the umpire explained what was going on, *Brooks* promptly dropped his bat and joined in the applause.

Then, down in the left-field corner at Fenway Park—what I refer to as No-Man's Land, where some of baseball's worst line drives have been hit— some leather-lunged fan stood up and started to sing, "God Bless America." No sooner did he start than everybody in that old ball park was singing. You've never heard it sung so loud by people who were crying. Emotional? *Unforgettable.* Definitely not just another day at the park.

—*Chuck Thompson*

My most memorable moment in an old ball park involves a public address announcer, 1987. It's Reggie Jackson's last year in baseball, and we're at Fenway for Reggie's last game there. As Jackson comes to the plate in the ninth inning, everyone knows this is the last time he ever hits at Fenway. So the late, great Sherm Feller, in his remarkably unique style, simply said, "Number 44, Mr. October." That's how he introduced Reggie. What a wonderful moment. Great player, P.A. announcer, great park.

—*Ted Robinson*

In 1970, Seattle's Pilots moved to Milwaukee. In '77, the expansion Mariners were born as baseball came back to Seattle. Their home was the Kingdome, which is not a ball park. There are no elements, no effect on the baseball. Going indoors is a pain in the ass on a beautiful day. Say it's 75 degrees, clear skies, I'm sitting on my deck watching the boats race up and down the lake, listening to the birds in the background, and I can see beautiful Mount Rainier. Oh, for a place like Fenway Park. You can see the grass grow, Fenway smells, you can see Ted Williams, Babe Ruth playing there. I darn near genuflect when I walk through the gates.

—*Dave Niehaus*

The Pilots played their only year in Seattle at Sick Stadium, where the visiting broadcaster sat looking down the first-base line. Daylight baseball was wonderful, 'cause Mount Rainier was right there. Sometimes it was better to watch than the game. But the park was aptly named. Would you believe that Boog Powell had one inside-the-park home run in his career? He did it here. Looking down the first-base line, I could see center field, shortstop, right field, first and second basemen. But you know how I had to follow anything that went by the third baseman into left field? A mirror was hung up. That's right, you had to look into it and refract the play. A funny kind of way to do baseball. You might even call it sick.

—*Chuck Thompson*

There'll never be a better broadcast booth than Tiger Stadium. You're so close to the game you can hear the umpire and hitter talk and the spikes digging in. But the proximity makes you vulnerable to foul balls. One afternoon, I'm with Bill King on A's TV when Luis Polonia fouls the game's first pitch back. Our stage manager, Carl Young, was standing in the three feet of space between Bill and myself, and the foul smacks him on the right shoulder. Carl starts rubbing, and the A's all look up because they know how close we are when, lo and behold, Polonia fouls the *second* pitch straight back between us and hits Carl in the same place. The dugout's roaring, and so I pick up a white towel just sitting there and wave it. Almost never do two straight pitches come to the same spot. The moral: When you come to Tiger Stadium, bring a white flag or a baseball glove.

—*Ted Robinson*

The 1984 World Series, my Padres are playing Detroit. We're at Tiger Stadium, and the Tigers have just won the title. The game's over, and we got about 15 minutes more time to fill on the post-game show. The fans go on the field, spill all over, then look up at the broadcast booth. In Detroit it's only about 30 feet from the field to the booth, so somebody picks up the idea of "target practice." A couple dozen people start pelting us with clods of grass. Hey, it's not enough they've just beaten the Padres; this adds insult to injury. We close the screen, and I fall on my hands. We finish amid blitzkrieg from the air. I should have sent 'em the dry cleaning bill.

—Jerry Coleman

Have you ever been to Wrigley Field in Chicago? If you haven't, you've missed a temple. I'm not talking about today's fancy things. This was when you went to the ball park in the daytime and saw baseball without lights. In this day of computerized scoreboards and electronic message boards, Wrigley Field is still as refreshing as a pretty girl in a flimsy dress on a windy day.

I started baseball dreaming before World War II, listening to Bob Elson do the Cubs. I hadn't made the bigs, so what I knew of baseball was stands wrapping around the crowd which looks over the field to a brick wall covered with ivy. In the old days, street cars came clanging up and down Clark Street. Even on a weekday afternoon, you'd get 35,000 to see two last-place teams. I looked quickly to the scoreboard, worked by men who inning by inning gave scores of other games. The suspense built, waiting to see the Cardinal score, or games in the other league. Sometimes guys running it brought a 6-pack. Then they might miss a couple innings. One night, they must have inhaled some hard stuff; the numbers started appearing upside down.

A scoreboard that screams, flashes, and blinks isn't baseball. I'll take that old-time religion. Sort of a hymn to baseball: "How Great Thou Art."

—Jimmy Dudley

Every time I go to Wrigley Field, I think of my partner Whitey [Richie] Ashburn. Whitey was a character even in his playing days, and especially known for hitting foul balls. The Phillies were in Chicago, and a player who shall remain nameless went down to the batting cage. The guy came up and said, "Whitey, you hit a lot of foul balls. My wife, Madge, and I aren't getting along at all. You know where the wives sit here at Wrigley? Why don't you take a shot at her?"

Sure enough, the first time up, Whitey hits a screaming line drive behind the Cubs' dugout. This guy goes to the top step, waves a towel, and says, "Whitey, two rows back and one to the left and you got her." True story. Only with my pal.

—Harry Kalas

There's a rumor I like night life. But it's *day* baseball that makes the Cubs so popular. You saw that when baseball made the Cubs put lights in Wrigley Field [1988] because it had a contract with network television. If the Cubs were to win a division or pennant and make the World Series, they had to be able to present games at night. *Without* lights, TV would have moved post-season games to Milwaukee or St. Louis. Do you know what would have happened if the Cubs won a pennant and you had to go to St. Louis to watch? Mass riot. People almost rioted as it was when lights went in. The reason was that you go to California or Hawaii, and people watch Cubs games over the SuperStation [WGN-TV]. And they watch 'em in the afternoon. *That's* the magic of Wrigley Field.

Even with lights it's still a daytime park. We only play 18 night games a year. That's good, because people forget what made the Cubs. It isn't Harry Caray and Jack Brickhouse and all the press or anything; it's day ball. Generation after generation, a little kid leaves home, gets on the L, gets off at the park, and watches the game. By 6 he's home, and can you imagine the excitement of that youngster when he gets there! "Dad, you should have seen what Ryne Sandberg did—oh, Dwight Smith did—well, Rick . . . " and they talk. That kid grows up and has his own kids; same thing happens. Day baseball made the Cubs so loveable. More clubs should pay attention.

—Harry Caray

When I did "Game of the Week" [1983-89] with Tony Kubek and went to Milwaukee, we spent part of the broadcast extolling the best ball park food anywhere: the bratwurst with red sauce at County Stadium. They have a formula that makes it taste like another planet—pour beer on the grill and seep it in sauerkraut, add secret sauce—no one knows the formula, it's in a vault. NBC'd put us on camera, and I'd say it's now an official game because we have the bratwurst. We'd start inhaling and have to alternate play-by-play because one of us would have a mouthful.

This became semi-legendary, especially in Wisconsin, to where the concessionaire at County Stadium would send vats of bratwurst to my home in giant industrial size. I'd get jars of the secret sauce, but also letters from Cub fans who were insulted that I didn't say Wrigley Field had better hot dogs.

Anyway, I get a letter from a guy named Ma Pesh in Stevens Point, Wisconsin. Ma Pesh wants to challenge me to a bratwurst-eating contest. He enclosed a Polaroid of himself, and I'm telling ya', the guy had to tip the Toledos at about 430.

Ma wears bib overalls, he's got a big beard, looks like Junior Samples, and says he holds the record for bratwurst consumption at County Stadium. Claims he consumed the most brats ever in a game between the Brewers and Orioles in August 1972, and goes on to say this was even more surprising to Ma and his friends because before then he'd never eaten well against Baltimore. I mean, you know, what do ya' say? I wrote back to Ma Pesh and he wrote back to me and now we're pen pals.

—Bob Costas

It's funny how one park links the good, bad, and ugly—for me, County Stadium. Head scout Tom Sheehan took over as Giant manager for Bill Rigney when Rig was fired in 1960. Rig was in second place, and Sheehan managed to finish fifth. A nice man, but not cut out to be a manager. One night in Milwaukee the winning run's at third base, nobody out, and Stu Miller comes in to pitch. Tom goes to the mound and gathers his infield—he was the manager, right?—but instead asks, "We've got Eddie Mathews, [Hank] Aaron, and [Joe] Adcock coming up. What should I do?"

Shortstop Eddie Bressoud said, "I'd pitch to Mathews, walk Aaron, then pitch to Adcock." So Sheehan says, "Fine," walks back to the dugout, and sees Mathews whack the first pitch for a hit to win the game. Sheehan's comment wasn't that he asked Bressoud what to do, but "I have the dumbest shortstop in baseball to want to pitch to that guy." Not long for the managerial world. In that same park, Warren Spahn pitched a no-hitter against the Giants on April 28, 1961. Two days later, Willie Mays hit four home runs and could have had five! 'Bout his third time up, Mays broke his bat and still slammed the ball up against the center-field fence. Five swings, five times up, four homers, and another ball hit 400 feet.

In the ninth inning, Jimmy Davenport comes up and makes the final out with Willie on deck, and Braves' fans boo him 'cause they want to see Mays hit. I'm not sure anybody will ever hit five homers in one game. I am sure not a person in County Stadium didn't think Mays couldn't park Number 5.

—*Lon Simmons*

Like Lon, I described Willie's great day in 1961. But I liked better 1954's performance by the Braves' Joe Adcock at Ebbets Field. Adcock loved to hit there, and this day smacked four homers and just missed a fifth when he hit the center-field fence a couple of feet below the top of the wall. Big Joe went to second base with a double for a record total of 18 bases in a game! But he paid for it the next day when he was beaned by Clem Labine and collapsed at home plate. Our booth was so close I can still hear the crack of the ball against Adcock's head. It scared the hell out of everybody. A plastic batting helmet saved Joe's life. Two days, and what a roller coaster. No wonder Red Barber said, "Anything can happen at Ebbets Field, and usually does." True, really, of all the old parks.

—*Earl Gillespie*

In late 1957 came the bombshell that the Dodgers are moving to Los Angeles. I'm third man on the wheel with Vin Scully and Al Helfer, so I don't know whether I'm going. But a few days later [owner] Walter O'Malley asked me to go west, and I couldn't wait to pack. I'd lived in Texas for many years and always wanted to live in California. Now I was, and in a new era for baseball because the Dodgers and Giants moved together. Out came the Dodgers of Ebbets Field: [Gil] Hodges and Pee Wee Reese and [Jim] Gilliam and Duke Snider, Carl Furillo, Carl Erskine. We played our first game at Seals Stadium in San Francisco, and then opened in L.A. [Their 1958-61 home, Memorial Coliseum, had a 251-feet left-field foul pole and 94,600-seat capacity. "It's the only place," went a favorite *mot*, "that can hold almost 100,000 people and two outfielders."] What a feeling to bring this historic team almost en masse and be received as we were.

It's still special to think about, the Dodgers' Opening Day parade, Roy Campanella Night [on May 9, 1959, the stadium lights were turned off, and 93,103 lit matches to salute No. 39], and spectacular crowds at the Coliseum. Each night was like *Alice in Wonderland*. Our years there were fantastic. Then, in '62 we moved to Dodger Stadium. I'll never forget my first visit, coming out of the dugout and looking up at this jewel. I'm sure hearts were breaking in Brooklyn. But I talked with Walter O'Malley, and he was as pleased as a person could possibly be.

—Jerry Doggett

California just took to us, right from the start—crucial because we hadn't known what to expect. The move had been such a jolt, like starting over. I'd established myself for eight years in New York. Everything I cherished was there. But there wasn't any real decision because I loved being with the team, and loved my job. I was like the bride whose husband has been transferred. She might not want to go, but she goes.

At the Coliseum, people were so far removed from the playing field that I guess my voice gave them some feeling of connection with the game. Although people were aware of some of the superstars, they weren't aware of the rank-and-file ball players. So they brought their radios to hear me tell them. Then it became a habit after we left for Dodger Stadium, where you *could* follow the action. I always thought it was strange knowing that thousands of people are listening to you describe a play they are watching.

—Vin Scully

After the Giants and Dodgers came west, crazy things kept happening like they had at Ebbets Field and the Polo Grounds. That was especially true when we played in L.A., and usually Willie Mays was in the middle. Memorial Coliseum wasn't built for baseball. At night, the lights were lousy. By day, the sun field blinded you. One afternoon, Felipe Alou was playing right field, there was a runner at third base, and a fly ball was hit his way. Alou lost it in the sun, but Mays covered so much ground that he sprinted over, caught the ball in straightaway *right* field, threw to the plate, and kept the guy from scoring.

Later, the writers asked Willie if that was a planned play! I think the only plan was the Good Lord's when he gave us Mr. Mays.

—Lon Simmons

Another park Willie owned was Connie Mack Stadium [Shibe Park, pre-1953] in Philadelphia. Whenever Mays ran from first to third, he'd slow down to try and draw a throw so that the guy who hit the ball could go to second. If you got lucky, maybe the ball'd be thrown away and Mays could score. One day, Don Demeter was playing left field when, on a hit and run, a line drive reached him on a hop. Ordinarily, a runner in that situation stops at second. Not Mays. He got such a jump that he rounded second and was headed for third even as the ball got to Demeter. Don picked up the ball, looked at Mays, and Willie sort of slowed down to try to draw the throw. You could see Demeter thinking, "You're not tricking *me!*" So he threw the ball to second to thwart the hitter. What happens? Mays rounds third and scored. You heard me. Willie scored from first on a one-hop single to left field. He'd rather have *always* been in Philadelphia.

—Lon Simmons

Today, you can't get a ticket to Braves' games. In the late 1970s, you could literally sit in the booth and count the people at Atlanta-Fulton County Stadium. I'm there one night doing the Giants with Lon Simmons—great voice, sense of humor, among the best-ever. It's my first big-league job, and I've got jitters, though there aren't many folks there to share my anxiety.

Lon was the Number One guy, so I did the third, fourth, and seventh innings. I try to sit down to start my play-by-play, when I lose my balance, the collapsible chair in the booth collapses, and, as I reach to break my fall, I stuck my left hand in the middle of the chair. The chair collapsed onto my finger for a severe gash, and I start bleeding. Lon says, "Hey, don't worry, just get it taken care of." I said, "No way, man." All of a sudden I'm looking at this as a player might if he got hurt and felt that he had to stay in the lineup.

Lon was kind enough to go get a cup filled with ice. He sat it on the table, I stuck my hand in the cup, and for two innings did the play-by-play as the cup soon looked like strawberry soda. After the game, I got a couple stitches, and it's OK. And the most important thing was that pain didn't beat me. I got those innings in! Today I'd see a doctor right away. When you're young and foolish, priorities take a different turn. Times change. Just look at the Braves' crowds then, and now.

—Joe Angel

I've worked in three markets where one guy exemplified the work ethic. Nolan Ryan in Houston: How about his fifth no-hitter in 1981? Andre Dawson in Chicago. Don Mattingly in New York. And ball parks that in an age of cookie-cutters are uniquely their own. I know that the Astrodome now isn't the Astrodome then; I hate how they ditched the exploding score-board to build 10,000 crummy football seats. Also, natural grass would help. But the Dome's been positive for baseball in Houston, the most intimate of the indoor parks.

Wrigley Field is the quintessential baseball experience: electric, close, alive. Still has the concept of knotholers—people watching across the street [from rooftop homes]. It's a national treasure, like Fenway or Yankee Stadium. The Stadium looks different since its [disastrous 1974-75] renovation, but still hallowed ground. Where else to step on the same turf as Ruth and Gehrig and Mantle? It's the fiber of what baseball is supposed to be. People talk about the Yankees moving. Let them remember that you don't buy history in an MTV store—or New Jersey.

—*Dewayne Staats*

Even indoor ball can leave footprints. The most unusual thing I've seen occurred in 1984 in the Metrodome. Frank Viola is the Twins' pitcher. One of the all-time flakes, Mickey Hatcher, was playing first. Great guy, but weird things would happen. Tim Laudner was catching. At bat, Dave Kingman, a big right-handed hitter who took enormous cuts that sometimes led to titanic homers. Most times he'd strike out, but often hit what became known as Dave Kingman Pop-ups. Straight up, seemed in orbit, unbelievably high.

Viola throws, Kingman takes that undercut swing, and we get a typical Kingman Pop-up. Now, the Metrodome has two roofs: one on top and, below it, a false ceiling with ventilation holes each a little bigger than a baseball. Once the ball gets past a certain height, you lose it, and look at fielders to find the ball. OK. I'm doing play-by-play and start looking at the infield. Hatcher and the second basemen are circling around, so I know it's on the right-hand side. Actually, the entire *team* is waiting for the ball to come down. Only it doesn't. And now everybody starts running because they don't know where it is. Maybe the ball'll hit 'em on the head! Nobody can figure what's going on. It hadn't happened before, never will again.

Then we learn the unbelievable: The ball went *through* the false ceiling and a tiny ventilation hole and got lodged up on top of the ceiling. There it stayed, never to come down! The umpires call time. Too bad there's no ground rule. They meet for 10 minutes, but what can they do? They can pretend the ball went in the seats, or call no play. No way the defense could have caught it. Finally, in their infinite wisdom, they give Dave a ground-rule double, a decision I still can't figure. Next day the Twins milk it for PR. What goes up's got to come down, and they enlist Hatcher to prove it. Mickey in his flakiness said, "Sure, I'll cooperate." So the news goes out that Mickey's going to put himself at first base and prove the law of gravity.

A guy on the roof puts a baseball over the ventilation hole and drops it to Mickey. Funny, a big moment, but duck soup for sure. What Mickey forgot is that the guy dropped the ball with no spin, so it became a giant knuckleball, wiggling all over the place on the way down. All of a sudden, Hatcher sees the ball moving and darting and jiggling, and he starts doing the same thing. It keeps dropping and getting heavier, and, well, Hatcher never caught it, never got in position. He put the glove up, and the ball missed it and landed on his toe! He's in pain. The crowd's in hysterics. It could only happen to Mickey and, believe me, only in the Dome.

—Joe Angel

I've always loved differences between fans. When I arrived in Baltimore [1983, after stretches in Oakland, Texas, and Boston], the Orioles had finished second the year before—made a great stretch run to the last weekend. They won the first three games of a four-game series with Milwaukee, then lost the pennant on the final day. The next year, they have a huge function at the Inner Harbor the day before Opening Day. Must be 50,000 people all going nuts at the arrival of the Orioles. I was astounded!

In Boston, even if the Sox made the Series and lost, everybody'd talk about, "What a bunch of losers they are [assuming a Boston accent], those Sox have broken my heart since I was a kid." Red Sox' fans are knowledgeable and rightly demanding. But the affection between Orioles' fans and players is probably more pronounced than in any other city.

I'd compare it to a small town that reacts to its college football team. I remember Billy Ripken going to Texas [1993]. What was he? A .231 hitter, but played hard. Got his uniform dirty, and people loved him. You don't find that anywhere else. People ask me, "How do Oriole fans compare to the Red Sox'?" Well, now that they're outdrawing them by a million per year, you have to ask, "How do Boston fans compare to the Orioles'?"

—Jon Miller

My favorite experience was the Orioles' final game at Memorial Stadium [October 6, 1991] the year before moving to Camden Yards. The post-game farewell was the most wrenching feeling I've had at a ball park. If you haven't seen it, I would invite you to write to the Orioles and ask for their videotape. You'll be crying because of what happened *after* the final out—and without a word being said over the P.A. system.

First, the background music began from "Field of Dreams." Then, the first man emerged from the dugout to take his position: Brooks Robinson, at third base. Followed by outfielder Frank Robinson, followed by pitcher Jim Palmer. This is how the Orioles said good-bye to Memorial Stadium, asking to come back to Baltimore all former players who could possibly be there. The crowd didn't know this. When it happened, they were stunned.

One after another the players came out—no introduction, just dressed in their era's uniform—and found their position. [Luis] Aparicio went to shortstop. The first basemen, second basemen, catchers, outfielders—each together. More than 75 players positioned around the field, and that music kept rolling. Working with Jon Miller, I looked with binoculars at fellows like Brooks and Boog Powell, and they were, like we were, drained. It was hard to keep from breaking down completely. The thing is that there was no cheering, none. Instead, thunderous applause, and enough tears for a river.

When I left the park that afternoon, I didn't pass a dry eye as I walked to my car. Whoever said "There's no crying in baseball" would have changed his mind that day.

—*Chuck Thompson*

Today, name a ball park, and a mascot comes to mind. The Rockies were in Philadelphia for our last '93 game there when, without warning, the Phillie Phanatic crashed through the back of the broadcast booth. I was working with Duane Kuiper as the Phanatic came between us, threw all of our notes up in the air, climbed over the ledge outside, and worked his way around the stadium. Sign of the times: Boston doesn't have the only green monster.

—*Charlie Jones*

In baseball the park's a participant. Take Pete Runnels, a left-hand batter who slapped the ball to the opposite field. When Pete played for the [1951-57] Senators, he'd make out to the left field [a trolley ride of 387 feet at Griffith Stadium]. He gets traded to Boston and starts tatooing the ball off that left-field fence [Fenway Park's 315-feet Green Monster, shrouding pitchers with a blanket of doom]. Wins two batting titles. It's like another guy. Clark Kent turns into Superman on a train ride to Boston from Washington.

—*Bob Wolff*

I love the photo of Mickey Mantle catching a fly ball in front of Yankee Stadium's right-center field auxiliary scoreboard. Top of the eighth inning, two outs, fifth game of the World Series. The Yankees already have two runs off Sal Maglie, one of them Mantle's homer in the fourth inning. October 8, 1956. Dodgers-Yankees. Don Larsen's about to complete his perfect game.

The photo shows Mantle, the grass and bleachers, that look of fall in the East, shadows cutting the outfield. Its colors are vivid, completely distinctive. Could this be anyplace but Yankee Stadium? Could Crosley Field be anyplace but Cincinnati? Ebbets Field anyplace save Brooklyn, or Camden Yards elsewhere than Baltimore? Why do you think people go to Camden Yards and will even when the Orioles don't contend? Why do the Red Sox sell out first place or last? Or fans see the Cubs at Wrigley Field? Because they like the ambience, the baseball *feel*.

Compare this with Veterans Stadium, Three Rivers, Riverfront Stadium: places with all the individuality and collective soul of a Kmart. Why can't the idiots who run baseball get it? The answer to their future lies in the past.

—*Bob Costas*

CHAPTER FIVE

LEGEND IN YOUR OWN TIME

TED WILLIAMS

*T*he first big-league game I attended was August 30, 1960—Ted Williams'
42nd birthday—against the Tigers, at Fenway Park. Eleven years earlier,
my parents had watched a Red Sox-Indians' game at Fenway on their honey-
moon. Now I saw on my father's face why Williams became John Wayne in
baseball woolies for a generation of Americans.

I still recall Williams lofting amid waves of noise to deep right field. I took
home a charged puzzlement as to his effect on the crowd. Only retrospect told
that in his day (or should I say my father's), Williams was the most volcanic
athlete since the Babe. He threw tantrums, spit at fans, reviled the press, and
was a dazzling interview. As Curt Gowdy said, "Where would you find another
like him in a million years?"

I first met Teddy Ballgame in 1966 as he and Casey Stengel were inducted
at Cooperstown. Visiting the Glimmerglass, Williams wrote an acceptance
speech longhand the night before that many call the finest in Hall of Fame history. Later, Ted was besieged for autographs. "I'm not signing, you pushy kids.
Learn some manners." Eclipsing voice, his roar stunned them into silence.
"Know who I'm signing? Kids outside the circle who aren't rude." And, jostling
pen and paper, he pushed his way toward me.

Hooked from there to eternity, I never forgot the honest outrage of this part-
child and part-Gibraltar. When No. 9 retired, Ed Linn wrote, "And now Boston
knows how England felt when it lost India." Pray that Gibraltar
crumbles and, yes, the Rockies tumble before America forgets the seasons of The
Kid.

In the early '50s, the Red Sox and Boston Braves broadcast home games—but no road, too expensive. Then [owner] Tom Yawkey decided he wanted to have every Sox game on radio, and have his own guy; Jim Britt had been doing the Braves as well. Given a choice, Britt, to his regret, chose the Braves. So in '51 Yawkey taps the guy who'd been working in New York with Mel Allen.

By 1954, Curt Gowdy was an enormously popular play-by-play guy. When his partner, Bob Delaney, left to join the Giants, I auditioned for his job and won. Curt was a great talent, but demanding. He'd learned a lot from Allen—Mel insisted you get it right—and right away started tutoring me. Here I was, a young twangy Oklahoman amid foreign tongues. Curt and I were together six years. I'm glad I stuck it out, even if the Sox weren't competitive. What made it worthwhile was a guy I would have hated to miss. I'll never forget Gowdy telling me that first year in spring training as I was trying to get acquainted, "You haven't seen anything until you've seen Ted Williams."

The Kid—now, and four decades later.

—Bob Murphy

When I was a [Braves'] rookie in 1950, we played the Red Sox in a city series, and I got a chance to pitch. It's late in the game, and Williams comes to the plate. I thought I'd try to get a curveball over the outside corner. Instead, Ted hit one in the seats; it's rolled to the Kenmore Hotel by now. The game is over, and we're walking through the clubhouse. Billy Southworth was our manager, and he was trying to make me feel good, build my confidence, but that's not how it came out. He put his arm around me and said, "Don't worry, he's hit them off better pitchers than you." I'll never forget that—and I've tried.

—Ernie Johnson

No one forgets a Presidential opener. My first was in the '50s, at Griffith Stadium, against Boston. The Red Sox trained in Arizona, so I hadn't seen them that spring, and I wanted to find out about Williams. I asked the Boston newspaper guys, "What kind of a spring did Ted have?" They said, "Fantastic. Must have hit over .400, but the unusual thing is that he didn't hit a homer."

The first time Williams came to bat, Opening Day, I recite this story: Great average in the spring, but no power. I no sooner spoke than the ball disappears over the tree along the high wall in deep center field. The next day I came to Griffith Stadium—oh, about three hours before the game— and the Sox are taking batting practice. And out of the visitors' dugout comes Ted shouting about this big-nosed, loud-mouthed, bald-headed broadcaster that didn't know his something from his something. I'm in the Senators' dugout. So I thought, I don't want him to get a sore throat from hollering at me, might as well go over and let him unload. He steps into the batting cage and rips me up and down—"no power" this and that—and I just stood there. With Ted it was a good idea to listen. Finally he stopped and turned and spit and looked at me. "Kid," he said, "it's the first bleepin' ball I've hit all spring." Then he went back to his business.

I'll never forget that spring training. Mr. Williams hit a few home runs after that, I recall.

—*Chuck Thompson*

Nineteen fifty-two was the Braves' last year in Boston. We're playing the Red Sox in spring training, and Vern Bickford is pitching. Vern was a proven starter. I guess that's why he felt he could do something I'd never seen. First time up, Bickford gets Williams out. In the third, he tells us in the dugout, "Ted is up this inning. I'm gonna' see how far that big donkey can hit one." We all said, "What are you gonna' do?" He said, "Lay it in there about 3/4 speed and see what happens." We're on the edge of our seats. Bickford goes out—here comes Ted—and Vern laid the first pitch in there, a 3/4 speed fastball. Sometimes, in batting practice, you hit one in the ground or otherwise screw up a lollypop pitch. Not here. Williams hit that ball so far it went past the light towers in right-center field. Maybe the longest-ever home run in Bradenton. We're roaring as the inning ends. Bickford comes back and says, "Well, I got my answer."

—*Ernie Johnson*

The first day of '54 spring training, Ted broke his collarbone diving for a ball. He missed the first five weeks of the season and didn't play until the Red Sox were playing a double-header in Detroit, always a magnificent park for Number Nine. Ted played both games, went 8 for 9, hit two or three home runs. And the only time he made out was when Al Kaline climbed the fence in right field to rob him of another.

Williams was everything people said about him: explosive, temperamental, dramatic. He often called his shots. Cal McLish told how he fanned Ted once a couple of times, and Williams said in the dugout, "The next time I'm up, he's gonna' throw me that side-arm slow curve and I'll hit it in the upper deck." That's exactly where he parked it. Ted could be sick or have an injury, but the very first day back he'd hit a home run. It was uncanny. I remember a monster shot he hit off Tom Morgan into the center-field seats at Fenway. His Sox were sometimes bad, but never boring. "Old Rubber Arm" Ellis Kinder was on those '50s clubs. Ellis was a reliever who stayed out all night— *night* after night. One morning they picked him up off the sidewalk at 5 o'clock in Chicago, said, "Well, so much for using him in today's double-header." All Ellis did was save both games. Came on in the first game, worked about four innings in the second.

It was a different breed of cat in those days, but always fun. The Red Sox still have New England all to themselves. Nobody has more loyal fans. Even with Williams, they've needed it over the years. 'Course, he's a reason they've *been* so loyal.

—*Bob Murphy*

T om Yawkey loved Williams like his own son, but once he gave him hell. Williams was very unselfish. Mickey Mantle would come up to him—Al Kaline when he was 20—everyone'd ask for tips on hitting. Ted would help any way he could. Finally, Yawkey called up and said, "Why are you aiding the enemy?"

Williams' answer was really profound. "Look, T.A., when you're a block away from a major league ball park and hear the crowd roar, somebody's just hit the baseball! It's exciting. Fans get a home run or double or triple or run-down play or a cut-off. It's all action and involves hitting." Ted always complained about this house in Baltimore up on a hill that had lights on at night, bitched to the league office about how it hurt his hitting. He had every park analyzed as to the background. He loved Fenway because of the high wall in center where that white ball came in off a green background.

Always, it was, "Hitting! More hitting!" A perfect game to Ted was 20 to 18.

—*Curt Gowdy*

Ted Williams was the only player I ever saw who stopped batting practice by himself. People in the opposite dugout came up on the steps. His teammates paused to watch. It was like a one-man pre-game show. Mesmerizing. Ted was also moody. He could be the most convivial guy stepping into the batting cage. If he didn't do well, he'd come out storming, "Get out of my way!" I'd wait till he cooled off, then resume our conversation. I loved to talk to Ted off-camera, and each year when Boston came to town I approached him for an interview. The reaction was always the same: "Hm." He'd grimace, recoil.

In 1956, I met Williams in spring training. He treated me like a leper, so I forced the issue. "Ted, you're a friend, and yet when you see me approaching you try to hide. So here's my deal. If you hit 25 homers by August 15, or you're batting .340, you go on with me." He agreed, shook hands. That August, Ted misplayed a ball at Fenway, was booed, and spit at fans in the lower boxes. The Sox fined him $5,000—Ted's front-page news. His next stop was D.C., and he's hitting over .340. I tell Ted, "According to our handshake, you said you'd appear with me if you hit that figure. You're hitting it." Silence. I went on: "One proviso. As a reporter, I've got to ask if you feel remorse about spitting. If you don't want to go on, tell me." More silence. Finally, Ted says, "Hell, what time's the show? Ask anything you want."

Back then everything was live. I start the show knowing that whatever happens is news because Ted's only speaking to me. A few minutes into it, a fan goes on the field and says, "Bob, good to see ya.'" I said, "We're doing a show!" He says, "Is that Ted Williams?" I answer, "Yeah, but we're in the middle of a show!" I'm trying to get this guy away, to no avail, all the while smiling so people don't think I'm upset. Ted's *not* smiling. The camera on him shows Williams dying from the controversy and this fan. Finally, I resume our talk, and he apologizes for spitting. "It just happened. I erupted." A great show, but I'm heartbroken. What do I do with the fan?

Each morning I looked at tape to see how the prior day's film came out. This morning I didn't want to because I was so upset about the fan spoiling my interview. I ask my colleagues to watch. First, I hear titters, then roars, then gales of laughter at the guy—and Williams going apopletic on camera. I go in to peek, and even I started to laugh. So I took that tape and one I did with Mickey Mantle and showed 'em to the Colgate Palmolive Company. I said, "Would you like to sponsor my shows around the country?" They looked at the two pieces—in essence, my pilot—and said, "Absolutely." From that came pre-game shows with the Yankees, Red Sox, and Athletics. I'll always be indebted to Mr. Williams. But then, I'm not alone.

—*Bob Wolff*

Ted's eyes tested perfect in the marine air force. They couldn't believe how good his sight was. I've duck-hunted with him when he says, "There are two ducks coming at 3 o'clock." I have good eyes, and I'd say, "Where?" Two minutes *later,* they'd show up.

Ted is the best fisherman I've ever seen. He got to like me because I'd talk fishing instead of baseball. Once, though, I asked, "Ted, your war with the media, why'd you do it?" Bobby Doerr [Hall of Fame, 1988] was probably his closest friend on the ball club. Williams called him "Silent Captain of the Red Sox." One of the two sweetest men I have met in baseball; the other, King Kong Keller with the Yankees. Doerr told me that when Ted hit a home run in his rookie year, he'd take his cap off and wave it to the fans rounding the bases. The next year, they started to boo Williams for hitting fewer home runs, and Ted got mad. To him, they were fair-weather.

Ted couldn't stand a phoney—"a politician," he'd say. So he stopped tipping his cap and never did again. He was too stubborn to go halfway to meet the Red Sox' fans. The irony is that he thought they were the best baseball fans on earth.

—*Curt Gowdy*

I'm asked who most impressed me among the stars of baseball? There are many; don't forget I was a baseball nut. But a player did things up in Boston that made him No. 1. Every time he got a chance, he'd visit hospitals, and take baseballs autographed by the greatest hitter of all time. As he finished he told the nuns, "God bless you ladies in your love for kids. Don't tell anybody, especially a newswriter, that I was here." He had a bad taste for them. Keep the kids happy and talk baseball is what he loved. Ted Williams, my hero.

Ted was a great flyer in World War II [also, Korea]. He had the sight of a bird, could land a fighter plane on a dime. I think his vision helped him hit so many homers [521]. If you want to learn about Ted, ask Herb Score. One day Cleveland was leading the Red Sox in the ninth inning. In the last half, Ted came to bat with the bases loaded. The count goes to 3-2. The next pitch was a blazing Score fastball that Williams hit onto the Massachusetts

Turnpike. After the game, Score went over to Ted and said, "See ya' later, slug-ger." Ted looked up and said, "Herbie, do me a favor, will ya', buddy. Don't ever throw me a fastball on a count of three and two." Isn't that something? Williams was the most unselfish guy in baseball.

My first year [1948] I was new to baseball and followed Ted around because he knew everybody. One day he was in a conversation, so I walked up and said "hi" to the group and turned to Williams. "Mr. Williams, would you be the guest on my pre-game show today? I'd sure appreciate it." He looked down at me with that great height of his and said, "Why, you little skinhead, I thought you were never gonna' ask me." I was his man after that for a long, long time. One of the best friends I ever had. I'm sure the nuns feel the same.

—Jimmy Dudley

I interviewed Ted quite a few times over WGN-TV at Comiskey Park, and he was never reluctant to share his knowledge or philosophy of hitting. The last time I saw him was at O'Hare Airport. Doggone if [broadcaster] Jack Brickhouse and I don't run into him, and he said, "Hey, you know a guy I've been thinking about is [then-Cubs' slugger Dave] Kingman. Here's my phone number. I'll be there only two days before going to Canada. Would he mind calling me?" I think, "Are you kidding? What hitter in his right mind wouldn't welcome the chance to get help from you?"

I wondered what Ted would tell him. "You can't be afraid not to get two strikes," he said. "If he'd be more patient, not swing at every pitch, he could put 30 points on his average." That day I saw Kingman at the Hilton pool and gave him the news. Other Cubs were amazed. "*Williams* wants him to call?" I told Dave to do it now. The next morning I saw him—still hadn't called. The upshot was that he never called the greatest hitter in the world. Later, I told [Ron] Santo, [Billy] Williams, and Glenn Beckert. They couldn't believe Kingman hadn't phoned. Then we thought a moment and, knowing Dave, we could.

Once, I said, "Ted, you never take your eyes off the pitcher from the time he starts his windup till you swing." He said, "Neither did Ty Cobb." Williams took off his cap. "Look at this," he said. "Cobb would put a hole in his cap only 1/4 inch wide. He'd put the cap back on, and all Ty could see through that tiny hole was the pitcher. It forced him to concentrate." Ted didn't have a cap like that. Somehow he survived.

—Vince Lloyd

After playing in, calling, and viewing thousands of baseball games, batting practice had little appeal to me. I used it only to visit players. The exception was when we televised a Red Sox' game on CBS-TV's "Game of the Week." Then I'd go to the park to watch Williams take batting practice. His skills were unbelievable.

Diz[zy Dean] and I went to Boston to televise the Red Sox on Saturday and Sunday. We arrived Friday night and met at the Kenmore Hotel, where Ted lived. He learns we're there and comes down from his room. I mention to Ted that earlier that week I'd visited a hospital in the Midwest and met one of his biggest fans, a little boy suffering from leukemia, about 10 years old. The nurses loved him. Each day in the corridor, they sat him on the floor with a little wooden bat and got on their hands and knees and rolled a ball to him. He'd hit it, and as it rolled they exclaimed, "Oh, that's a double. That's a triple. That's a home run." If it was a homer, it was hit by Ted!

The little boy's room was filled with Williams memorabilia, and he asked me to say hello to Ted. I'm leaving when the nurses corralled me in the hallway and asked if I could get the young man an autographed ball or cap from Ted. I said, "No problem," and now let me tell you about a side of Ted Williams that you don't know about. He tells me in the bar, "OK, Bud, alright, fine, I'll tell ya' what I'm gonna' do. I'll fly in and see this boy"—he flew his own plane—"but on two conditions, and I mean this sincerely. I want to be met at the airport by the boy's mother and father *only*. Any media or other gathering, and I'll just touch down and then take right off again." The second condition was that we were never to mention it on the air.

One of the most heartwarming stories of my broadcasting career, and I couldn't tell it. The young boy died later in the year, but he enjoyed the greatest day of his life: a visit with his hero.

—*Bud Blattner*

I get to the park, and equipment manager Johnny Orlando said, "Listen, this is The Kid's last game. He's gonna' retire after today [September 28]." [In 1960, Williams batted .316 and smashed 29 homers and, at 42, declined to tip his cap. He also exited as only a deity could, with a home run in his final time at bat.] It was Boston's last home game, but we had a season-ending series in New York. Johnny said, "Yawkey said OK. Ted's got a chest cold, so he wants to call it quits." I went to Ted—nobody knew he wasn't going to New York—and said, "Is this your last day?" Ted said, "Yeah, don't mention it till the game starts." Before the game, we had a little ceremony behind home plate. Mayor Hines gave him a Revere Bowl and made a speech. Then I got up.

I'd been late getting to the ball park—did some commercials downtown and the recorder didn't work. So I got hell when I got there 30 minutes before the game. Bill Crowley, the Sox' publicity director, said, "You don't have a note." I said, "I don't need any about Williams." I stepped to the mike and said, "Today we honor a man who in my opinion and many of yours was the greatest hitter who ever lived. I didn't get to see Ty Cobb, Paul Waner, or Rogers Hornsby, who hit .400 four or five times, but I don't see how they could be better than Ted Williams. I could have pages of batting records up here, but what really made Ted was pride. He had an intense pride that every time up he wanted to produce a hit. Not only for himself, but for the fans at Fenway whom he secretly loved, who stood behind him amid ups and downs. Pride is what made him go and why he's here. The greatest hitter of all time, Ted Williams."

Williams grabbed me and said, "I want a copy. That's one of the nicest tributes to me ever." I said, "I don't have a copy." He says, "Oh, shit"—vintage Ted!—and walks to home plate. His first words were, "Well, I want to thank the knights of the keyboard," his sarcastic salute to writers in the press box. Then he thanked Tom Yawkey and [Sox' ex-general manager] Joe Cronin and his teammates. But most of all he wanted to thank the New England fans who cherished him—and they did. You had to understand Ted, a perfectionist who got mad at himself more than anybody. If you know a perfectionist, you know how they are. All the ashtrays have to be clean, everything in a row. I think New England forgave him more than he did himself.

Finally, the game starts. Ted goes out his first three times up. His third time, he nearly had one, a long fly to right against the bullpen. In the eighth inning, he's up against Jack Fisher. Today, they say Fisher grooved it. He didn't. It wasn't a good pitch. Williams never swung at a bad pitch. His thesis was, get a good pitch to hit, and you'll be a better hitter; don't swing unless it's a strike. This time he did, and when I heard the crack of the bat and the ball started toward right field, I knew it was gone. ["The count one and one on Williams," Gowdy's call began. "Everybody quiet here at Fenway Park after they gave him a standing ovation of two minutes, knowing that this is probably his last time at-bat. One out, nobody on, last of the eighth inning.

Jack Fisher into his windup, here's the pitch. Williams swings, and there's a long drive to deep right! That ball is going, and it is gone! A home run for Ted Williams in his last time at bat in the major leagues!"]

I was choked up. My heart was pounding, and, as he rounded first and headed to second, I made the statement about Ted's last time at bat. The media didn't say much about it then, but years later they replayed it at the 1986 World Series between the Mets and Red Sox, and made a big to do. "How did you know it was his last at-bat? He was supposed to play the Yankees in New York." "Because Ted told me," I said. Icons are like that.

—*Curt Gowdy*

One last Williams story. In the late 1980s, they had a tribute to Ted. David Hartman of "Good Morning America" came up to emcee. Thirteen public friends of Ted came together in a theatre with about 6,000 people, to raise money for the Jimmy Fund [New England's cancer charity]. Each of us was interviewed by Hartman for about five minutes. I look over and said, "That's John Glenn, the astronaut and senator from Ohio. What's he doing here?" I introduced myself: "Senator, I'm Curt Gowdy. I used to broadcast Red Sox' games. What's your connection with Ted?"

Glenn says, "I was his flight commander in Korea, and that's how I got to be an astronaut, through my air force background. Williams used to fly a wing for me." I said, "What kind of a pilot was he?" And Glenn says, "The best I ever saw."

—*Curt Gowdy*

CHAPTER SIX

DOIN' WHAT COMES NATURALLY

BOOTH FUNNIES

In Jack Benny's old TV show, a bank robber accosts our hero. Pointing a gun, he demands, "Your money or your life." Benny pauses before replying, "I'm thinking, I'm thinking." His leitmotiv was cheapness, like Johnny Carson's golf swing, Phyllis Diller's cackle, or Barbara Bush's pearls.

Mel Allen's name, even apart from voice, screams "How About That!" Harry Caray's "Take Me out to the Ball Game" denotes half-anthem and half-command. Jerry Coleman evokes Colemanisms. Bob Elson, a monotone. Joe Garagiola, humor etching continuity on the transient pulp of life. Think of "It's outa' here!" or "My, oh, my!" or "Hey-hey!" or "Kiss it good-bye!" Each identifies a specific Voice.

To me, the Miss America pageant will always mean Bert Parks. It is true Bert could not sing, act, nor dance adroitly—also, that millions would not go to bed until Parks crooned, "There she is" to the winner. My hometown would no sooner miss Miss America than burn the American flag. Faux pas or trademark phrase, broadcast calling cards draw you toward them—from laughter, never wandering far away.

Debating baseball's all-time bloopers, you think of Ralph Kiner saying, "Today is Father's Day. So to all you fathers in the audience, Happy Birthday." Or Ralph saying as he goes to commercial, "Now I'll turn it over to Tim MacArthur," and McCarver having the presence to reply, "It's McCarver, but like MacArthur I shall return after this break." They're good, but pale beside what happened at a mid-week game at Busch Stadium in 1977. I'm 25, and trying to hang around the booth to absorb as much as I could—really, just hoping to be around Jack Buck.

This day, the Cardinals are hosting the Cubs. Forgettable except that it's National Dairy Day, one of your huge promotions. Fans flock from nearby states for the festivities. They put on the screen, "Welcome, members of the National Dairy Council," and the game starts. The booth in St. Louis is two-tiered, and, if you're behind them, Jack would be on your left, Mike Shannon's in the middle, and to the right is Bob Starr. The game moves to the fourth inning, and the National Dairy Council president shows up and is waved down by Buck who is bored with the proceedings. Buck starts to schmooze with him on the air.

Buck says, "How do you like St. Louis?" The guy says, "Jack, it's great. We haven't seen the National League in Milwaukee since the Braves left." Buck says, "That's wonderful, head up to the Hill, get a nice Italian meal." We now turn to a woman from the National Dairy Council who's with this guy. Well-constructed. Wears a bathing suit with white high heels as if she were in a beauty pageant, except that the ribbon going across her doesn't say "Miss Wisconsin" but "Miss Cheesecake."

Ken Reitz comes to bat as Miss Cheesecake comes sashaying down the steps of the booth with a goodwill offering from the National Dairy Council. Three tiny cheesecakes, one for each broadcaster. Curve to Reitz as she places one in front of Buck, one for Shannon, and a third in front of Starr. She then makes her egress to much attention all around. Reitz flies to left as Buck leans across Shannon and says to Starr, "Hey, what do ya' think of Miss Cheesecake?" Apparently distracted, Starr thinks Buck asked, "What do you think of *this* cheesecake?" So he says, "I'll tell ya', Jack, I'd like to try a piece of that right now."

For my money, there is the greatest moment in baseball broadcast history, eclipsing Russ Hodges' call of Bobby Thomson's homer or anything else. To this day, Starr doesn't know what it was he said, or why it was so funny. The booth fell silent for 15 seconds until they were composed enough to speak—on radio, a true eternity of dead air.

—*Bob Costas*

Bobby Costas has told the cheesecake story at banquets, on "The Tonight Show," in a *Playboy* interview, *ad infinitum*. We're good friends, but he's never told the story right, so in this historic book I am pleased to set the record straight!

Each year at Busch Stadium a group of area bakers get together for a night at the ball park. They come upstairs to our booth—large, double-level, with a three-step stairway down to where we were. On the far left was producer Tommy Barton. Jack [Buck] sat next to him, Mike Shannon in the middle, and I'm to the right. If Mike wasn't involved, he'd get up and let the person interviewed sit in his chair. That's what he did as the head of the retail bakers came upstairs with goodies and a young lady in a nice little outfit with a sash across her that said "Miss Cheesecake." She was, I suppose, 17 or 18 years old. Miss Cheesecake sat down, and Jack talked to her for a few minutes while doing play-by-play. After a few minutes, she was excused.

Keep in mind the great distance between Jack and me—he's to the far left, I'm far right—and that we usually kept a hand over our ear and worked without headsets, which were uncomfortable. There also was a retail baker guy, over my left shoulder, holding a box of cheesecake. Jack says, "Do you like cheesecake, Bob?" And I said, "Yes, I do, very much." Then he says what I think is, "How do you like *this* cheesecake?" meaning the cheesecake this guy is holding, and I said, "Jack, I haven't had any yet, but it looks good enough to eat."

With that, Jack chokes his way through the last hitter in the lineup. I noticed Tommy Barton was turning his face to the wall in hysterics. Jack finished the half inning, we break for the spot, and he says, "Do you know what you said?" I said, "Yeah, you asked me if I like cheesecake. I said yes, and you asked me if I liked this cheesecake." He said, "No, no, I asked how you liked *Miss* Cheesecake?" We went from there. I got home that night, and my wife Brenda's waiting for me. "Tell me I didn't hear what I think I heard on the air tonight in the first inning." There you have it, the true story of Miss Cheesecake.

—Bob Starr

For years in the late '30s, I'd leave the CBS office in afternoon, drive uptown to Yankee Stadium or the Polo Grounds, sit alone, and, you know, really broadcast to myself. "Man," I thought, "I'd give anything to do baseball." Then along came Ivory Soap.

In those days the principal announcer—for the Yankees, Arch McDonald—did seven innings. His assistant only did the third and seventh. In May 1939, I still wasn't a Yankee broadcaster, but I knew how, each day, Ivory Soap was plugged in the third inning. It was all afternoon games then, and a lot of ladies listened. Arch's assistant leans forward and says, "Ladies, before we go to the bottom of the third"—and he got real coy, he was going to talk to women—"gather around your sets, 'cause I want to talk to you about *Ovary* Soap."

Suddenly, he realized what he'd said and burst out laughing. He made three efforts, and, every time, for some reason, it came out "Ovary Soap." And then he'd roar. He was fired the next day, and I replaced him. I guess people think of me and "How about that!" But when I think of broadcasting, it's soap that comes to mind. Guess which brand I still use?

—*Mel Allen*

A lot of fans knew me by terms like "The string is out" [a 3-2 count] and "stay-alive fouls" or "Come on down to the old ball orchard." Probably the most famous was "So long and lots of good luck, ya' heah?" A lot of these were southern expressions. I used to date a gal from North Carolina, and every time I said, "So long," she said, "Now don't forget to call me, ya' heah?" But the expression that meant the most was at the start of a game where I said, "Hello, baseball fans everywhere." I'd get letters addressed, "Hello, Baseball Fans Everywhere, Cleveland, Ohio."

You don't forget gaffes. One day I came on the air by saying, "And leading off Boston is Detroit." *What?* When I broke in, everything was live. I interviewed A's manager Jimmy Dykes on our post-game show where guests got an electric razor. After the interview, I said, "Thanks for being my guest, and let me give you a beautiful Schick electric razor." Jimmy came back so quick that the station didn't have time to cut him off. "Thanks," he said, "I'm just glad it's not a straight razor. Watching some of these turkeys play baseball can drive you to cut your throat."

—*Jimmy Dudley*

In the Baltimore suburbs, I lived a couple houses from a wonderful guy named Sharman. Solid Christian, great family. He fancied himself a pretty good putter, read books about it. Truth was that he wasn't any better than I was. And like any golfer, he had some real frustrations.

What made it funny is that when Bob missed putts, he wouldn't swear but always say the same thing. He'd be in his back yard; then I'd hear, "Go to War, Miss Agnes!" Bob had missed another putt. I'd hear this, and hear it, and didn't know what it meant. But I loved it, picked it up, and used it for something exciting on the field. It just snowballed; fans liked it. Over the years, they've come up and said, "Chuck, Go to War, Miss Agnes!" If I had a dime for every time, I'd own my own battleship.

—Chuck Thompson

Dizzy Dean knew pitching, about the only baseball thing that interested him. He had a very limited formal education ["I graduated second grade," said the Hall of Fame pitcher, "and didn't do too good in first, either"] but had a master's degree in both back pockets on the mound.

One pitcher that intrigued him was the Yankees' Eddie Lopat. On one of our Saturday "Game of the Week" telecasts, the Yankees faced the Indians and Lopat was to pitch, so Diz was unusually up. Now, if you recall Lopat [AKA "The Junkman"], he had no overpowering stuff. So Dean started the broadcast by saying, "Friends, Eddie Lopat is a great pitcher. Now what I want you to do is to watch a few hitters and see if you can tell why he gets everybody out, and if you can't, well, Ol' Diz'll tell ya." Lopat faced two hitters, recorded two easy outs, and Diz said, "Figured it out? If you ain't, I'm gonna' tell ya'.

"First, Eddie Lopat has great control, and, second, he's got testicle fortitude." Diz hesitated a moment and said, "Well, I think ya' know what I mean. He's got guts." Never broke stride, and I don't think ever realized what he'd said. A case where Diz's "fracturing the King's English" took on a whole new bent.

—Bud Blattner

Byrum Saam broke me in as a Phillies' announcer after I retired as a player. He hired me, and we had a hell of a run. I don't think any announcer meant as much to a city for as long as By [Philadelphia 1938-75]. He had a laid-back image but a great sense of humor. Even if some was unintentional.

By would say the wrong thing at the wrong time, totally innocent, and wouldn't realize what he'd said. We played the Expos in 1969—their first year in Montreal—and By says, "You know, 85 percent of the people here speak French, but they're nice people anyway." The two parts of the sentence were totally unrelated. But that was By; he'd say things, and when they caused a fuss, he'd wonder why.

Late in his career, By had trouble with his eyes. That was especially true on Astroturf, where when it fades it's hard for *anyone* to see the ball, especially at night. By would watch the fielders, look at the umpire's call, and take hints from there. It didn't always work. One time we were in the new St. Louis park when a batter hit one toward the bleachers, and By couldn't see it. He thought the guy had hit a grounder, started talking, then realized what had happened. I'll never forget his call. "There's a ground ball to short-stop . . . , and it's gone!"

Who else could go on like that, booming out that great voice and entertaining the fans? No wonder people loved him.

—*Richie Ashburn*

I covered two World Series for NBC Radio. One was in 1965. The other was '59, Dodgers-White Sox, and I was assigned with Mel Allen. Our first two games were at Comiskey Park, and then we flew to Los Angeles. What a sight the Coliseum was: All those people [three straight record 92,000-plus crowds], that ridiculous left-field screen [251 feet from home plate], a riot of noise and color.

Before Game Five, Mel set the stage on the air, then turned it over to me for the first inning. I'm looking at my notes as he gives what I later learned was a spectacular introduction. He winds up, "Now, here from Philadelphia is the affable, able, and amiable announcer: the great Byrum Saam." I just hear the "Byrum Saam" part and respond, "Right you are, Mel." You can imagine the reaction *that* got.

In 1990, I won the Ford C. Frick Award [for career broadcast excellence] and was inducted at Cooperstown. Before the ceremonies, friends hosted a cocktail party at the Otesaga Hotel. I look at the napkins, and there's writing on them. Each read, "Right you are, Mel."

—*Byrum Saam*

I was born at 1909 LaSalle Street in St. Louis. Probably I'm the only kid born on that block that didn't go to jail. Suddenly, I find myself a poor orphan kid broadcasting the Cardinals. The first thing I realized is that I couldn't use on the air profanity that was common on the street. So I started using the term "Holy Cow!" which was popular. Over the years, [Braves' 1953-63 Voice] Earl Gillespie and Phil Rizzuto of the Yankees said they used it before me. Gillespie wasn't even broadcasting when I started. And the reason I know I was first to use "Holy Cow!" on a major-league broadcast is that I said it in a game that Phil played!

In my early years on radio, a lot of towns had two big-league teams. A rule said you couldn't broadcast the road game, only whoever was at home. So one day I did a *Browns'* game from Sportsman's Park, and Rizzuto is playing shortstop. The only guy that heard Phil say "Holy Cow!" before I did was second baseman Gerry Priddy of the Yankees, because when Rizzuto tossed the ball to Priddy and he didn't catch it, Phil would say, "Holy Cow! You should have held that ball!"

At this point, I'm up in the booth. I say that Rizzuto said, "Holy Cow, Gerry, why didn't you catch the ball?" It was an expression probably thousands of people used daily. I said it on the air, and have been saying it ever since.

—Harry Caray

In '62, Phil Rizzuto has been retired six years as a player. He's doing games with Red Barber and Mel Allen, and the Yankees play a 22-inning Sunday game in Detroit. Mickey Mantle comes out in the eighth to rest his legs. He's replaced by his caddie, Jack Reed, who finishes out the game in center field and hits the only home run of his major league career in the 22nd as the Yankees win.

Now, Phil is notorious for leaving early. A lot of times when the game ends, he'll say, "The Yankees beat the Angels, 4-3. Totals and highlights in a minute"; and you actually hear the mike jiggle as he hooks it back into the stand and gets ready to leave because someone else is handling the post-game show. On this occasion in '62, Phil finishes in about the eighth inning, gives it back to Mel, and leaves to try to catch a flight back to New York, the last one out of Detroit. Phil lands at LaGuardia, gets his car out of parking, and starts driving across the George Washington Bridge to go home to New Jersey.

Keep in mind it's now hours after the game should have ended. Phil puts on the radio and, surprise, hears Red doing play-by-play—Mel's on TV—neither can even go to the bathroom because there's no other announcer. Rizzuto's listening to the game that he started to broadcast in Detroit earlier in the day! I've heard Phil tell the story. He sits on the bridge and says, "Holy Cow! What am I gonna' do? Should I turn around and fly back to Detroit? No, that probably doesn't make much sense." He keeps driving home to [wife] Cora.

One day I drop by the booth, we start talking, and I'm looking over Phil's shoulder at his scorecard. For a strikeout, he's got a slash. For a single and a sacrifice, he's got "WW." They go to commercial, and I say, "Phil, I've seen a lot of different ways to keep score. What's WW?" He says, "Wasn't watching." That's our Scooter.

—*Bob Costas*

Words can turn more ways than a screwball. The Red Sox used to train in Sarasota, Florida, and we had a ceremony at home plate to open spring training. The mayor was going to throw out the first ball. Just about that time, our press steward came up to see what we wanted to drink. I tried to tell him but couldn't get near enough. So he wrote down the name of what he thought I wanted, and handed it to me. Just then, the mayor readied to throw out the first ball. I look at the steward's writing and say, "Here is the Mayor, Mike Shake." That's what he was going to order for me, a milkshake.

—*Curt Gowdy*

The events down the line now seem to blend into one singular joyful experience embracing 40 years. Amid the cobwebs is how early in your career the sportscaster may render an expression, without presence of plan, that registers with the audience.

Eventually you become aware of the favorable response and incorporate it in subsequent broadcasts. Finally, that innocent expression becomes your identification tag that stays with you forever. A "Catbird Seat" for Red Barber. "Holy Cow!"—Harry Caray or Phil Rizzuto. "How about that!"—Mel Allen. "Oh, my!" for Dick Enberg. "Pod-nuh," you think of Dizzy Dean.

It happened to me during my days with basketball's St. Louis Hawks. One constant over the years is the difficulty deciding whether the official's called a blocking or a charging foul. Usually, I wouldn't interpret the infraction before the official because, well, you're incorrect about 50 percent of the time. So one night while doing a Hawks' game from Madison Square Garden, I mentioned a foul, waited until the official ruled, and then said—this came out of nowhere—"they are walking the wrong way." My interpretation—it just happened—and I didn't give it another thought until I returned to St. Louis and found that I had mail up to my ears as fans said they liked it.

Thereafter, I included the expression once a broadcast. It became my epitaph, then and now. On the street corner, I'd be greeted with "Hi, Bud, they're walking the right way." Even now, I'll speak at a banquet, and a chorus comes from the back of the room. Can I explain it? No, I just enjoy it.

—*Bud Blattner*

After graduating from school in 1972, I went to a small TV station north of San Francisco and noticed that nobody was doing the National Hockey League California Golden Seals. Charlie Finley was their owner, and I sent him a letter saying, "We'd be happy to televise your games." One day, he called and said OK. We put some cameras and the director and cameraman into our truck, televised the game on tape, and ran it back the next day.

Now, I had memorized the rule book. I'd memorized names and numbers, the history of the league, because this was big-time hockey and I was 20 years old. And they kept calling during the game from down in the truck saying, "Hey, you sound like you've been doing this for years." Nice, huh? It was about then that I mispronounced "puck." You can do that in baseball, right? "He's under it, and he drops the fall, er, ah, ball." And nobody says anything. Hockey's different. Since then, my recommendation to any young broadcaster is to always refer to the puck as an "it."

—*Jon Miller*

Jerry Coleman is famous for saying things like "Winfield is on first base, and he's always a threat to grow." Or Glenn Beckert is finishing his career with the Padres, and Jerry says, "We just found out that Glenn has been waived, and we hope that before he packs his bags and heads home, he'll stop by the booth so we can kiss him good bye. He's that kind a guy."

I think it's good that baseball breeds bonds of that sort. But to me Jerry's greatest moment happened in the late 1970s. Dave Winfield was acrobatic and graceful. At 6-6, he'd leap outstretched to rob guys of home runs. This occasion, he was playing left field for the Padres when a drive is hit and Dave leaps as high as he can. The ball tips off his glove and vanishes over the fence. Coleman waits for the tumult to subdue, the batter rounds the bases, and then he says, "If Winfield had made that play, they'd be throwing babies from the upper deck."

I didn't know this had become the time-honored means of expressing joy at the ball park: hurling an infant to its doom on the diamond below. I'm still waiting to find out what Jerry meant.

—*Bob Costas*

It's funny. When I reflect back on my years of play-by-play, I don't remember the good stuff, just the crazy. My first real *faux pas* happened in Cleveland Stadium in 1963, a Sunday double-header. It was my first year as Yankee broadcaster, and Birdie Tebbetts was managing the Indians. As I went upstairs to the booth, I said, "You starting [Sam] McDowell and [Jack] Kralick?" Birdie nods, "Yep." Both were lefties. The first game starts, and we're rolling good. Phil and Mel are on the air with me, and I say, "Look at McDowell out there!" Sam was a strikeout pitcher with erratic control, but his control this day was astounding.

Finally, about the *sixth* inning, mind you, we got a call from the control room of our TV station, WPIX, New York. "Are you sure," they said, "that's McDowell?" At the time, Phil and I were on TV. We look at Bill Kane, our statistician, and he says, "In New York, they say Kralick is pitching." In Cleveland, the Indians' radio booth was next door. Bob Neal and Jimmy Dudley were their announcers, and I lipsync to Bob, "Who's pitching?" He said, "Jack Kralick." I can't believe it! We've had the wrong pitcher for six innings, and none of our announcers knew it.

Now, Phil and I were a couple of ex-jocks. We started to giggle. We had to tell viewers that we'd had the wrong pitcher for six innings, and we did. "Oh, our terrible mistake." Then it suddenly dawns on us: Somebody has to tell Mel. Neither Phil nor I wanted to, so poor Kane got the job. Mel is doing radio as Kane moseys over and whispers in his ear. I swear that Mel's head went straight up in the air and it came down over his hands. For 30 seconds he didn't move. Phil and I were a couple of kids; to us, the whole thing was hysterical. Mel was a professional; a root canal would have brought a bigger laugh.

—*Jerry Coleman*

One of my early interviews in the Yankee days was in Baltimore. Brooks Robinson's wife and, I think, Dave McNally's wife and I are talking about problems that ladies have with their husbands being away all the time. Finally, near the end of the interview, I said, "I guess you ladies kind of wear the pants when your husbands are gone." Dave McNally's wife pops up with, "And we take them off when they come home." Dead silence. I don't know whether we were on black-and-white or color television, but I turned beet red and, in my usual marvelous way of overcoming things, I started to stutter. Oh, dear, the things that happen.

—*Jerry Coleman*

For many years, my Houston broadcaster partner was Loel Passe [chanting "Now you're chunkin'," "He breezed him one more time," and "Hot ziggety dog and good ol' sassafras tea"]. Together, we saw a lot—and did lots live. One day came the kind of incident all broadcasters dread. I interviewed J.R. Richard and asked, "If you had to throw a pitch in a tight situation, what would you throw?" J.R. said, "Well, Gene, I'd throw him a slider." And as he moved his hand across the groin area, he added, "I'd put it right in there, cock high."

—Gene Elston

People don't know this, but I've sung "Take Me Out to the Ball Game" for years. It's the only song I know the words to, so wherever I've been, I sing it, but nobody ever heard me.

In late '75, Bill Veeck buys the White Sox. One day he looks over and sees me as our organist, Nancy Faust, is playing "Take Me Out to the Ball Game." He's reading my lips, I'm singing, and only our producer hears me. Bill looks beneath the booth and, again lip-reading, sees that fans are hearing me mumble. The next night, without my knowing it, Veeck hides a P.A. microphone and, oops, my voice comes roaring back at me along with everyone else. Afterward I ask him, "What was that about?" Bill said, "I've been looking for 40 years, and as soon as I heard you, I knew you were the guy I was looking for."

I began to puff up with flattery, and he said, "As soon as I heard ya', I realized that no matter where the fan was sitting—the bleachers, a grandstand, a box seat—hearing you, he knew he could sing better and so he'd join in. If you had a *good* singing voice, you'd intimidate them and they wouldn't take part." All this gives you an idea of Bill Veeck's public relations mind. Boy, I wish baseball had more like him today.

—Harry Caray

People kid me about the wild clothes I wear. I guess it started when *Sports Illustrated* was planning a story on me. They told me they were going to take pictures one night at the park, so I show up in a Hawaiian shirt and shorts. Not too bright, I'm afraid. Come to think of it, the shirt was *very* bright. That was the first time I'd dressed like that at the ball park. After that, I figured what the heck. If the shirt fits, wear it.

—Jon Miller

Ralph Kiner has been my partner in the Mets' broadcasting booth since 1983, a wonderful person with whom to work. Understated sense of humor, and ability to laugh at his malaprops. In that first year, I'd been in the booth for about three months with Ralph when one night he said, "And now, I'd like to turn the play-by-play over to my good friend, Tim MacArthur."

I said, "Ralph, you're probably thinking of General MacArthur."

Ralph said, "What did I say?"

I said, "You said, 'Tim MacArther.' It's McCarver."

He said, "Well, close enough."

The Mets lost by something like 9 to 1—no surprise; they lost over 90 games that year [68-94]—and afterward Ralph was seeking post-game comments on camera. I said, "Ralph, earlier in the broadcast we talked about General MacArthur, and one of his favorite lines was 'Chance favors a prepared man.' Obviously the Mets weren't prepared tonight because they were just blown out." Ralph turned toward the camera and brilliantly said, "MacArthur also said, 'I shall return,' and we'll be right back after this."

—Tim McCarver

Another of Ralph's wonderful moments came the day we were going to a commercial that involved a new sponsor, American Cyanamid. Now, that word "Cyanamid" you need to look at more than once before you say it on the air, because it can be tricky. We got the call to do the commercial, and Ralph was handed the note American Cyanamid, and he says, "We'll be right back after this word from American Cyanide." We were actually saying that the Mets were playing bad enough that cyanide pills were prescribed.

—Tim McCarver

It was a thrill to follow the entire career of Michael Jack Schmidt and call all but a handful of his home runs. [No. 20 won 10 Gold Gloves, was three-time Most Valuable Player, topped the National League a record eight times in homers, and led Philadelphia to its only world title. Only six players surpass Schmidt's 548 homers.]

Mike's five hundredth was a great thrill—April 18, 1987—whacking a two-out, three-run, ninth-inning blast which gave the Phillies an 8-6 win. It's funny because when I was in Houston in the '60s, I called Eddie Mathews' No. 500 at Candlestick off Juan Marichal and didn't realize the significance of it at the time. In Mathews' case, not even the beat writers built it up. Eddie had spent most of his career with the Braves and wasn't really a Houston home product. I remember congratulating him in the clubhouse. For most of the guys, it was, "So the guy hit another home run"; big deal.

Another difference is that I didn't use "It's outa' here!" for Mathews. That came after I went to Philadelphia. I was standing around the cage watching batting practice, and [Greg] Luzinski launched one toward the upper deck. Larry Bowa said, "Wow, that ball's way out of here!" I thought, "Hey, that's got kind of a nice ring to it." So "Outa' here!" was born that day for a Phillies' home run, and "Outa' here!" it remains.

—Harry Kalas

One final Kinerism. In 1983, a reliever named Bert Graff entered a game. Any broadcaster will tell you his nightmare is the month of September. So many new players come up, and you're trying to research them and learn to pronounce their names. As Bert Graff came into the game, Ralph was having difficulty seeing his number. At a time like this, it's protocol for the analyst to try to find out [the number] and help your partner. Ralph couldn't see who it was. My problem was that I couldn't say on the air, "It's Bert Graff," because it's not your place to say that. So I wrote down "Graff," and Ralph said, "I beg your pardon, Frank Graff is in the game." At that point, I wrote "Bert" on some paper. The next thing I hear Ralph say is that "Frank Bert" is in the game! I'm shaking my head "no" when Ralph says, "Check that, it's Bert Frank." Mr. Kiner's ways are wondrous.

—Tim McCarver

In broadcasting, once you say it, that's it. We've all said things we wish we could take back. Early in my career, I did a post-game show and would say, "The Dodgers with Drysdale beat the Giants this afternoon." One day, I was giving a Washington Senators' score. They had a pitcher by the name of Cox—you guessed it. I said, "The Senators with Cox this afternoon beat the Yankees." Instantly, I knew what I'd said. I didn't know what to do, so just kept on talking.

Years later, [Braves' Voice] Skip Caray and I were doing a game in Philadelphia. It's the bottom of the seventh, two outs, and Mike Schmidt is the Phils' third baseman. Skip says, "Here's the pitch. A bouncing ball to third. Shitz is up with it, and throws to first in time." We break to commercial, I'm chuckling to myself, and I knew what Skip was hoping, that no one heard his goof or maybe didn't believe it when he did.

We came back in the top of the eighth, and I couldn't let him get away with this. He gives the upcoming batters, and before the first pitch, I said, "Skip, who plays third for Philadelphia?" He was beside himself, still tells the story. You can't broadcast and be too straitlaced without going crazy.

—Ernie Johnson

In 1968, I retired as a player—a popular decision—joined the Braves' front office, and started on the rubber-chicken circuit. I did stand-up stuff about my career, anything for a laugh. When I was getting started as an announcer, anyone who saw me play knows I had plenty of material.

After I joined ABC [1976], Al Michaels asked if I'd ever been thrown out of a game. "No," I said, "but I got thrown into a couple without notice." Al liked my five greatest thrills as a player. Getting out of a rundown. Driving home the winning run by walking with the bases full. Watching a fan in the upper deck. Showing up for most games. And catching the games on radio that I didn't show up for. But it was worth it. Once, my son struck out three times in a Little League game. The biggest thrill a ballplayer can have is when your son takes after you.

Al is a great guy. He understood me as a person. One game, he asked about my father. I told him, "Oh, my dad came from the old country. He was on the soccer team." That made Al wonder if dad played goalie. I said, "He didn't play anything. He just blew up the balls. That's where I get a lot of my talent."

—Bob Uecker

I was doing a game in St. Louis—gosh, my first or second year with the Giants—and the great Lindsey Nelson was in the TV booth and I was alone on radio. We were at bat, and a pitcher named Pedro Borbon one way or another managed to reach first base. Billy North came up next and singles into right field. Pedro goes around to third—runners at the corners.

Now, as we all do, I'm writing this down in my book, and by the time I look up and start to say, "OK, so here's the story," I look around and there's no Borbon! It sort of came out: I said, "Pedro Borbon is missing." He wasn't there, and I had no idea what happened. I look at our engineer, Lee Jones, and he shrugs; *he* doesn't know. This is now a very sinking feeling. We've gone from runners from first and third to a runner at first, and the guy at third isn't LOB—he's MIA.

Lee finally gets up and goes to the press box and—you can't fake it—I say, "Folks, I don't know what's going on, but I'll try to find out." After a few minutes, which seemed like an eternity, this message came over the press box P.A.: "Attention, media, Pedro Borbon was ruled out for missing second base on an appeal." All of which occurred as I stared at my scorebook. No hole was deep enough for me just then.

—*Hank Greenwald*

In 1981, I did Milwaukee Brewer games on select television, which was paid TV with a little box, and worked with one of the most colorful people I've ever known. Tom Collins and I had our season interrupted like everyone else by the baseball strike—we only did about 10 games—but the most memorable game came on an afternoon in early October. It was a split season, and that day the Brewers won something for the first time in their history, beating the Tigers, 2-1, to take the second-half crown. People still marvel at my call: "The Brewers win the second half! The Brewers win the second half!" OK, so it didn't have the same ring as Russ Hodges' "The Giants win the pennant!" In baseball, you take what you can get.

—*Joe Castiglione*

People like when you poke fun at yourself. Often, there's a lot to poke fun at. I was doing an Indians' game in Kansas City and about to describe a catch by Rocky Colavito. What I wanted to say was, "There goes Rocky against the wall." Instead, it came out, "There goes Wally against the rock." I caught the error and tried to redeem myself. "For those of you who like statistics," I said, "that was my 12th fluff of the year. It puts me in third place in the American League."

—*Ken Coleman*

In Boston, I've worked with two great partners whose musical awareness ended around 1953. Both Ken Coleman and Bob Starr still think that "Walking in the Rain" tops the charts. No knowledge of Bill Haley and the

Comets, let alone the Beatles or Stones or Whitney Houston. The night [April 29, 1986] that Roger Clemens struck out 20 Mariners to set a big-league record, Ken was reading from the Red Sox' yearbook around the second inning. It had just come out; listed players' favorite activities, foods, and musicians; and Ken said, "Roger's favorite singer is Steve Nicks." I said, "Ken, I believe that's Stevie Nicks." Ken said, "Well, I know him well. I call him Steve." And I said, "Uh, Ken, Stevie is a girl." Later, Roger sent up a big wall-size poster of Stevie Nicks which we kept in our booth the rest of the season. Today, Ken can still break me up by saying, "Stevie is a girl."

—*Joe Castiglione*

Every broadcaster has a certain signature. One Memorial Day, the Pirates had a great comeback to beat the Dodgers. Next year, they did the same thing against the Cubs. I said on the spur of the moment, "It's Memorial Day all over again!" Just happened in the sweep of emotion. It's amazing how many fans come up and make some reference to Memorial Day even in the dead of winter.

—*Lanny Frattare*

My, oh, my" is my trademark that was extemporaneous. It just sort of evolved. That's not the case with my home-run call. In 1977, I had a common home-run call— "It's gone!" or something—which isn't good because that call is part of an announcer's signature. In 1978, J. Michael Kenyon from the Seattle *Post-Intelligencer* and I were in Arizona, the radio was on, and some group [Seals and Croft] was singing something about "fly away." I said that is exactly what a baseball does. I knew it was good, and I've been using it ever since. But there are variations. When a crucial homer is hit, I always wait a beat or two. Then I let it go, real big. And that's all, for a while. I know the value of silence. Or a few listeners wish I did.

—*Dave Niehaus*

On the road, you rely on home-team camera people and stage managers, and one job is to fill in the out-of-town score sheet with information off the ticker. We're in Texas a few years back and had a young lady who'd never done this before. During the game, John Blake, the Rangers' PR guy, announced on the press-box intercom that somewhere a pitcher was throwing a no-hitter. I heard "no-hitter" with my headset on, took it off, and said to the young lady, "Did you hear that announcement?" She hadn't, so I said, "Will you go and ask John Blake what he just said?" She came back and said, "The no-hitter isn't happening in our game." I said, "No kidding." She just didn't understand the concept.

That's OK. No one understood *me* in a 1990 ESPN game I did with Ray Knight. Dwight Evans came up with I believe 2,299 career hits. I wanted to say, "He's one hit shy of 2,300." Instead, it came out, "Here's Dwight Evans who's one ship high of 2,300." Ray kind of snickered; and the guys in the truck said, "Oops"; and I knew what I'd said, so, laughing, I continued, "I did say he's one hit shy of 2,300, didn't I?" Ray said, "Oh, absolutely, we all heard it." A couple weeks later I'm in Texas with the Red Sox when a man came up and said, "Will you do me a favor?" I say sure. He says, "Just say 'one hit shy' for me."

Broadcasters don't get away with a thing.

—Sean McDonough

You may wonder where stuff comes from about me being nuts. People have me saying that "Rick Folkers is throwing up in the bull pen." What I said was, "He's throwing them up," meaning just tossing softly, but guys read that as Folkers losing it in the bull pen. [Among the Burma Road of Colemanisms: "On the mound is Randy Jones, the left-hander with the Karl Marx hairdo." "He slides into second with a stand-up double." "Sometimes big trees grow out of acorns. I think I heard that from a squirrel."]

Once, somebody said, "Did you say it that way?" He was referring to when I said, "The flags are blowing out in San Francisco." People claim I said, "The fags are blowing out," but I didn't say that, never would. [What Jerry did: "This is the only afternoon day game in the National League," "Next up for the Cardinals is Barry Carry Garry Templeton," and "The way he's swinging, he won't get a hit until the twentieth century."]

I still remember the playoffs with [CBS Radio's] Jack Buck. A ground ball was hit to Mike Schmidt. I said, "Ground ball, Shitz up with it. Over to first, got him." Sad that I didn't slur "Schmidt." I said a clear "s-h-i-t"—and it wasn't a first. Mike's name gives me fits. The inning's over; I tried not to focus on it. Jack looked at me and said, "You know you said shit?" I said, "Yeah." After that, I got his name right, but too late for the 20 to 30 million people listening to the playoffs. They probably said, "Nah, he didn't say that, wouldn't say that, would he?" Just another of my highlights.

I used to worry about these Colemanisms. Now I figure they add to my sex appeal. I say that even though there's some guy here in southern California who's monitored every broadcast and wrote down everything I said wrong. If I find him, I may put him on the next rocket to the moon.

—Jerry Coleman

Watching late-night baseball highlights, I'd see ESPN's Chris Berman and hear his game accounts in which he uses names of players. "Tim 'Purple' Raines steals a base." Or "Oddibe 'Young Again' McDowell makes a great play." But I never heard "Billy 'Free' Sample."

No matter how quickly I left the ball park or how late I stayed up to watch the repeat shows, I never caught a game story with my nickname. Finally, toward the end of my career, I had a game in which I did everything but collect tickets. I get in front of the TV set and tune in to Berman and ESPN, and what happens? Gayle Gardner read the game summary! I finished my career without ever hearing Berman read my name, but at the 1987 World Series, I spotted him in a hall and introduced myself before he said, "Billy 'Free' Sample." I feel much better now, thank you. For all I know he could have been saying "urine."

—Billy Sample

In 1962, here's this new team, the Mets, and we're competing with the Yankees on New York TV—and we got to get attention. So I stop at a men's clothing store at 49th and Broadway and say, "Show me all the jackets you got you can't sell." The guy goes into the back and comes out with seven jackets, and I bought all of 'em. They were *dreadful*—horrible patterns—and I started wearing a different one each night. A month later, I got into a cab in Manhattan and the cabbie says, "Hey, mack, you're the guy with all those jackets, aren't you?" I told a friend, "See, he doesn't know my name, but he knows what I do. It pays to advertise."

It got to where I'd use time on the road hunting for jackets [ultimately, owning more than 350. Andy Rooney said that of his World War II army friends, only Lindsey was better dressed then than now]. Bob and Ralph [Mets' mikemen Murphy and Kiner, respectively] looked around. And my family started. My daughter Nancy went overseas and bought me a jacket in Shannon, Ireland. She got to customs, and the customs man was a baseball fan. He thought he'd put her on a little bit and said, "*Nobody* would wear a jacket like this." And she said, proudly, "My daddy will."

When I went into the Hall of Fame [1988], they asked if I'd bring a jacket. I didn't know at the time why they asked. When I was ready to take the podium, they whispered, "May we have the jacket?" So I left the jacket at Cooperstown. My legacy, if you will.

—*Lindsey Nelson*

People ask why I entered broadcasting. I point to why I'm famous: my career with the [1962-67] Braves, Cardinals, and Phillies. A .200 average helped. I could always talk, which is good. I never was the brightest student. My dad spent more time in the high school principal's office than I did in class. Even now, old friends are amazed that I made something of myself. They think back on me not graduating from 11th grade and those three years in the pen—oh, never mind.

I knew early where I was headed. I'd sit in the bullpen and talk into a beer cup. Of course, a lot of the stuff you couldn't say on radio. My managers didn't want me in the game. Hell, they didn't want me on the bench. So they exiled me to the bullpen. One week I played four straight days for Philadelphia. Talk about a miracle. Kids ask me who I played for. I say, "Nobody, but I sat for a lot of clubs." I had to fight players to get in games—and fans who wanted to get me out.

One day this fan got to me. He was saying things that would have killed my parents. The worst thing is that I couldn't argue with what he said. But, finally, I'd had enough. So I dove into the stands and took him on. Figured I had the advantage, had my chest protector and shin guards on. Hey, I'm no fool. Even with these tools, the guy hit me, and they arrested him for assault. Then they arrested me for impersonating a player.

—*Bob Uecker*

My first year, I'm talking to Cookie Lavagetto on the air when all of a sudden comes the National Anthem, and I don't know what to do. The viewers can hear the music. Should I keep going or shut up? The director should have cut me off and shown the flag or something, but we hadn't discussed this in advance. So I thought, Better keep talking, and interviewed Cookie through the entire song. Afterward, CBS got letters about this broadcaster who blabbed through the National Anthem. Believe me, today when the Anthem starts—I don't care whether I'm taping, talking, or eating a banana—I stop in mid-stride.

—*Jerry Coleman*

CHAPTER SEVEN

WHERE YOU LEAD

MANAGERS

Some baseball skippers burn out like supernovas. Others wear mediocrity so clearly as to flaunt a scarlet M. Great skippers defy both laws by climbing upward and enduring onward: John McGraw, Bill McKechnie, Miller Huggins, "Senior" Al Lopez. None banked the embers of their big-league fire.

One pyromaniac was Leo Durocher. "Show me a good loser, and I'll show you an idiot." Charlie Dressen bubbled egomania. "Just keep 'em close," he told his players. "I'll think of something." Connie Mack—Athletics' owner, patriarch, and 1901-1950 manager—presaged Gil Hodges and Walter Alston as sport's Quiet Man. Once asked what the Miracle Mets' '69 pennant proved, Gil said, "Can't be done," and laughed. Later, Alston pondered what he'd learned in baseball. "You make out your lineup card, sit back, and some very strange things happen."

I had just begun college when my first magazine piece appeared. "Down on the Farm, Marse Joe Doesn't Seem So Bad" etched the man Ted Williams called "the best I played against or for." Many dub Joseph Vincent McCarthy—10 pennants and seven world titles, Hall of Fame '57—the greatest manager of all time.

Crossing him, players feared losing not only jobs, but legs, arms, and perhaps life itself. "Sometimes," McCarthy said, "I think I'm in the greatest business in the world. Then you lose four straight and want to change places with a farmer." It was a sentiment shared by 1973-79 Phillies' manager Danny Ozark. "I give up," he said of a three-game Atlanta sweep. "Those games were beyond my apprehension."

Birdie Tebbetts was a great baseball man. Heck of a player, good catcher, tremendous sense of humor. He showed that while managing at Memorial Stadium one day, even as his baseball knowledge seemed to slip a gear.

Birdie called for a relief pitcher. He warmed up, and Tebbetts is back in the dugout. The pitcher threw ball one to his first hitter, and promptly followed it with ball two. Birdie jumps out, runs to the mound, and points to the bull pen. With that, the umpires reminded him of a simple baseball rule: No manager can take a pitcher out till he's faced at least one batter. Sorry, Birdie, no way he can come out now.

Tebbetts looked around, looked at the umps, nodded, smiled, and left the mound. Whereupon every step he looked like a guy swimming the breast-stroke—you know, flapping his arms in front of him, all the way to the dugout. As soon as the game was over, the media jumped on the elevator, raced to the clubhouse, and we talked to Birdie about trying to get a relief pitcher out of the game before he pitches to a batter. And what was that arm motion after you'd found out what you'd done?

Birdie's response was, "I was swimming through a sea of my own stupidity."

—*Chuck Thompson*

During my first few 1950s spring trainings with the Braves, I wasn't far removed from the four years I played in the old Wisconsin State League. I think I'm the only guy who played that long in Class D—so much for my talent. Manager Charlie Grimm was a favorite, maybe because he let me work out with the club. I had my own Braves' uniform and on the back my number, 0. Wes Covington saw me make a couple running catches in the outfield and asked some of the guys, "Who the hell is working out in left field [his position]?" Once, I was pitching batting practice when Joe Adcock hit a liner right past my ear—sounded like a rocket. Grimm yelled, "Time out," and said, "That's it, Earl, if that ball hits you in the mouth, your career's over." Smart guy. I threw down my glove, and went back to the mike.

—*Earl Gillespie*

In baseball everyone's a critic. Ask a manager. When I was broadcasting the [1948-67] Indians, an elderly lady who lived south of Cleveland was a baseball nut. Al Lopez was our manager. She didn't dislike him but wouldn't stop lecturing. She set a big picture of Al on her kitchen table, and also had one of those rulers that teachers used to slap your hand or the back of your neck. This lady'd sit there and say to Al's picture, "Lopez, you better do as I tell you, or I'm gonna' use this ruler right on your big head"—and she did. The Indians finished high that year, but Al Lopez's head and face photo looked like he'd been run over by a truck. "Now, Lopez, you take that pitcher out. I want to see Bob Feller in the game." Or, "Bring in [Ray] Narleski. He's [catcher] Jim Hegan's kind of pitcher." I got to meet her one time when we stopped by her house. Whoever said women are the weaker sex should have confronted this belle.

—Jimmy Dudley

I had the only fight of my career when I broadcast for the [1950-53] New York Giants. You'll never guess who it was against. Their manager was a street-smart hustler who needed the bright lights. The problem was that Leo Durocher also needed his court—and court jester.

The Giants were coming home by train from Chicago. My partner, Russ Hodges, and I were sitting in my compartment. I was reading the paper—but not for long. Leo strolls into the compartment and says, "Hi, what's going on?" Russ says, "Oh, nothing much. Have a seat." I looked up and said hello.

The next thing I saw was Durocher's fist smacking into my paper and knocking the pages into my face. That was Leo, trying to prove he could bully—read, own—me. Mrs. Harwell will tell you that I'm a mild and lazy guy. I was that way long before Steve Martin became a wild and crazy guy. Not now. I was steamed. Maybe because I knew Durocher picked on other guys and, if they took it, they became his stooges.

I jumped up and wrapped Leo in a bear hug. At first he tried to get away. Then he grabbed my arm, and we fell to the floor. Our fight will never rival Young Stribling against Max Schmeling. After a while we quit. Leo was in so many wars he probably didn't recall that fight. For me, its memory is as sturdy as the house by the side of the road.

—Ernie Harwell

When Juan Marichal debuted in professional baseball in the late '50s, he spoke little English and had an interpreter, his shortstop. One day Juan was in the bull pen, and the bases were loaded and no one out. Buddy Kerr was manager and brought Juan in to relieve, and as he walks away the shortstop called to Buddy, "Juan wants to know where you want him to throw the ball."

Kerr was amazed. Here comes a kid in his first professional game, the bases loaded and nobody out, and he asks the skipper where he wants him to throw the ball. So Kerr answers on a lark, "Well, low and outside corner is pretty good." Naturally, he's funnin'. Not Juan. Nine low and outside corners later, he struck out the side on nine pitches and got out of the inning without anybody scoring. Juan'd come into spring training ready to throw on a dime. No one could hit a thimble like number 27.

—*Lon Simmons*

Gil Hodges became manager of the Washington team in May of 1963, taking over for Mickey Vernon, who'd been too decent a guy to handle the team's cast-offs and ne'er-do-wells. Gil was picked by George Selkirk, our new general manager and Yankee outfielder who bristled at his nickname, "Twinkle Toes." The change didn't produce miracles—the Senators lost 106 in 1963—but it was clear Gil would be in charge and knew how baseball should be played. He fretted quietly when his players threw to the wrong base, missed the cut-off men, screwed up run-down plays, and misran the bases—which, believe me, happened about every game.

Hodges had the devout, strong image that inspired a Brooklyn priest to urge the congregation to pray for him when he slumped in the ['52] World Series. He brought in some old Dodger friends as coaches. One, Rube Walker, had a special place in Gil's heart. Rube could take his mind off the woes of enduring this inept gang of ballplayers. We were playing golf one off day—Gil, Rube and I think pitching coach Sid Hudson was the fourth—and Hodges made a good putt on the ninth hole to win the front nine and go one up. Walker said, "I'm gonna write a book on the life of Gil Hodges entitled *Nice Guy, My Ass.*"

Jim King was a regular outfielder in our first years from Elkins, Arkansas, and had an earthy southern humor. After a two-week road trip, he said, "I hope my wife's not in the bathtub when I get home." Why? "Because I don't want to get this new suit wet." Gil liked that. He needed all the laughs that he could get.

—*Dan Daniels*

Of all the places I played, Philadelphia was toughest. Its fans are so bad that when there's no game scheduled they go out to the airport and boo good landings. But it also had maybe the best manager, Gene Mauch. Gene'd always fight for his players. Sometimes he'd even fight *them*. In 1965 I was traded to his Phillies. Later I was dealt away, and Gene tried to cushion the blow by letting me stay in one game. I got a double, a whole career in one swing. Afterward, he called me into the clubhouse and told me I'd been traded. I said, "For who?" He said, "Gene Oliver." That did it. We went at it like Ali versus Liston.

I was sad to leave because Gene was the manager who best understood me. When I was with the Phillies, he'd say, "Get a bat, and stop this rally." Or, "Forget the bat, and try for a walk." Like me, Gene took it personally when, as a hitter, I'd look at the third-base coach and he'd turn his back. And the catcher, instead of giving a signal to his pitcher, would yell out what he wanted.

I wouldn't say the other clubs regarded me lightly, but it never was reassuring to go up in the ninth inning, look into the visitors' dugout, and see everybody in street clothes. Gene stuck up for me when nobody else would. Even my mom was critical of my play. She'd always say, "Why don't you get a job?" Dad, on the other hand, was a real fan. He booed me, too.

—*Bob Uecker*

Twenty-seven years, going strong, with the Expos, and Gene Mauch was a big part of 'em. He was the Expos' manager the first game they played—April 8, 1969. It was gloomy at Shea Stadium, but sunlit across Canada. The first big-league game with a team from outside the continental United States. Being an American, I was new to Montreal, but it was moving to hear the Canadian National Anthem and see through binoculars the tears of our owner, Charles Bronfman, and face of Montreal's then-Mayor, Jean Drapeau, in the box seats beside the dugout. They realized how much this baseball moment meant to the people of Canada. They also liked the final score: Expos 11, Mets 10.

We all learned baseball from the Expos' first [1969-75] manager, not to mention his sense of humor. Gene'd use one-liners to get across a message. We got a young pitcher from the Mets by the name of Steve Renko—started out well, then tailed off. This was in the early '70s, when facial hair was frowned upon, and Renko decided to grow sideburns. He let 'em grow a while, but Gene didn't like this and also the slump Renko was in. So he said, "Steve, I see the sideburns are going down and the ERA is going up." That's all the Little General had to do.

The next day the sideburns were gone. What's not is Gene's memory. What a baseball ambassador in those unforgettable first years.

—*Dave Van Horne*

One of my favorite stories is about a former manager, Sam Mele, whose Twins were in an awful batting slump. At that time, Sam's good friend and Twins' scout Del Wilber was searching for big-league talent. One day Wilber spotted a great young pitcher—another Koufax, surely. He corralled the kid after the game, rushed him to the hotel, locked him in a room, and got on the phone to Mele.

"Sam," he said, "I've found the greatest young pitcher in America for the Twins. I wouldn't have believed it if I hadn't seen it. He struck out every man who came to bat, 27 straight men in nine innings. Only one guy even fouled a pitch off. The pitcher is right here with me now. What should I do?"

Mele didn't blink. "Sign up the guy who got the foul," he said. "We need hitters."

—Ernie Harwell

If you ask him his most embarrassing baseball moment, Paul Blair will mention Tiger Stadium. He was a runner at third base. Frank Robinson was the batter. Frank took a swing, missed, and couldn't hold onto the bat.

Anyone in baseball knows the terrible experience of seeing a bat fly into the seats. Frank's bat went end-over-end into the seats down the third-base side as the park just froze. All of us said a prayer that no harm was done, including Blair, who turned and stared at the stands. Robinson's worried, so he starts that way, too.

Now, when Frank swung and missed, Tiger catcher Bill Freehan caught the ball. So, all of a sudden, I see Freehan start up the third-base line because Paul was standing there looking into the seats. He tapped Blair on the shoulder and showed him the baseball. "Paulie," he said, "look at what I've got."

Paul is called out. He starts arguing with the third-base umpire. "You can't call me out." The umpire says, "You're out."

Paul says, "You can't do that." He answers, "Why not?"

Blair says, "Because when I get to the dugout, [Earl] Weaver's going to kill me."

—Chuck Thompson

Earl was such a great part of the Orioles [winning a World Series, four pennants, six divisions, and 2,541 games in 1968-82 and '85-6]. He handled the 25-man roster as well as anyone. One of Weaver's favorite guys was Pat Kelly. Pat was a very religious player. As a matter of fact, today he's a minister and helps prisoners and underprivileged children in Baltimore.

One day, Kelly hits a home run, and he trots around the bases with that great big smile on his face. He came to home plate, and as he tagged it, raised his right arm and pointed to the heavens. When he got to the dugout, Weaver greeted him on the top steps and said, "Hey, what's this pointin' all about?"

Kelly explained, "Earl, without the Good Lord up there, I wouldn't be able to do that." Weaver looked at him and said, "Kel, the Good Lord didn't do too much for the guy who threw the ball, now, did He?"

In the clubhouse one day at Milwaukee, Weaver did it again. Kelly was talking to some of the players about his favorite subject, the Lord. The thing that Earl heard walking by was Kelly's remark that, "[We should] walk on the righteous side, and that's the way to live." And Kelly looked up and said, "Isn't that right, Skip?"

Weaver looked at him and said, "Kel, a walk with the bases loaded would be just as good"—and kept on going.

—Chuck Thompson

Nobody got more from his players than Earl. Once he was suspended for three games, starting Friday. He said he'd keep off our case till we lost. We win on Friday, win Saturday, then lose Sunday. Monday, our fearless leader addresses us in the clubhouse. "I knew the pressure would get to you."

Once, we were in Oakland against Vida Blue. The first batter pulls Vida down the left-field line—man, it's gone. Only it's foul by a foot. Weaver pounds the wall. "Darn it," he said—OK, he didn't say "darn"—"should be one to nothing." The next pitch is hit the same place, again, foul by a foot. Weaver's beside himself. "Darn it, should be one to nothing." Next pitch is hit the same place, but this time it's *fair* by a foot. You think Earl is satisfied? He says, "Darn it, should be *three* to nothing." One of a kind.

—Ken Singleton

One night in 1976 the Cardinals were in Philadelphia. It was Red Schoendienst's last year as manager—made difficult by the fact that [Cardinals' reliever "The Mad Hungarian"] Al Hrabosky suddenly wasn't as feared and unhittable as in the past. It's the bottom of the ninth, and the Redbirds have a one-run lead. The Phillies get guys at first and second, Al comes into the game, and he has to face Garry Maddox, Mike Schmidt, and Greg Luzinski with the tying and winning runs on.

The pitch to Maddox, and Garry hits it as far as you can at Veterans Stadium and still keep it in the court. Bake McBride sprints over, catches it, bangs into the wall, scrambles to his feet, fires the ball in. *One* out. Schmidt stands in and hits a rocket up the middle. The shortstop dives to his left, spears the ball, scrambles to his feet. Runners hold, *two* out. In steps Greg Luzinski, who hits a bullet back through the mound and hits Hrabosky on what seems to be every part of his anatomy. Al scrambles after it, throws to first, retires Luzinski, and the Cardinals win by a run.

Later, a reporter in the clubhouse comes up to Red and asks, "What did you think of Hrabosky's performance?" Without looking up, Red says, "Well, I thought we had everybody played right except maybe Al was a little shallow on Luzinski."

—Bob Starr

Sparky Anderson [1979– Tigers' manager] is in a class by himself among managers I've broadcast. I've had great access to him, I think, because I'd played. On a whole, he was more trusting. Managers can be hesitant to talk fully to career broadcasters, but he knows I can say things on the air that he didn't say and attribute them to him! Example. In 1993, the Tigers got Eric Davis from the Dodgers, and the release came out 15 minutes before airtime. I raced down to Sparky's office to get quotes and found 30 to 40 guys there. Couldn't get near enough to see or hear. But I went on the air and invented four or five Sparky quotes about Davis. I knew him that well.

Next day at breakfast, I told Sparky what I'd said. "Yeah, that's probably what I'd have said," he laughed. "You read me pretty well." I knew that he'd want everybody to believe Eric Davis was the one guy he wanted. Anybody who doesn't know that baseball is a people business is messing in the wrong game.

—George Kell

When Sparky was fired as Reds' manager in '78, I said that I didn't understand why, and I stand by that view. Yet John McNamara came in and did a great job of taking them to the National League West title. Mac overcame the controversy of Sparky's firing. We also shared an unforgettable night.

Starting with Al Michaels, who preceded me, the Reds have had an off-season radio program—"Reds Line"—the original baseball talk show. It's tradition that our first program after the World Series features the Reds' manager. So it was with Mac in 1979. I arrived at the WLW studio, then and still the Reds' radio flagship, and am introduced to a young woman reporter with a man I assume to be a photographer. They say they're from *Ohio Magazine* and want to do a story about our show, ask if it was OK to hang around the studio while the show's on to get its flavor. No problem. I assume everything was on the up and up.

Six o'clock rolls around, and we're on the air. I sit on one side of a table, and John sits across from me. The woman reporter and photographer are there, and our producer is fielding calls. A guy phones in about a report that the Reds may get Ron Guidry from the Yankees. As Mac began to answer, I see the lady stand up and cross her arms and peel her sweater off, and she's topless. Well, Mac was dumbfounded, can't talk. I tried to carry on, but, trying to answer the question about Guidry, Mac stammered so long that finally he looked at me and said, "Marty, *help.*"

I said, "Mac, I can't do a whole lot for you, pal, you're on your own." Soon, we go to a commercial break. Later we found that this had been set up by Bob Trumpy. People know Bob as NBC's top NFL analyst. Then he was doing a WLW talk show and had planned this whole thing, hiring an exotic dancer from Kentucky across the river. My only regret is that [partner] Joe Nuxhall had a previous commitment and couldn't be there. He'd have had an even tougher time dealing with this situation! Player, manager, or announcer—in some cases *all* distinctions blur.

—Marty Brennaman

Astro manager Harry Walker [1968-72] was often labeled baseball's greatest teacher. You and your wife could be having lunch in the coffee shop, and he'd be giving batting tips. Yet he didn't know players by name, saying, "You there, on the end of the bench, pinch-hit." And he'd never leave well enough alone.

That was especially true of Jim Wynn. Jim was a "take your cuts" kind of hitter. That didn't placate Harry. Wynn had great power for a little guy, but when he'd hit homers, Walker told him to hit to the opposite field. He'd get on base more, and Harry wanted him to bat lead-off and steal bases. Wynn would shake his head, then try to comply. In 1969, he walked 148 times to tie a league record. But Jimmy'd say, "They're never satisfied with what I do." That lack of support hurt him; look at his roller-coaster years.

Harry'd been around a long time and knew how to take a lot of grief, which was good, because the players gave him plenty. Pitcher Larry Dierker rode Walker night and day. Harry'd sit at the front of our bus with a hat over his face as the players in back, led by Larry's writing, sang verses. Almost all went back to Walker. One went, "Now Harry Walker is the one that manages this crew. He doesn't like it when we drink and fight and smoke and screw. But when we win our game each day, then what the hell can Harry say?" The tag-line was, "It makes a fellow proud to be an Astro." I never asked Harry if he liked the thought, or tune.

—Gene Elston

Years back there was an awful lot of drinking on flights, especially commercial. Any delays at the airport, and guys'd get pumped up more at the bar. So it wasn't uncommon to file onto a bus and find trouble.

In the early '70s, Leo Durocher was Astro manager and had his usual seat in the front as Don Wilson got on the bus and stepped to the top step. Durocher says, "Hi, Don, how ya' doing?" Wilson came back with the retort, "It's none of your business, mother-f_____," and went to the back of the bus. Durocher was stunned. He may have been aggressive as manager of [1939-46 and '48] Brooklyn and the [1948-55] Giants, but not at Houston—he was older. Leo sits there a moment or two, then looks over to Grady Hatton, a coach sitting across the aisle, and says, "*What* did he call me?"

Grady said nothing, just hunched his shoulders. So Leo asked some people behind him—including me, two seats away—"What did he call me?" More silence. After a while, he got up and walked slowly to the back. Durocher says, "What did you call me?" Wilson replied, "I called you a mother-f_____." You could hear a pin drop. Durocher says, "Would you say that again?" Don says, "I called you a mother-f_____." And thus began a lot of shuffling. It stops, and Leo returned to the front and sat down and was silent—just looked to Grady. At last I heard him say, "I want you to report this incident to Spec Richardson"—our general manager—"and see that that guy is fined." I guess Leo had changed. The effect of alcohol doesn't.

—Gene Elston

Whitey Herzog managed the Cardinals a long time [1980-90] and is the best manager I've been around. He kept players' respect while being one of the players. He'd criticize them, yet they liked him. [1991-94 Angels' manager] Buck Rogers is a lot like Whitey but got fired because people said he was too critical of pitchers. Whitey was tougher but got away with it. Baseball's funny.

Another manager I worked with is Rocky Bridges—used to play with the Tigers—bigger in humor than talent on the field. Rocky was Hawaii manager in the early '70s. Had his fun, let players have theirs, didn't have control. Which leads me to Maury Wills. I was in Seattle when Maury had his brief, ill-fated stint [25-56] as manager in late 1980 and early '81. Bizarre. Maury deserted an exhibition game early to catch a plane to L.A. with his girlfriend—left the team with no manager. One time, he had the groundskeepers at the Kingdome move the batter's box around the plate— tried to adjust the dimensions of the field!

Maury's habit was to show up late for games; he'd walk in as the Mariners completed batting practice. Once, Dave Niehaus and I were in the clubhouse in Oakland at the manager's door. We're antsy to get the lineup so we can get to work. Maury walks in, everybody's on the field, and he starts to undress to get into uniform. He's got a completely blank lineup card in front of him and says, "Fellows, what batting order should I use? Why don't you make out the lineup for tonight's game?" Dave and I were just smart enough to give each other a look and suggest to Maury that he'd better do it. And he was *serious*. Something you can't say about his tenure.

—*Ken Wilson*

I've been with some bad clubs. Do you realize that I came to Seattle in 1977, and this club could go 162-0 two straight years and *still* be under .500? That was also true where I started in the bigs—California—and met one of the more colorful characters in baseball history, although he isn't credited as such: Harold "Lefty" Phillips, who managed the [1969-71] Angels.

Lefty rivaled Dizzy Dean in the way he fractured English. We were play-ing the Twins at Minnesota and had lost a bunch in a row and led by a run with two outs in the last of the ninth. The bases were loaded, Jim Fregosi's our shortstop, and the batter hit a two-hopper. You couldn't place a fungo any better. It goes between Jim's legs, two runs score, we lose. The next day I'm standing around the batting cage, Lefty had a pot belly, chewed tobacco, and the juice's dripping down his mouth, and he said, "David," and I said "What?" and he said, "You know the error by the Dago last night. That was the goddamned Coup de Ville."

He'd say, "That's water over the bridge." Sort of what I thought when Gene Autry, who owned them in my Angel days, got up to speak in 1981 as I introduced him at a banquet. I said, "Here's this living legend"—which he certainly is—and he got up and says, "Well, goddamnit, David, you call a hell of a game, not the game I'm watching, but a hell of a game."

—*Dave Niehaus*

Frank Lucchesi was Phillies' manager in the early 1970s. Once, he had a meeting when he felt the players were getting the upper hand. Frank thought it was necessary to bridle the players and get them back into his fold. So he opened the meeting with some choice words. "I've been reading a lot of things in the papers," he stated, "that you guys—so-called anonymous sources—have been saying about me, and I want you all to know that nobody makes a scrapgoat out of Frank Lucchesi." That's right, *scrapgoat*.

—*Tim McCarver*

I was with Dick Williams, whom I love dearly, in California and then here [Seattle]. A realist, knows what's going on. One year, we closed out the year in Texas against the Rangers, won the last four games, and ended on a high note of Williams' [1986-88] Mariner tenure. We're at the airport and Dick called me over and I was smiling, looking forward to next year. He says, "You know what?" and I said, "What, Skip?" and he said, "We're still horse-shit." And he was right.

—*Dave Niehaus*

One night during a three-game series in Atlanta, Tommy Lasorda was guest speaker at a benefit dinner. Next day at noon, he talked to a Braves' Booster Club luncheon. Lunch ends, and I see a familiar-looking, pudgy left-hander throwing 3 o'clock batting practice to the Dodgers' utility players. I know his Dodger Blue rhetoric gets old, but the man works so hard at promoting baseball that he gets the benefit of the doubt. What separates Tommy from the rest is you can't name a better motivator. It's amazing because, by October, teams have played over 190 times. How many variations of the same speech can move an athlete?

To me, motivation means more than giving a Knute Rockne speech. I'll never forget the second-guessing Tommy got after pitching to Jack Clark with a base open in Game Six of the 1985 League Championship series. [Making Hades of the City of the Angels, Clark promptly whacked a three-run homer to beat Los Angeles, 7-5, and put St. Louis in the World Series.]

Broadcaster Pete Van Wieren tells how after giving up Clark's homer in '85, reliever Tom Niedenfuer was dejectedly sitting by his locker with no idea of going to the post-game interviews. Seeing this, Lasorda approached him and convinced him that the primary reason the Dodgers made the playoffs was Tom and his 19 saves. Bingo—he got up from the locker and went to the interview room. You may say that any manager would console a player after a tough loss, but most take a loss of that magnitude so personally that thinking of someone else is inconceivable. This is as part of Tommy as the bravado and pasta. ["I'm on a seafood diet," he said, "I eat all the food I can see."] Trust me. There's nobody like Lasorda.

—Billy Sample

I've seen Lou Piniella manage in the National League [1990-92 Reds] and American [Seattle, 1993-], but I remember him as a fine hitter with the late-'70s Yankees and how they'd come to the Kingdome and draw because no team has more fans in Seattle than them. This is when the Yankees had Tommy John and a lot of guys, including Lou, in their mid-to-late 30s. I said on the air that this team's good but aging, and then I listed the players getting up in years.

I didn't think about it until the next night at, oh, I would say, 5:15. I'm sitting alone in the dugout at the Kingdome, and Piniella comes up and says to somebody, "Is this the guy?" and he says, "Yeah, that's him," and Piniella had fire in his eyes, his bat in his hand, and he came up to me. "Are you the guy that said that our team is too old?" he says. I said, "No, I didn't say anything about your team being too old." He says, "I ought to punch your head off," and he starts attacking me with the bat.

He's in front of me, I'm up against the wall, and it took two or three Yankee players to restrain Lou. When people say that Piniella is intense, I know firsthand. Others have threatened to attack me as a broadcaster, but this was a rare time somebody did. And I've never forgotten, because I see Lou and figure it's best to keep distance from him. We haven't visited in a while.

—Ken Wilson

CHAPTER EIGHT

JUST THE WAY YOU ARE

CASEY STENGEL

*B*y *reputation, Casey Stengel was a clown and semigrammarian when named Yankees' manager in 1949. Only once in nine previous big-league years had he placed above fifth. "I became a major-league manager in several cities and was discharged," Casey later told a U.S. Senate committee. "We call it discharged because there was no question I had to leave."*

The Ol' Perfessor will never leave America's psychic memory. His 1949-60 Yankees won an unmatched 10 pennants and seven World Series. His 1962 Mets also lost 120 games. Across the land, Stengel became the very face of baseball. Few more enlarged its family of avid big-league fans.

Rambling—that is, Stengelese—hid a street-smart hardness. "If we can make losing popular," Casey said in '62, "I'm for it." That summer, the writers gave him a birthday cake. "They'd have given you one, too," he told Marv Throneberry, "but they were afraid you'd drop it." Fired by the Yankees, Stengel barbed, "I'll never make the mistake of being 70 again."

In 1992, Richard Nixon said, "If I had it to do over again, I'd name Casey secretary of state. The essence of diplomacy is to confuse the opposition. The opposition never knew what Casey was talking about. Stengel always knew." Paid by the word, the Ol' Perfessor would have owned the world.

F or years Joe McCarthy had things his way with the Yankees or worked with people who didn't care about showmanship. But in 1945, Larry MacPhail left Brooklyn to buy the Yankees [with Dan Topping and Del

Webb]. He and McCarthy didn't get along, so McCarthy left, Bill Dickey succeeded him, and left in September [replaced by scout Johnny Neun]. Three
managers in 1946. No wonder the Red Sox won the pennant.

In 1949, along comes Casey Stengel, and he wouldn't have had to win a
pennant to catch the fancy of America. He rambled worse than I do, didn't
obey periods at the end of sentences, ran them together, as he did eras that
he'd known. Ask him a question, and he'd start out 'bout when he was a
minor leaguer in Montgomery, Alabama, and talk about every club he played
with in the minors and the fans who gave him dinner, before he would
answer the question which was—by now, *you'd* forgotten—"How did you
like playing under [Giants' manager] John McGraw?"

Casey had a great way of handling things. In spring training, he'd leave
the bench and talk to a veteran player about how that player could improve
himself. Actually, he did it so the man sitting *next* to him who was a *rookie*
could learn by indirection. Someone'd ask Casey a story, and he'd reply: He
was with the Boston Braves when they released him, played for several clubs,
then was asked if he'd manage and be president of a minor-league team and
play some. And Casey said that was better than going to California, where he
lived. He went to the minors but didn't like it and didn't know what to do.
So, as manager, he fired himself as a player. As president, he fired himself as
manager. Then, he resigned as president!

Gave up three jobs like that and went to Toledo, then to Oakland, which
was then in the minors. And that's where Del Webb, who knew Casey, said,
"Let's have him manage our team."

Now, everybody thought this was ridiculous. Casey'd had bad teams
with the Braves and used to joke around. His answer was that "with the
clowns I had as players, that's the only way you can survive." With the
Yankees, he knew they had good players and a chance to win the pennant. He
not only won in '49, but five [1949-53] straight Series. Never been done
before or since. I don't know which I loved more, that or the philosopher
who befuddled, taught, and always made you laugh.

—*Mel Allen*

Casey was one of my favorite people. We were in St. Petersburg in spring
training, and one night I and some media guys were listening to Casey
tell stories. It was late in the morning when the bar closed, and we all left to
go to our rooms. As we approached the elevator and the doors opened, the
operator standing there—back then, elevators weren't run by buttons—
greeted Stengel and the two or three of us who got on.

Casey pulled a baseball out of his pocket and told the operator, "I got to give this ball to a kid tomorrow. Do me a favor. If any of the guys come in, get him to sign the ball and give it to me at breakfast, will ya'?"

The elevator operator said he would. And he did, because the next morning Stengel was the first guy at breakfast, and the elevator operator came over and handed him the baseball. It had four or five signatures of Yankee ballplayers who arrived, uh, late that night. Stengel took the baseball, thanked the man, and promptly fined all of those Yankee ballplayers who signed the baseball $50 for breaking curfew.

—*Chuck Thompson*

For years I had a funny habit. I was doing a game at Tiger Stadium when somebody hit a foul ball and I said on a whim, "It was nabbed by a guy from Alma, Michigan." It caught on, and as I walked through the stands folks'd say, "Hey, Ernie, let a guy from Hope grab one tonight," or "Have somebody from Saginaw catch one, will ya'?" [Hearing Harwell at age 10, I recall thinking, "Boy, he has a lot of friends."]

People ask how I've known names of these towns, and I kid 'em that I study seating charts, or that I've even added a computer that goes through all the names. It goes back to Casey Stengel.

When Casey managed the Mets, a young prospect came up and said, "I'm a great player, and I think I can play for you." Casey says, "OK, what are your credentials?"

He said, "Mr. Stengel, my senior year in college I hit 40 home runs. I knocked in 85 runs. I was a pitcher, threw five no-hitters and won 10 games, had an earned run average of 1.30, and I run the 100-yard dash in 9.7."

Casey said, "That's amazing. Don't you have any weaknesses?" And the kid said, "Well, I do lie a little."

That's what I do. I lie a little. And I owe it all to Casey.

—*Ernie Harwell*

I got a letter once. "You seem to know these fellas that played a long time ago, but did you ever meet a fellow named Casey Stengel?" I laughed through my shoes. Anybody that's ever been in baseball and didn't meet Casey should hang up his glove.

Stengel was a fair major league ballplayer who later parlayed flair, a brilliant baseball mind, and a way with words into immortality. Noting Stengel's age and how long he'd been in baseball [ultimately, 54 years from Pie

Traynor to Tom Seaver], a young reporter asked Casey if he'd known Abe Lincoln. Stengel replied, "No, son, but you give me his batting average and I'll tell ya' how to pitch to him."

Almost always, Casey had to beat the Indians to win the pennant. Almost always, he did. [The 1951-56 Tribe finished second five of six years.] Each year, he'd pick up Country Slaughter or Johnny Mize, or replace Bobby Brown with Billy Martin. A fringe player here, an injury healing better there, and we'd have won—I counted—about six pennants in a row.

Before one Yankee-Indian series, a *Cleveland News* writer asked Casey what he thought of [manager] Al Lopez's plan to use only three starters—Bob Lemon, Mike Garcia, and Early Wynn—in the last month of the season. Stengel said, "Well, I always knew it couldn't be done, but somehow, it don't always work." If you figure that out, let me know. One day, Casey gave a photographer permission to take a picture of [outfielder] Jackie Jensen, swimming with his wife, former Olympic star Zoe Ann Olsen. Then he added, "If Jensen don't come up, tell somebody, will ya'?"

Stengelese made you swear English was Casey's only foreign language.

—*Jimmy Dudley*

In the early '70s the Orioles and A's played some great American League Championship Series games. One night, league officials gathered in Jack London Square in Oakland at a restaurant called the Elegant Farmer. And at this great table were dignitaries including Mr. Stengel.

Casey was telling stories and had a death grip on a glass of scotch. All of a sudden the double doors to the restaurant opened, and in comes [A's owner] Charles Finley leading his ever-loving mule, Charlie O. He walked that mule right over to the American League table and, as fate would have it, the mule kind of put his head down and nudged Casey.

Stengel grabbed the glass, turned around, and looked up at the mule, and says, "A very remarkable horse. He hasn't seen me for a year, and still remembers."

—*Chuck Thompson*

Once, the Yankees came to Washington from Baltimore on a Saturday night, and we checked into the Shoreham Hotel. I'm going to my room when I see Casey sitting there with a huge frown. I said, "What's the matter, Skipper?" I thought he wasn't feeling well. He said, "They didn't tell me this was a blue town." Casey liked to have a couple after a ball game, or four or six or eight. He could go to bed at 3 o'clock and be up at 6:30, fresh as a daisy. That's why he's got trouble: The bars had closed at midnight.

I said, "Skipper, don't worry about it. I carry a fifth of scotch with me in my bag"—rarely used it, if I wanted a drink I went downstairs—"in case of an emergency, and *this* is an emergency." Casey would smile at writers because their stories became part of history, but seldom at announcers. That's why it was unusual that Casey now showed a great grin. People talk about records. I said to Casey, "Have a drink if you don't mind coming up." And, boy, I never saw anybody move that fast.

We get in the elevator, go to my room, take out the bottle of scotch, call for soda and ice. Casey made some comment about the game we'd played in Baltimore, then said, "We don't have to wait on ice, do we?" I said, "No, Skipper." And Casey had two straight before the ice and soda arrived. I had one that I sipped on and then a second, and I kept looking at my watch. It's 2:30 in the morning, and the bottle is getting down, and I said, "Don't we have a double-header this afternoon, Skip?" and he said, "Yep," and picked up the bottle and poured another drink.

Finally, there's the last drop, and Casey said, "I better go." It's after 3, and he takes 15 more minutes at the door. I wish I'd recorded his Stengelese—and also pass on his grasp of baseball. He'd take a [Hank] Bauer and [Gene] Woodling, and platoon 'em in right. Gene would have four hits and come up again. They'd change pitchers and bring in a lefty. Casey'd send Bauer up to hit, and Woodling would storm into the clubhouse. Casey knew this, and how it motivated. When he became Mets' manager, one of the first people he got to play for him was Gene Woodling. If that's a clown, you need a new dictionary.

—*Mel Allen*

When the New York Metropolitans entered the National League in '62, I auditioned with a tape of Roger Maris' 60th home run hit off Jack Fisher that I'd called as an Orioles' announcer. The Mets wanted three things in a broadcast team. One, somebody with a national reputation. That was Lindsey Nelson. Second, a former National League—preferably, New York—star. They talked to people like Pee Wee Reese and Bobby Thomson, but then listened to Ralph Kiner's '61 White Sox radio work and got excited. And third, I guess, a professional, which turned out to be me.

The three of us met, and went to spring training in St. Petersburg. Early in '62, Lindsey, Ralph, and I decided that the best thing we could do was get acquainted with Casey. So we start hanging out with him, and found that the

Mets' manager was indefatigable. After 10 days we're hiding behind potted palms in the hotel lobby. He was over 70 years old and running us into the ground! A month doesn't go by that I don't think of Casey. Today, Tommy Lasorda is the best salesman for a club, but, then, the Mets *were* Stengel. Kids won't believe this of the New York media, but Casey had them in another palm: his hand.

Those '62 Mets went 40-120, but no one could tear Casey down until a broken hip and age. Over the years, the Mets have won and lost, but at least it's big-league ball. If you've ever done a minor league game, you know what a thrill the majors are. Our philosophy was, If we're not having a good time, how can our audience? That's what sustained us from Marvelous Marv through Tom Seaver. And it all began with Stengel.

—Bob Murphy

Dick Young was the New York *Daily News* baseball writer who coined the term, "Amazin' Mets." And they were. [Nelson said of the Mets, "They were the last age of innocence. They played for fun. They weren't capable of playing for anything else."] Roger Craig loses 24 games. Jimmy Piersall hits a homer and runs backward around the bases. Marv Throneberry smacks a triple and is called out for missing one and probably two bases. One day Hobie Landrith homered down the Polo Grounds' short foul line. Later, Casey started talking about the 1964 move to Shea Stadium. "Ain't that somethin'! Just just when my fellers learn how to hit in this ball park, they're gonna' tear the thing down."

—Ralph Kiner

Brother Kiner refers to Marv Throneberry—the earliest Met prototype and their perfect metaphor: no talent of any kind—and alludes to the day Marv lined a ball into the right-field corner, rounded first, and headed for second. The ball eluded George Altman, and Marv slid with a flourish into third. Then the afterword: The Cubs pulled an appeal play. First-base umpire Tom Gorman called Marv out for missing first base. Casey charged Gorman, but was intercepted by coach Cookie Lavagetto at first base. Cookie said something, and it wasn't long before Casey returned quietly to the dugout.

The game ended—another Mets' defeat—whereupon I went to Casey's office in the clubhouse beyond center field. "Skipper," I said, "it looked like you were about to begin a war with Gorman until you got to Lavagetto. What'd he tell you?"

Casey smiled. "Mr. Lavagetto said, 'Don't argue too long, Skipper, he missed second, too.'"

—*Lindsey Nelson*

Whitey Ashburn played for Stengel on those '62 Mets, hit .306, and did 'em proud—named the team Most Valuable Player. As his gift, Whitey got a boat, and, after that wretched season, which aptly ended with Joe Pignatano hitting into a triple play against the Cubs, he went back home to Philadelphia. What happened next was the perfect finish. Stengel must have loved it. Whitey took the boat out on the Delaware River, and it sunk.

—*Harry Kalas*

In Year Two of the Mets' existence, Stengel made his first return to the park where he'd been fired. It was the 1963 Mayor Trophy's Game at Yankee Stadium, and how he hated the Yankees. As did our fans. My wife and two daughters came with their cowbells and horns, and the Yankees stopped them at the gate and confiscated the stuff. Despised? The Yankees were *reviled*!

There were 50,000 people there that night, and 49,000 were for the Mets. We come to the sixth inning and, incredibly, the Mets are ahead. The Stadium is in a frenzy, and Stengel calls down to the bull pen. "Who do you want?" the coach asked. "Ken MacKenzie?" He was mediocre, the kind of pitcher you see in an exhibition game. Not in *this* game. "No," Casey said. "Then who?" the coach asked. "Carl Willey?" being sarcastic. Casey answered, "Damn right I do." Carl Willey was our best pitcher, and Casey was using him to nail down an *exhibition*!

The Mets won, and I've never seen anything like the reaction of their fans. This lousy second-year team beating the *Yankees*—unbelievable. It took me two hours that night to get from Yankee Stadium to the Triborough Bridge. Traffic couldn't move, people couldn't dance, David had killed Goliath. That was Stengel—what he brought to the Mets.

—*Lindsey Nelson*

When I think of Casey Stengel, I remember the 1966 All-Star Game. It was played at our new park [Busch Stadium] in St. Louis. The temperature was 103 on the field, and it registered 130. They asked Casey, "What do you think of the new ball park?" He said, "It sure holds the heat well."

—*Jack Buck*

There's nobody ever been like Casey. The Mets' magic came from this man who spread more happiness than anyone I've ever known. He was the *happiest* man I've ever known, because he was doing exactly what he wanted.

I remember the first time we visited the Astrodome [1965]. I called play-by-play from the roof in a gondola high above second base. "What about my man up there?" Stengel asked [umpire] Tom Gorman. "What man?" Gorman said. "My man Lindsey. What if the ball hits him?" Gorman looked up and shrugged. "Well, if the ball hits the roof, it's in play, so I guess if it hits Lindsey, it's in play, too."

"How about that?" Casey said. "That's the first time my man Lindsey was ever a ground rule." That was Casey Stengel.

At first, Casey hadn't known my name. In fact, he really didn't deal in them because he couldn't remember names and he quit trying. He didn't know who you were, and he didn't care. Just hang around and listen and learn baseball. And he'll keep you entertained. One year, Casey confused my name with Bob Miller's all season. He'd tell the writers, "Miller pitches tomorrow, and Nelson pitches the next day." And he'd get it all mixed up. Joe Pignatano joined us in August as a bull pen coach. That first night he was in the bull pen when the phone rang in the seventh inning. Joe picked it up, and it was the Old Man. He said, "Get Nelson up."

Well, Pignatano knew there was no Nelson on the Mets' team. He also knew he wasn't going to argue with Casey. So he took a ball, and he put it on the rubber in the bull pen and said, "*Nelson!*" Bob Miller got up and started throwing. He said, "I'm Nelson," and he was. That was Casey, too. Amazin'.

—*Lindsey Nelson*

CHAPTER NINE

SUMMER SIDE OF LIFE

AT HOME/ON THE ROAD

*D*riftless is the lot of a radio/TV baseball man. Games blur into seasons, and decades into careers. The announcer boards a plane, jets to the next city, hops the team bus, and treks to the hotel. He checks in, finds his room, unpacks, and marvels at walls more cookie-cutter than Three Rivers Stadium. He sleeps, phones, makes notes, interviews, and is interviewed. Then, the bus trip to the park. Dugout banter, on-air chitchat, the game. Finally, the gnawing night.

"The road'll make a bum of the best of 'em," a writer named Dan M. Daniel cried of baseball's itinerance. "And, kid," he told a colleague, sagely, "you ain't the best." Radio/TV men resort to movies, museums, books, and other treats—anything to dent boredom. Contrast it with the homefront's pressure of family, friends, and public speaking.

Ernie Harwell visited old pals in every city. Harry Caray never met a bar he didn't like. Mel Allen chattered about baseball, or spent days doing commercial spots. Bob Wolff made a list of household names he wished to meet—then, say, in Kansas City, near Independence, phoned Harry S Truman out of the blue. Say hello to what Voices reminisce about between and outside the lines.

I saw the movie *Bull Durham*—and swear I saw every player in my stay in the minor leagues. At Topeka in 1949, the team rode a refurbished school bus. Each team was allowed 17 players, and they paid a player $50 a month to drive. One year we had a brawl over who'd get picked. Sometimes the bus'd only go 40 miles an hour—and that was *down*hill—or broke down and about 12 guys pushed it to the first service station. Primitive—you had to love baseball. To me the minors are its heart and soul.

Take a look at Joe Magoto, who owned Muskogee, Oklahoma's, Western Association team in the early 1950s. Joe was typical of minor-league owners. He ran some drugstores and thought baseball was good for the community. He also had a pitcher by the name of Eddie Lubanski, a little guy from Michigan with a tremendous fastball—just kinda' overwhelmed the league.

By July, Eddie had a great record. One day, he walks into Mr. Magoto's office and says, "I'm quitting baseball—going back to Detroit—my salary, please." Magoto said, "What do you mean?" They argue, and Magoto pulls a gun from his desk. "You're not leaving," he said. "You pitch on your next assignment." Lubanski had been married just before the season. He leaves, gets his wife, packs, and goes home. Eddie went back to Detroit and became one of the great pro bowlers on the circuit. For a guy who didn't want to travel, he made a lot of money bowling.

—*Merle Harmon*

The minors are so personal. I got my start with the Triple-A Syracuse Chiefs. My three years we never finished higher than sixth, I believe. Actually, I hate announcers who say "we"—but in the minors you felt like it. The players were my age and weren't prima donnas because they weren't making money, either—and we all had the same dream, to reach the majors. You'd read promos to sell tickets, and were forbidden to call it cold—it was always a beautiful night, even if freezing you'd preface it with, "You may want to bring a jacket"—because we never knew if someone was driving around and this might spur 'em to stop by.

Tex Simone was our general manager. Every day he'd be on the tractor mowing the grass outside the ball park in his shirt and tie. The minors have more of a family feeling—which doesn't mean no bad blood. Sometimes I doubled as official scorer. They had a radio in the scoreboard booth and I'd say, "That will be an error on the shortstop"—and you'd see an "E" flash on the scoreboard. They're more sensitive to scoring decisions down there— guys think that this hit or error will keep them from the bigs. Manny Castillo had played for Seattle and was on his way down. One day I gave him an error and he said, "I'll hit 10 of those and see how many you stop." I said, "I'm not a Triple-A third baseman and you are—and you should have stopped it." Tony Fernandez once gave the bird to the official scorer from shortstop because he didn't like a call. I wasn't the official scorer but felt his finger. We arbiters stick together.

Our team had a lot of born-again Christians. On bus rides you'd sit next to players, and one would recite passages from the Bible and point out things about life he thought I should know. Now, I consider myself a religious person—a practicing Catholic—but I'd see this guy on road trips coming into the hotel late at night, often in the company of a lovely-looking lady in various minor-league posts. One day on the bus he's preaching. I finally ask, "Not that I doubt your sincerity, but how do you explain these women you go in and out of hotels with?" He said, "It's my weakness." I think the term is "rationalize."

—*Sean McDonough*

Movies tell a lot about baseball. I was proud to play Grover Cleveland Alexander [in the 1952 movie, *The Winning Team*]. Alex is in the Hall of Fame and deservedly so [winning a National League record 90 shutouts and league-tying 373 games. Among Alexander's big-league marks: four one-hitters and 16 shutouts in 1915 and '16, respectively]. Everyone knows that 1926 World Series, when he won two games, received the greatest ovation anyone ever got, and was called on in the seventh inning with the bases loaded and one of baseball's best hitters [Tony Lazzeri] up. He came in and saved the final game.

A bad habit of Alex's was widely heralded in that picture and it took something away from his luster. But what I regret is that the studio was afraid to reveal what was behind his habit. Alex was an epileptic. And when he was arrested and picked up for being drunk in a gutter, as he once was, he wasn't drunk at all. But he took that rather than admit the disease that plagued him all his life.

Early in his career, Alex was hit in the head by a catcher's throw. So he was out of baseball for a while, and they didn't know whether forever, because of double vision. He kept trying to find some way he could pitch. Finally, he went to a minor-league club and asked for a tryout, and the manager went to the plate and said, "Go on out on the mound and throw a few." Alex broke three of his ribs on the first pitch. The experiment had been to close one eye and throw—Alex figured that way he'd be OK. A friend with him when they were thrown out of the ball park said, "What happened?" And Alex said, "I closed the wrong eye."

—*Ronald Reagan*

In the late '40s I was still an active baseball player, but in the off-season did minor-league TV hockey games of the St. Louis Flyers. Believe me, we were all television amateurs then—announcers and production—it was a feat just to memorize visiting players' names. Now, the first part of the game I'd usually use the player's last name until I became more familiar with it—then go whole hog and use the first. This night the Flyers played the Cleveland Barons—and Cleveland had a great defenseman by the name of Dick. Things went swimmingly until the second period when I'm fed his first name—Harry. Well, in the heat of battle and without further thought I had Harry Dick in the penalty box and I had Harry Dick jammed into the boards, and of course my engineer and my assistant were doubled over with laughter and I'm sure that the bars carrying the game felt the same. My only thought was why anyone would have to carry the burden of such a name—and secondly, why anyone would want to be an announcer.

—*Bud Blattner*

Years go by and some guys never get a break. My pal Whitey Ashburn got two in one at-bat. Whitey hit a foul ball that hit a Phillies' season-ticket holder right in the coconut. They put her on a stretcher and took her to a hospital near old Connie Mack Stadium. Being the good guy that he is, Whitey went to visit her the next day and here she was with her head all bandaged. Then, he saw that her leg was suspended from the foot of the bed in traction and he said, "Gee, I know I got you in the head with that foul ball, but what on earth happened to your leg?" She said, "Richie, you won't believe this—but as they were carrying me off on the stretcher you hit *another* foul ball that hit me and broke a bone in my knee."

—*Harry Kalas*

Two little ladies went into the ball park about the fifth inning and sat down behind a priest. "What's the score, Father?" they said. The priest said, "Nothing-nothing." One lady said to the other, "Oh, good, we haven't missed anything." We go to the eighth inning, and a pinch hitter bats for the local team. He makes the sign of the cross before stepping into the box. The little old lady leaned over and said, "Father, Father, will that help?" The priest turned around and said, "Not if he can't hit."

—*Ernie Johnson*

You know, sometimes mistakes seem scripted Above. Take Bill
Mazeroski's ninth-inning homer to win the 1960 World Series. I was on
the air [NBC Radio, from Forbes Field] for the last half of Game Seven and
when Maz hit it, I was so excited I gave the wrong score. "The Pirates win it,
10 to 0!" Actually, it was 10 to 9 over the Yankees, but nobody noticed
because everybody was berserk. I also had the wrong pitcher throwing—Art
Ditmar instead of Ralph Terry!

Later, the Pirates put out a souvenir album narrated by Bob Prince, and
asked if I wanted a voice-over correction. I said, "Hey, I said it, so keep it."
Next year I came into Pittsburgh as a "Game of the Week" announcer and
heard 'em play this record over and over as a promotion. I kept hearing the
wrong score and pitcher, but feeling it was the right thing I'd done.

That final game of the Series was tough for the Junior Circuit.
Afterward, we're driving to the airport with the NBC group and another
limo had pulled off the road with a flat. Nobody knew who it was and somebody joked, "Probably the American League." And by golly it was. Mr. [A.L.
President Joe] Cronin and his executives had blown a tire on the way to the
airport.

—*Chuck Thompson*

I broadcast the first football game between Army and Air Force. Yankee
Stadium, 1959. I miss those college games. Michigan-Ohio State was a
thrill in Columbus or Ann Arbor. I loved the carnival air on campus—
reminds me now in '52 I began doing Kansas University network hoops
games and met maybe America's first full-time coach, the legendary
Dr. Forrest C. [Fhog] Allen. We'd travel by train. When the players were
tucked in, he'd open his compartment door and knock on mine and start
talking basketball.

That year his great team of 1951 had pretty much graduated. On the '52
team was a guy by the name of Dean Smith. Kansas goes to New Orleans to
play Tulane and then to Baton Rouge to play LSU and its great star, Bob
Pettit, with a team one guy called "two bantam-legged roosters, two football
players, and a crane." Kansas loses to Tulane, and is a heavy underdog at
LSU.

I'll never forget the pre-game meal at LSU. Dr. Allen was grand at moti-
vating players. "You made bad passes at Tulane," he began. "You gotta' see
things happen—improve your eyesight—don't go to movies—rest your eyes.

You got to see the lanes—have peripheral vision—see to the right and left." He went on about eyesight and segued into a tale about "a great boxer who was briefly heavyweight champion. Could have been even better—but didn't last 'cause he couldn't see the punches coming."

Max Baer was the champion, and Dr. Allen was just warming up. "They kept telling Max, 'You gotta' improve your eyesight to stay as champion—take care of those eyes.'" By now the players are hanging on every word. "They told Max to go to California and lay on the sand and look at the stars. But Max went there and laid the stars and looked at the sand." Suddenly, the kids' mouths opened as wide as their eyes—and they started to laugh and the tension vanished. Doc's medicine worked every time.

—*Merle Harmon*

Another story from *The Winning Team* is about Nancy and me. We were engaged and waiting for the picture to end to get married. She came out on the set one day, and I said, "How would you like to have a baseball autographed by all these great ballplayers?" Oh, she thought that would be great. I started out, looked back, and there were tears in her eyes, and she was standing there. And I said, "What?" And she said, "Can't I go get them?"

—*Ronald Reagan*

Players get asked why they quit baseball. My main reason came my last year in spring training—1960 with the Indians. I was pitching middle relief—that's where you wind up if you can't start and you can't finish. I was in the bullpen warming up and this 18-year-old boy who'd just signed a contract was catching. Now, when a pitcher warms up with his catcher he uses a lot of hand signs to communicate. I'd thrown my fastball, and wanted to throw the curve, so I threw the glove down to my side—the signal which to everyone in ball means, "OK, I'm gonna' start throwing my curve." This kid stands up, looks at me, and is wondering what's going on. He kneels in his crouch and yells, "Don't worry, dad. Throw anything you want. I'll figure it out on the way down." I knew then it was time to hang 'em up.

—*Ernie Johnson*

As a player I loved leisure time. In the 1964 World Series, the Cardinals had three Dixieland bands playing before Game One. One entertained, then took a break—then another started. When the first band stopped, I grabbed its tuba. I was going to blow it, but then I figured, "What do I have to prove? People already know I have a lot of hot air." I come up with a brain storm—use the tuba to catch fly balls. So I start shagging and, I mean, it's tough. I didn't catch many, but a lot clinked off the metal. Typical. The Cardinals docked me for a new tuba. I wasn't bitter. I just decided to concentrate on what I did best.

My specialty was catching the knuckleball. One time Joe and Phil Niekro were pitching, and their parents were sitting in seats behind home plate. Trying to catch the knuckler, I saw more of them in a game than Joe and Phil did all weekend. I loved catching. Sure, I held the big-league record for passed balls. But it had a good side. I got to meet a lot of people in the box seats. I'm still proud of my technique. I'd just wait till the knuckleball stopped rolling and then I'd pick it up.

—*Bob Uecker*

L et me tell you about the craziest 24 hours of my life. All year the National League 1965 pennant race had been unbelievable. We come to the last week, and it's still up for grabs. Locally, I was the Braves' announcer—but also doing network baseball for ABC, and this was playing havoc with our schedule because we were supposed to air our last game on the final Saturday. As the week went by I didn't know *where* I was supposed to go.

On Friday the Braves were in Los Angeles, whose Dodgers were in first place. But the Giants were still alive, and playing Cincinnati at night. That morning, I began to get calls from the ABC people as to how, where, and when I would broadcast the next day. At first the message was, "Stay by the phone in your hotel room—we'll get this straightened out." Then they started saying go to this game, that one, or another.

Finally, ABC decided that if the Dodgers won and the Reds beat the Giants, L.A. would clinch at least a tie and I should go to Cleveland for a game. If the Dodgers lost I'd go to San Francisco. There was also a chance I'd be going through Chicago to Minnesota, where ABC could highlight the A.L. champion Twins. The only place I wouldn't be on Saturday—even if the race was tied—was L.A., where I was, since for me to do the Braves on network TV would be a conflict of interest.

By Friday night, I had plane reservations to San Francisco, Chicago, Cleveland, and the last plane leaves at a quarter past midnight. But I'll only know where I'm going when I find out how the Dodgers do. Wouldn't you know, our game is scoreless. It goes into the tenth inning, and I say, "I've got to leave." I rushed out, caught a cab, and told the driver, "Put the game on, will you?" We got to the airport and the game's in the twelfth inning—still scoreless. I *still* don't know where I'm going.

The cabbie couldn't believe it—"Which terminal you going to?" I said, "I don't know. Let's pull over to the side of the road and listen to the game." We're sitting there, the meter's wild, and at last the game ends. L.A. has clinched a tie. I look at my piece of paper with various flight possibilities written on it, and I think, "Let's see, this means I go to Cleveland." So I say, "Take me to United, quick."

I check in and the flight's ready to leave. I jump over the conveyer belt, vault through the baggage room, run to the plane, the doors close, I sit down, and the plane taxies down the runway. I sigh, then look at my paper again and I can't believe it. "God, I'm going to the wrong *town*," I said. "I'm supposed to be in *San Francisco*." With that, I panicked—the whole thing was so confused.

Hours later I get to Cleveland—by now, I didn't know who I was. So I call the hotel in Cleveland where the ABC people stayed. When I got through to some of our folks they told me, "Yes, Merle, this is your destination." In the wee hours of the morning, we finally resolve this theatre of the absurd. You'll forgive me if since then I've been partial to trains.

—*Merle Harmon*

Baseball broadcasting has its ups and downs. The good is you get to know famous people. I have a son, Little Duke. Named him after Duke Zeibert, the Washington restaurant owner. Maybe he'll be an announcer or a politician—either way helps get good tables. The flip side is the travel. When the season starts, my wife, Janine, says, "Have a good day, honey. Listen, any time you're in town, stop by. Call first." Each spring I tell her, "I'm Jon Miller, your husband. See you in October."

—*Jon Miller*

Our early Royals' teams weren't good [134-190 in 1969-70]. Often it was hard to even warrant a guest for our 10-minute pre-game show. But by August '69 everybody had made it except a utility infielder who rarely played, Juan Rios. One day, Juan gets into a game, gets three hits, is the star of the game. Going to the park next day I decided to have him on, but Juan spoke and knew little English. I knew he'd need an interpreter. Bingo! Jackie Hernandez, our regular shortstop, loved doing stuff like that. I ask, "Do you think Juan would consent to going on if you interpreted?" Jackie says, "Yeah, and I'll be glad to help out."

At old Municipal Stadium, we interviewed people in the dugout bullpens down the right-field line. I start the tape and say, "Jackie Hernandez will interpret for Juan Rios who's our star of the game. Jackie, ask Juan for his feelings on last night's game." I held the microphone in front of Jackie and in Spanish he asks a few words. I'm thinking, "God, just let this work out." Then, I put the mike in front of Juan, and his eyes lit up as he starts talking. Juan giggles, Jackie laughs, Juan talks—all in Spanish.

I'm thinking this is great. Then I look at our producer, Ed Shepherd, and Shep's kinda' nodding like this is OK, we'll fill our time. Juan went on another 45 seconds and then stopped. I put the mike back in front of Jackie and he says to me, "Juan said he feels great." Panic. Shep drops his tape recorder. This guy has just told me his life story—and that *can't* be all he said. I guess baseball loses something in the translation.

—*Denny Matthews*

In 1973, Chicago's NBC-TV affiliate, WMAQ, called me. Their sports director, Johnny Morris, was taking a sabbatical to visit Europe—so they asked if I could move to Chicago, replace him for the football season, and do the 5 and 10 o'clock sports. I lived there four months in the executive house hotel doing shows Monday through Friday. For a while I also did Cincinnati baseball, and Minnesota football on weekends. Each night on the late show I did a sports commentary—something I'd always wanted. This was a big deal back before the explosion of sports talk shows—and being a rabid sports city made Chicago perfect.

The downside is that each night the phone rang off the walls from viewers who vehemently disagreed and threatened me with anything short of bodily harm. After several weeks, I got tired of it and couldn't figure out a way out. I didn't want to hang up, nor ignore their calls, so I came up with what I thought was an ingenious answer. I invented a fictitious twin brother named Bill Jones and made him producer of my nightly show. Each night after the show I'd retreat to my office which I shared with Greg Gumbel, then rather new in the industry. Greg would do weekends, write for me, and clue me in on things in Chicago because he knew all the people there—and is one of the nicest people in the world, comes over exactly as he is.

Anyway, in the office my twin brother answered the phone, "Hi, this is Bill Jones, may I help you?"

The voice at the other end would say something like, "Let me speak to that idiot Charlie Jones."

I'd say, "Charlie has left. I'm his twin brother Bill, who produced the show. Can I help?"

To which the caller'd say, "I thought you sounded like him. Do you know what that son of a bitch said on the air?"

I answered, "I know, I know what he did, I tried to get him to take it out but he's such a stubborn son of a bitch he just wouldn't do it." The man on the other end said, "Yeah, you're right. You're not like him at all." We'd have a pleasant visit, and agree that my twin brother *was* an idiot. The caller got to vent his anger—which didn't upset me because it wasn't me he was criticizing. It was Charlie, the talent, not me, Bill Jones.

—*Charlie Jones*

In baseball you get some great practical jokers. One of the best engineered our broadcasts in San Francisco—Mike Markward.

We were playing an afternoon game at Candlestick and Mike arrived early to hook up a tape machine to the TV monitor in our booth. At that time I did only radio—but each time a game was televised they'd put a TV monitor in our booth, and this game was being televised back to Cincinnati. Back then these machines were huge, and our booth in Candlestick was a tight fit for three guys—but Mike compensated by putting the machine on the floor and hooking it up to the monitor. This was all unbeknownst to [partner] Joe Nuxhall. The game starts and I start laughing. Finally, during break Joe said, "What the hell's so funny?" I said, "For some reason I'm in that type of mood." There was a much better reason which Joe later found big-time.

We get to the 7th inning having watched video replays all game. As we come out of break, I say, "The Reds are leading the Giants, 4-2, and now with play-by-play, Joe Nuxhall." The Reds put a couple of guys on base when up on the monitor pops a scene from the X-rated video *Deep Throat*. I'm laughing so hard that tears roll down my face. Bob Hertzel of the *Cincinnati Enquirer* had come by and he was in stitches, too. This made it hard for Joe to tell his audience on the Reds Radio Network what was happening on the field. Even funnier was that the scene from the video was rather, uh, graphic—and Joe thought that due to an electronic glitch what we saw on the video was being seen by people in Cincinnati and on the Reds Television Network.

You can imagine the trouble Joe had doing his half-inning with Linda Lovelace on the monitor. Only later did he find he'd been the subject of an elaborate joke. The next time somebody calls baseball "G-rated"—call Joe collect.

—*Marty Brennaman*

The Cardinals were in Pittsburgh about 1978 when a game was called at 5 o'clock—rain. We head back to the Hilton Hotel from the ball park and enter a friendly tap. I was keeping Napa Valley in the black at the time with my consumption of burgundy, but at about 11 I excuse myself and go upstairs to try to get some sleep. We have a golf game the next morning.

Sometime between 1 and 2, nature calls. Now, understand that I'm sleeping in the same uniform that I had on when I came into the world. I get up, half asleep, and take a left, walk from my bed to the bathroom, relieve myself, come out and take another left and walk out the front door of my room. The door slams shut behind me, and as I hear that noise I am wide awake and I am also absolutely without any clothes on. I'm standing outside the room totally nude and now trying to figure what the hell to do.

I know my only hope is to go down the hallway and put my ear up to each door. If I hear noise, I'll knock, and if someone approaches I'll say, "Don't open"—just ask 'em to call downstairs and send somebody up with a key. I'm about to start on this maneuver when I hear commotion down the hallway. I think, "Good Lord, someone's coming out of a room and I'm standing outside my door without any clothes on." Instead, it's a bellman who looks at me in absolute disbelief. I say, "I have a little problem here." Some later asked if I was referring to a physiological notation. He says, "I see that." I continue, "Do you have a pass key?" He says, "No, but I'll get one." He leaves without giving me his frock coat—goes about mid-thigh, would have worked fine—while he pursues the key. In about 40 seconds he comes back with a raincoat that doesn't fit, to wrap around me. Then he leaves again, comes back with a key, lets me back in the room, and bids me an affectionate good night.

The next morning, I get my wake-up call, and and I'm laying in bed thinking, did that really happen? I came to the realization that it did. I go downstairs, and there's our broadcasters, Jack Buck and Mike Shannon, producer Tom Barton, and our traveling secretary, Lee Thomas, plus Dick

Kaegel of the [*St. Louis*] *Post-Dispatch*. We have breakfast and I tell this story, and it wipes 'em out. Before long, we're disturbing the coffee shop. I don't think anything about it as Jack says, "Excuse me, I've got to run upstairs and get my golf shoes. I'll meet you guys at the cab out in front." We play golf, I come back, shower and shave, and call my wife. Brenda says, like in the Cheesecake Story [page 102], "Tell me that I didn't hear Jack Carney say what he said this morning after talking with Jack Buck."

What Jack had done when he got his shoes upstairs was call the late Jack Carney, a terrific KMOX on-air talent, and tell about me locking myself out of my room without any clothes on. If the 50,000 watts of clear channel KMOX weren't bad enough, that afternoon Dick Kaegel supplied the *coup de grace*. Ever been stripped naked in the paper?

—*Bob Starr*

NBC did Monday night games in the 1970s. One time a childhood hero of mine from growing up in Washington—Jim Simpson—and I made history on a backup game from Boston. It started raining about 15 minutes before air-time, so from the time we said hi I was interviewing people on the field as Jim did bridges upstairs. With us was the guy who really invented TV baseball—director Harry Coyle. He was there sort of on a lark—not at NBC's big game that night, Atlanta and Cincinnati.

Our game was only going to Atlanta and Cincinnati and Dayton, but we had to fill over an hour before the rain stopped. The game finally starts, Boston wins at a quarter to one, and we get off the air—at which point Coyle hears from broadcast center in New York that the stations in Atlanta, Dayton, and Cincinnati had left baseball at 11 for news and never came back. Jim and I had done a couple of hours of baseball going nowhere. For the next two hours we celebrated *somewhere*—the bar.

—*Jay Randolph*

The home team first baseman is having an awful day. In the first inning he grounds out, and a fan behind the dugout with a big mouth starts yelling. Third inning—he strikes out. Now the fan is really taking him apart. "Bum, you can't hit, go back to the minors!" Sixth inning—the first baseman hits into a double play, and he's beside himself. Looks over and sees the fan's mouth going faster than Rafer Johnson. Comes the ninth inning—he strikes out. By now the fan is bonkers. So the first baseman runs over and jumps right on the top of the dugout.

Now, he's about 6-foot-4, and he's looking down at the fan who's been on his case. The fan shrinks back like he doesn't want to be hit, and the first baseman says, "Lookit, I'm not gonna hit ya—just tell a story. When I was a boy I was brought up on a farm and we had a jackass and I treated him horribly. My dad used to tell me, 'Don't whip that jackass so bad. The way you're hitting him someday his spirit'll come back to haunt ya.' You know, I never believed my daddy until today."

—Ernie Johnson

One day my son Doug was a batboy for the Giants at Shea Stadium. Brett Butler was with the Giants then, and tried to beat out a bunt. As the batboy, Doug ran up to the batter's box and picked up Butler's bat, waiting for him to return. And as we've all done from time to time, he swings the bat to sense its feel in your hands. Rick Aguilera was the Met pitcher—and looking down toward the plate, sees this guy in the batter's box with a bat in his hands. There's not much size difference between my kid and Mr. Butler. And as Aguilera starts to look in for the sign and Doug stands there—Butler's still not back at the plate—he's about to get his first big-league at bat.

Finally, Aguilera realizes the batter isn't Butler. As Doug might say, "So close and yet so far."

—Hank Greenwald

We do Reds' baseball "down-home," mixing play-by-play with talk about my tomato plants and Joe Nuxhall's golf game and anything that comes to mind. I bring this up because a few years ago we were really into the World Wrestling Federation. I often said, "If you don't believe in the WWF, you don't believe in God, motherhood, and the flag." They'd come to Cincinnati with Hulk Hogan and Randy the "Macho Man" Savage and their other cast of characters, and I'd take my daughter Ashley and get first-row seats at Riverfront Coliseum to watch.

It was in September, I guess 1988, an afternoon game against the Padres. That night, the WWF was performing in the Coliseum next to our stadium, and I'd been contacted by a WWF official about whether we'd like to have

Randy Savage stop by our radio booth. Hell, yes. Not only was "Macho Man" a big name, but it told our listeners that we'd been telling the truth: We really *liked* pro wrestling. What added to its appeal was Randy's background: a former ballplayer in the Reds' organization—Poffo was then his name—who'd gone as high as Class-A Tampa in the Florida State League. So we awaited his arrival, assuming that he'd appear in jeans and a sweatshirt.

Instead, Randy showed up in one of his brightly colored outfits with cape to match, and, as soon as he appeared in the booth, not only the crowd but the players went wild. I'll never forget Eric Davis coming out from the dugout and making a pose with his arm cocked to show his muscles and Randy waving down. He ripped up a life-like poster of Hulk Hogan, and went through his whole act for us and folks who saw him in the stadium.

Now, I know what you're thinking. How did Mrs. Schott [Reds' owner Marge] take to this? Not too well. She expressed the view that this wasn't family entertainment. I disagreed. I loved the appeal that a Savage had for young people and how so many show up at wrestling matches around the country. She made it clear she didn't expect it to happen again. It hasn't, but that was one memorable afternoon. Gorgeous George must be smiling in his big wrestling ring in the sky.

—*Marty Brennaman*

In 1990, the Red Sox' Marty Barrett hurt his knee, wasn't playing much, lost his starting job, and wanted to be released. He had been publicly critical of general manager Lou Gorman and manager Joe Morgan. And my father [*The Boston Globe* columnist Will McDonough] wrote a column saying the Red Sox have given you a contract, treated you well, and you shouldn't be lambasting them. We were in Detroit, and I hadn't seen the column, but I hear Marty's voice say, "Hey, Sean." And I could tell this wasn't going to be nice. He said, "Tell your father he can kiss my ass." I said, "What are you talking about?" He told me about the column. I said, "Marty, I don't know anything about it." At which point he started in on me.

Marty says, "I laugh when I read these comparisons about you and Bob Costas. You're about as close to him as I am to Ryne Sandberg." I say, "Well, if that's supposed to be an insult, at least you know how far away you are from Sandberg." It's probably the most acrimonious conversation I've ever had with a player. I said, "Marty, if I had a problem with you, I wouldn't call your son at home and scream at him. I'd take it up with you. If you have a problem with my father, you should take it up with him." Instead, he verbally took it up with me.

A couple nights later, on the air, I said that they should pinch-hit for Marty. Nothing to do with our argument, just made sense. Next morning, I got a call from Marty's wife Robin, quite upset: "Why do you say these things about the players?" Blah-blah-blah. We talked for 45 minutes. I tried to explain that it was nothing personal. I liked Marty, still do. Sure, I was disappointed by our talk a couple days before, but I don't let that affect my broadcast. She wasn't appeased and finally hung up on me, the only time a player's wife has contacted me directly. I hate confrontation, but you have to stand by your word. Integrity is the greatest asset a broadcaster has.

—*Sean McDonough*

Baseball is pretty close-knit. In 1986, my wife, Randy, and I were expecting our first child. At spring training, we're at lunch with Kirby Puckett and his now-wife, Tonya, and Kirby says, "Do you know if it's a boy or a girl?" We say, "No." He says, "Have you picked a name?" Nope. He says, "How about Kirby? That works for a boy or a girl." I say, "Yeah, fine. Tell ya' what. If you're hitting .350 when the kid is born, we'll name him or her after you." Seemed safe. He'd never hit .300 for a full season.

Well, on due date, Kirby is hitting .397 to lead the majors. He calls and says, "You got a baby?" I said, "The baby's late. Actually, if the baby holds off for a while and you go into a slump, we can forget the whole thing." He's still hitting .372 when the child was born. The only way around it was double middle names: The birth certificate reads, "Keith Michael Kirby Costas." Keith's spent a lot of time on Kirby's lap in the dugout. When he was 3 and 1/2, he asked his nursery school teacher, "Do you know my dad?" She said, "I've seen him on television, but I don't think I've met him." Keith said, "Trust me, he's a goofball." Out of the mouths of babes.

—*Bob Costas*

In 1994, Fox-TV ran an exposé of Babe Ruth's "Called Shot" in the 1932 World Series. It explored a question still asked: Just before Babe hit his homer off [Cubs' pitcher] Charlie Root, did he predict it by pointing to the bleachers? Root was our pitching coach in Milwaukee for a couple years in the '50s.

Naturally, I asked him if Ruth had called his homer. His eyes narrowed, and he said, "If he had, next time up I'd have stuck the pitch right in his ear." Charlie Grimm was our manager, and he told me, "Boy, Root was mean out there. One time he knocked down three or four guys in a row." I don't think Ruth pointed to the outfield—the conclusion Fox reached, too.

Incidentally, Grimm was a great storyteller. Once, there was a runner on first base, and Lou Novikoff, "The Mad Russian," hit to the gap in right-center field. The runner at first rounded third and then held up and went back. Never looking, Novikoff rounded second with his head down and slid into third base. The problem is the other guy was standing there. Grimm was coaching and went over to him. "Lou, where the hell are ya' going?" Lou gets up, brushes himself off, and says, "Back to second if I can make it."

—*Ernie Johnson*

A ward events are part of a broadcaster's life. After my first year at ESPN, I won an ACE—the honor they have for programs on cable TV. I wasn't expecting it because I'd never won anything—so when they announced my name and I walked to the stage at the Beverly Wilshire Hotel in Beverly Hills I just said what was on my mind. I looked at the movie stars in the audience. And I said I was incredibly stunned to win with this room full of talented people—the tops in their professions. What was I, after all? I go to games and my best lines are, "Low, ball one" or probably the line that is my best— "Line driiiivve, foul!"

I'm sure that made all the people understand why I was there.

—*Jon Miller*

CHAPTER TEN

PIECE OF DREAMS

TEAMS 'R' US

Emile Lazarus' "Whoever wants to know the heart and mind of America had better learn baseball" has been replayed more than Pickett's Charge, "I Love Lucy," or Hitler's nap on D-Day. Yet, growing up, how does a body learn baseball? Often, through the wondrous process of falling in love with a team. As a child, to me the Yankees meant baseball's high deeds and Holy Days; Senators, cellar; Athletics, wretched of the earth. The White Sox denoted speed; Reds, power; Pirates, line drives; Mets, what I tuned to when the Yankees were rained out.

Rivalries stirred a special imagery. Cubs-Cardinals. Red Sox-Yankees. Baseball's Hatfields and McCoys: Giants vs. Dodgers. Bill Terry sniping, "Is Brooklyn still in the league?" Bobby Thomson forging "D-Day"—to Brooklyn-born comedian Phil Foster, "Dat Day." Juan Marichal clubbing John Roseboro. Willie McCovey owning Don Drysdale. All dispelled the notion that baseball is a non-contact sport.

Name a year. Nineteen twenty-seven equals Murderers' Row; '34, the Gas House Gang; '45, the last Cubbie pennant; 1968, The Year of the Tiger. Which was better, 1961 [Yankees] or '76 [Big Red Machine]? Could anything be worse than the '62 Mets? If "Mrs. Robinson" means "plastics," to millions, baseball means team.

Nineteen forty-five is when I started broadcasting major-league baseball. It's also when the Cubs were last in a World Series. Now, we're not talking some expansion team. This is one of the great names in baseball. They've won pennants [three in 1906-10 and every third year, 1929-38], been in World Series [10, losing eight], had players from Hack Wilson to Ernie Banks. They're not some Humpty Dumpty who's moved from one town to another. This is the Chicago National League Baseball Team. So what happened to the doggone law of averages? It's unbelievable; every guy we traded became an All-American All-Star. Can you explain it? Half-a-century without even being in the World Series? If America loves the underdog, it should marry the Cubs.

—Harry Caray

It's the final week of the 1950 season, and Joe DiMaggio was fighting to hit .300 as he hits a line shot to shortstop. Joe heads to the outfield, mumbling to himself as he always did, and Yogi Berra fires the ball down to second base. We're about ready to start the next inning. Now, Yogi had something of an erratic arm and air-mails his warm-up throw over my head by 10 feet. It sails into center field and hits DiMaggio right on the heel. He'd been injured there, and down he goes. Joe bounces up, turns around, and sees me. I'm the innocent victim, but he doesn't know it. So he one-hops his throw to me on purpose, yelling, "Hot dog, catch the ball." The ball hits me in the knee. *I* go down. *Joe's* down. Yogi's standing there at home plate with his arms at his side. I could have killed him. With the Yankees, you either won or lost; there was no second place. Winning the World Series was fun. Getting there wasn't.

—Jerry Coleman

With the old Washington Senators, I never had to mention who was winning or losing, just give the score. It wasn't that the Senators weren't playing well; other clubs played better. Storytelling is an art easier developed with a losing team. Less game drama means the sportscaster has to work harder to hold viewership with stories. The best insights are picked up from chatting with the players, so I'd arrive early to get a jump on the information gatherers. You'd also look for novelty.

One day, the Senators, as was their custom, trailed the A's by seven runs with an inning left. Mischievously, I imparted a secret to our small but dedicated TV audience. "I haven't resorted to this before," I told viewers in confidence, "but one of our cameras has a magic ray. If we focus on a fielder, the ray will so mesmerize him that the ball will go through, by, or over him. I should tell you, though, that this demands a concentrated thought process, for your telepathic brain waves have an effect on our magic camera. If even one of you isn't thinking 'hit' at all times, our rays can malfunction."

The result? Unbelievably, each player we showed on TV close-up succumbed to "magic rays." Through the shortstop's legs, past the third baseman—whatever we selected, the ball went there!

The runs pile up, and now the Senators trail by only one. The bases were loaded, Mickey Vernon up, and our camera turns on the first baseman. Vernon swung, a vicious liner toward right. The impossible's about to happen until the first baseman leaped and snared the final out for an amazing catch. After the shock, I saluted viewers for almost completing a miracle and mused that maybe one member of our loyal audience had to leave the TV at the critical moment, causing a blip in our magic ray and the last drive to be caught. Having learned the fantastic secret of how to win games, I said I'd call on them again to pull out a big victory when it counted. Those rays wouldn't hold up forever, and this power shouldn't be wasted on just any game.

That decisive game in a pennant chase never happened during my [1947-60] days in Washington. I didn't try "the magic ray trick" again. Maybe wisely—might have been embarrassing. But if the Senators get a franchise again, and I can locate the same camera and viewers, I'd be willing to come back and give it one more try, preferably in a World Series' seventh game.

—Bob Wolff

After 13 years of playing and broadcasting baseball—learning it inside and out—I finally earned my shot at the biggies. In spring 1953, the Braves [of Boston since 1876] moved to Milwaukee. I'd done the minor-league Brewers, and the late Fred Miller was president of our radio sponsor, the Miller Brewing Company. He said Earl Gillespie will be the Voice of the Milwaukee Braves, period!

My first game took place in St. Petersburg, a Yankees' exhibition. I was wet behind the ears and so excited I could barely breathe. I now belonged to that select group of 16 who were big-league Voices. Thus began an 11-year love affair at County Stadium. [The 1954-57 Braves *averaged* nearly 2.1 million fans, almost doubling the nearest team, in the big-league city with the fewest people. Said a writer of the Braves' 1957 world title, "It was the season of light."]

People talk about great teams, great years. That misses the point. I've always thought the essence of sport is community: bond between fan and team. The announcer can nurture but not invent it. I don't think that bond has ever been stronger than the '50s years of the Cinderella Braves.

—Earl Gillespie

The Red Sox had awful luck over the years, and nothing worse than Harry Agganis. He was of Greek descent, lived in Lynn [a Boston suburb], the Bo Jackson of his day. Paul Brown wanted him to succeed Otto Graham. But he was also a great baseball player. The Red Sox gave him a bonus, and sent Agganis to Louisville [American Association]. He came up to the Red Sox the next year in '54, and I'll never forget one home stand. Hit four homers into Fenway's right-field seats. Joe Cronin told me, "You know, Curty, Lou Gehrig came years here and never hit a home run."

Soon, Agganis started to pull the ball. We're talking All-Star first baseman for the next ten years. In 1955, he's hitting over .300 when he got pneumonia. They put him in the hospital, and one day he comes into the locker room drenched with sweat. "What the hell you doing?" I said. He said, "Working out." I said, "You're crazy. You just got out of the hospital." But he was desperate to play, and got on the plane with us for a western trip. One day they put him up as a pinch-hitter, and Jungle Jim Rivera robbed Harry of a base hit on a line drive. Next stop is Kansas City. I come out from breakfast as Agganis comes down the elevator with a suitcase in this hand.

Jack Fadden, the trainer, called me aside and said Harry had taken a turn for the worse. "What's the matter?" I said. "We don't know," Jack said. They sent him back to Boston, and he had a blood clot in his leg that went into his lungs and killed him. He was just 25 years old. New England, which revered him, was in shock. I did the eulogy, and kept thinking of that great smile on his face he had for everyone—and life.

—Curt Gowdy

I came up to the Yankees in 1939 and saw the 1940s McCarthy clubs, Casey winning five straight World Series, and a dynasty that no one's going to match [14 pennants and 9 world titles in 1949-64]. But the team that stands out is Ralph Houk's first year as manager in 1961. No Yankee team won as many games [109].

Six guys belt 20 or more homers: Maris, of course, with 61; Mickey, 54; Moose [Skowron], 28; and the catchers John Blanchard, Elston Howard, and

Yogi [Berra] popped, if I recall, at least 21. One day [Memorial Day] the Yankees bombed seven against the Red Sox. The club hit a record 240.

Look at Whitey Ford, whom Casey'd spotted between starts. Houk started him every day, and Whitey has his best year, 25 and 4. Jiminy Cricket, every day seemed like Luis Arroyo came out of the bull pen [15-5 and 29 saves in 65 games]. And what people don't remember is the defense. Yogi'd scare you sometimes in left, but caught what he got near. Mickey in center outran everything, and Roger was vastly underrated in right field—fine arm, covered ground. Man, could he play caroms off the wall. And the infield: Moose steady at first, [Tony] Kubek and [Bobby] Richardson up the middle, [Clete] Boyer the magician at third. I think that Ft. Knox had more holes.

What I'm saying is, Just add it up. The M & M Boys battling to beat Ruth's record of 61 homers [Mantle and Maris' 115 topped '27 Ruth and Gehrig's 107], the hitting blitz up and down the lineup, Detroit hanging tough till a terrific September series at Yankee Stadium. [Hordes jammed the triple tiers for a three-game Bombers' sweep.] For pure excitement, the day-in and -out thrills that lift baseball, there may not have been a season like it. Nor, by the way, a team as great as the '61 Yanks.

—*Mel Allen*

In late 1961, I became Voice of the expansion Mets. They were a fan's nightmare—and a broadcaster's dream. Every day made you do a dozen double-takes. As their first player in the draft the Mets chose catcher Hobie Landrith. Somebody asked Casey Stengel why. "If you ain't got no catcher," he said, "you get all passed balls." Once, Hobie got too close to the batter, who swung and whacked his head. What a catching crew. For his first pregame TV interview, Ralph Kiner wanted to start with an easy question for another catcher, Choo Choo Coleman. "Choo Choo," he asked, "how did you get that nickname?" Choo Choo: "I don't know."

One day, the Giants' Willie McCovey pulled two Roger Craig pitches into the right-field seats at the Polo Grounds. Stengel went to the mound. "At the end of this year, they're tearin' down this place," he told Craig. "And if you keep throwing inside fastballs, they're gonna' have a head start in the right-field stands." I learned quickly that Casey couldn't care less if you had anything to say. Being around him was egalitarian: No one had an identity. At his age, he'd met every new person he was interested in meeting. You took him on his terms or not at all.

Casey quickly *came* to terms with the '62 Mets. At first, he said, "We got to work on the little finesses: the pickoff of the runner with runners at first and second, and on the first baseman holding a runner in a bunt situation, breaking in and back to take a pickoff throw." That day, the Mets lost, 17-1. By evening Casey had begun to see the light, not liking what he saw. He spotted me and said, "The little finesses ain't gonna' be our problem."

—*Lindsey Nelson*

In 1962, the National League expanded to Houston. Our first spring training was at Apache Junction, located in the Arizona Desert, south of Mesa, where Geronimo's warriors roamed. The way our club—then named the Colt .45's—played, you'd think he warred on us. There's been talk over the years about the Astros being born with a curse. Possibly, it wasn't wise to train in the shadow of Superstition Mountain, where Indian spirits and an old Dutchman's ghost were said to guard a lost gold mine. The Colt .45's didn't have bad luck until the first inning of their very first exhibition game. Al Heist, their best outfielder, stepped in a hole and broke an ankle, ending his career.

All sorts of casualties come to mind. Don Wilson, who was accidentally asphyxiated in his garage. Another pitcher, Jim Umbricht, and traveling secretary Don Davidson, died of cancer. Walt Bond, to leukemia. Rookie Jay Doll pitched one big-league game and was killed next year in a car accident. Yet think of our marquee names: Bobby Shantz, Robin Roberts, Pete Runnels, Nellie Fox, Joe Pepitone, Jim Bouton, an Eddie Mathews, Don Larsen, and Bo Belinski. How come the team's whole hasn't matched the sum of its parts? Maybe we shouldn't have got those Indian spirits mad.

—*Gene Elston*

You hear tell that everyone loves an underdog. The '62 Mets were the biggest dog that ever was under. One of our problems was language. Spanish-speaking Elio Chacon was the shortstop. Slow Frank Thomas was in left, and Richie Ashburn played center. Richie was a Mets' exception: Some of his talent was not in the past tense.

These three players would often converge when a pop fly headed for short left-center field. "I got it!" Ashburn would yell. Thomas then stopped as Chacon ran over Richie as the ball fell safely. This went on a while before Ashburn went to bilingual Joe Christopher. "How do you say, 'I got it' in Spanish?" Joe told him to try, "Yo la tengo."

Soon, here came one of those pop flies. The three players converged. Ashburn's yelling, "Yo la tengo, yo la tengo!" Chacon stopped. And *Thomas* ran over him.

—Lindsey Nelson

The early-'60s .45's were awful but intriguing. We had a pitcher named George Brunet, who pitched into his fifties in Mexico. George was a vagabond who played for a bunch of clubs [26] in the major and minor leagues. Once, when the Braves traded Brunet to the Cardinals, the St. Louis publicity man caught hell from his wife after she intercepted a phone message telling him what time to "pick up that brunette from Milwaukee at the airport."

Brunet was like most of our players, past or before his prime. No one was *in* it. Rusty Staub was 19 when he came up to the bigs. He was playing first base when Hal Woodeshick picked off the runner. Unfortunately he also picked off Staub. Rusty said it was his fault, but that he was blameless when it happened again. We were playing the Mets, and Rusty told Woodeshick, "I'm going [toward the plate] on the first pitch, so, whatever you do, throw to the batter." According to Staub, Woodie nodded, Rusty charged in, and, the next thing he knew, Woodie threw over to first. It almost hit Staub in the ear.

Maybe the Astros' Pitching Disease stemmed from the time Turk Farrell faced Henry Aaron. Hank lined a drive back to the mound that hit Dick square in the forehead. The ball bounced off and was caught in center field for an out by Jimmy Wynn. Honest. Finally, I don't know when hair dryers came into vogue, but the first time I saw 'em in the clubhouse is when Joe Pepitone joined the Astros [1970]. After a game, I walk in and can't believe my eyes. Here's Pepitone, stark naked with gun holsters on, one on each hip, and in each gun holster he had a hair-dryer. A bald guy who introduced hair dryers to the major leagues.

—Gene Elston

Let me talk about magic and rebirth. In my early days the Red Sox were a great franchise. But by 1966 the bottom had fallen out. Finished ninth. Talk of leaving Boston. Only 8,324 showed up for Fenway's '67 opener to see a young pitcher, Jim Lonborg. Then we went to New York for its home opener, Whitey Ford against rookie Billy Rohr. Rohr had a no-hitter with two outs in the ninth before Elston Howard, later to join Boston, singled. Rohr didn't pitch long in the big leagues. He's now an attorney in Garden Grove, California, and wrote me a letter when he came back for the 20th reunion of the '67 team. It was lovely, about the closeness of that club.

What '67 did was recharge baseball in New England. In July we came home from a road trip, having won 10 games in a row, and 10,000 jammed the airport. Fans still tell me they followed the race by hearing Ned Martin and me on transistors at the beach. Dick Williams was a rookie manager—right man, time, and place—who said, "I never saw one man have a season like [Carl] Yastrzemski had." Incredible down the stretch, 7 for 8 the last two games against the Twins. The final day, our guys won the pennant and were almost torn to shreds by fans on the field.

Those last two months, a whole region went insane. One night, there was no score entering the tenth inning. Reggie Smith hit a triple and scored, and the Sox won—but not before a traffic jam. One man refused to drive through a Boston tunnel until he heard the outcome. Hundreds of cars were backed up. People talk about other upsets. Believe me, they're child's play compared to 1967.

—Ken Coleman

Nineteen sixty-eight is the only World Series where I saw every game, and how it happened is a tale in itself. I grew up loving the Tigers from 1954, and to finally see them as a college student, skipping class to go to Detroit and St. Louis for one of the great Series of our time—unbelievable. Bob Gibson against Denny McLain. Mickey Lolich and Roger Maris and Curt Flood and Al Kaline and Norm Cash. We had a station at the University of Michigan, and somehow another student and I got credentials in the clubhouse, press room, Series hotel. I'm 20 and in line to eat at Busch Stadium behind Curt Gowdy who's doing the Series for NBC. I look around; there's Ernie Harwell, Jack Buck. I'd never even seen a National League team play, and to see Gibson in his greatest year [22-9, 13 shutouts, 28 complete games, *nonpareil* 1.12 ERA]—nothing like starting at the top.

As we age, things stand out about a year. I remember July 1968, Friday night, Detroit, hot. I'm with my girlfriend in the bleachers because it's the only seat we can get, and Tom Matchick beats Baltimore with a ninth-inning homer that catches the overhang. Or skipping school to go from Ann Arbor to Detroit to see the Tigers clinch the pennant [September 17] against the Yankees. The game ends [Don Wert's single in the ninth inning scored Kaline to edge New York, 2-1: Detroit's first flag since 1945], and in two giant steps I went from eight rows up in the boxes to one foot hitting the top of the dugout to being on the field.

Lary Sorensen, the former pitcher, told later about being at that game and getting some sod from Tiger Stadium that he put in his refrigerator and kept over the years as a remembrance of 1968 and the pennant-clinching game and that great World Series. [Behind, three games to one, Detroit rallied to beat the Cardinals.] Just the climax of growing up a Tiger fan in maybe the best baseball town of all.

—*Ken Wilson*

Their first month, I knew the Expos were special. Their home opener— April 14, 1969—came six days after a first-ever game in New York. And the field was in terrible condition because the frost hadn't yet come out of the ground. When you stepped on the dirt portion of the infield, you sank like standing on a sponge—three, four inches deep. It was so bad, runners actually took their lead off first base by stepping on the infield grass to run to second. Yet no one complained, the Expos or Cardinals. They knew what a moment it was for all of Canada and major league baseball: the first game played outside of the continental U.S.

Three days later, Montreal went to Philadelphia before flying back to Jarry Park for their second home stand. And what happens? In my ninth game as a big-league announcer, Bill Stoneman pitches a no-hit game! Give me a break. Some guys spend a career and don't call a no-hitter. Sort of foretold how whatever this franchise would be; it would never be dull.

—*Dave Van Horne*

The Expos have baseball's only bilingual city. Most games are on French TV, but lots of people turn down the sound and listen to us on radio. It keeps you on our toes; they *see* on TV what you *call*. It makes me feel good walking down the street in Montreal and a gentleman comes up and says in halting English, "I learn something new each day."

Once, Dave [Van Horne] and I decided to have a contest—weird, since it was 2 Quebec time in the morning. We asked folks to write and said we'd give an autographed Expo ball to the one farthest from St. Catherine and Peel Streets. The winner was in Timmins, Ontario. Later, a man wrote who'd tuned in by short-wave in Oklahoma City. We got over 400 letters at that hour. It's not hard to have incentive with listeners like that.

—*Ken Singleton*

Sometimes you look back at the end of a particular activity and say, "Well, I made a mistake doing that. Maybe I should have done something else." It's like the woman who near the close of her life has run into family unhappiness and looks back and says, "Maybe I should have married John."

People do that with professions. They get to the end and say, "Gee, maybe I shoulda' done something else." I don't feel that way *a'tall*. I think baseball broadcasting is the best thing in the world. How couldn't I after October 16, 1969? The fifth and last game of the World Series at Shea Stadium. Curt Gowdy and I were doing it for NBC. If the Mets won the game and, thus, the Series, I'd do the locker room show. In the ninth inning, I left the booth for the clubhouse. That's when the enormity hit. After seven years of famine, this was the Mets' time of plenty, and I'd been there from the first.

I get to the elevator. I remember it had got stuck in the past. I realize this is no time to be pinned in there. So I raced down the ramp, fought the fans going crazy, and reached the dressing room in time to hear Curt describe the final three outs and say, "The Mets are champions of the world." I was on a platform in the center of the locker room, and the door burst open, and here they came! By the time I got done with the post-game craziness, it was past 4 o'clock. I told my wife and kids, "We don't have time to go home [Long Island], and, anyway, if we don't go into Manhattan, we'll miss the party" to be held at 7 for players, their families, and the rest.

So we got in the car and drove around Manhattan. Dancing in the streets. Confetti flying. Once in a while a cop would recognize me and go wild. What made the entire year marvelous was that the Mets may endure a thousand years, as Churchill would say, they may win a dozen championships, but they can only do it the first time once, and the first time was incomparable.

—*Lindsey Nelson*

The mid-'70s Reds were perhaps the best there ever was. Davey Concepcion was a guy lost in the shuffle amid all the stars. Probably the best shortstop of that time. When people talk about a player who "carried" a team. . . , Tony Perez had 90 or more RBIs over how many [11] straight years. Pete Rose, my baseball mentor. Joe Morgan made the Big Red Machine complete. General manager Bob Howsam got Joe prior to the 1972 season. He knew that with more Astroturf, you needed defense and speed. Morgan gave you that. Also a guy who walks just when you need somebody to get on base, did everything, off and on the field. There's a part of me that would love to see Joe manage, but another part that knows there's too much else happening in his life for Joe to commit.

Where do you stop with this team? Maybe with Johnny Bench; he made everything you knew was hard look easy. I remember when I was young. Catching was a non-glamorous position—the tools of ignorance. The worst kid was told to catch because he had to put all this stuff on. Plus, the Little League catcher doesn't do much because no one steals. The pitcher was a glamor guy; the shortstop, a glamor guy. The first baseman was always in the action—the center fielder. The catcher, who cared? Bench changed all that, did more to glamorize catching than anybody. Not to mention coming through in the clutch as much as anyone I've ever seen.

—Al Michaels

Most of the years I've done the Braves, they were terrible. One year in the 1970s, we're playing in San Diego, and Buzz Capra is on the mound, a great kid who could've been a star pitcher but hurt his arm. Biff Pocoroba was our catcher, and I think the runner at first base was Gene Richards. I was doing the game alone on radio, the Braves being a lonely item in those days.

Richards takes off from first as Biff fires to second. Capra turns to watch the play. Before he turns, the ball hits him in the forehead and I swear to God went 100 feet straight up in the air. Buzzy falls down, draped over the mound, as the ball lands and Richards slides into second. I'm trying not to laugh, because Capra was a friend and I was afraid he might be dead. But it was so typical of our team that I couldn't help it. Here I am trying to describe what happened, and I just couldn't. Thank heaven Buzzy was OK and was able to continue in the game, though you'd never know it from me. Laughter got us through a lot.

—Skip Caray

In late 1973, I left Cincinnati because free agency hit announcing before it hit the players. I went to San Francisco, whose Giants were so terrible that you had to joke about it. Fortunately, I worked with Lon Simmons. Both of us found humor in anything. We'd play Houston, and the attendance would come in, and I would say, "Here's tonight's attendance, Mr. and Mrs. Jim McAlpine of Palo Alto," or "Harvey Jones and his daughter have driven in from El Cerrito." One night the Padres are killing the Giants, and I lead to commercial at the end of the sixth inning by saying, "The score at the end of six is San Diego, 9, and the Giants, 9. Unfortunately, the Giants are playing in German."

When you're 25 games behind in July, humor keeps you sane. Just very unusual years after my time with the Big Red Machine.

—*Al Michaels*

The teams I love enfold the community. Take September 29, 1978. The Pirates began a weekend series against the first-place Phillies, trailing by 3 1/2 games with four games left. They had to win all four to play a make-up game the day after the season ended at Cincinnati. Win that, and the Bucs take the pennant. That Friday, the Pirates swept a double-header against the Phillies, 5-4 and 2-1. My good friend [reliever] Kent Tekulve won both games, and each ended in the bottom of the ninth. The Pirates win the first as Ed Ott tripled and scored on a Garry Maddox error—each a rarity. [Ralph Kiner: "Two-thirds of the earth is covered by water and the other third by Garry Maddox."] In Game Two Warren Brewster balked home Dave Parker with the winning run.

On Saturday, the Phillies won, 10-8, to clinch the pennant. Randy Lerch was the Phillies' pitcher and touched Don Robinson for two homers. But what I remember is Willie Stargell bombing a grand-slam home run in the bottom of the first. At that time, it seemed the Bucs are gonna' win. This miracle's about to happen. There was a football game at Pitt Stadium that afternoon, and I'm told there were thousands of radios tuned to the Pirates. When Willie hit his home run, a roar erupted. To me, that's what baseball is all about, a whole city riding on each pitch.

—*Lanny Frattare*

We're in Seattle's Kingdome. Lenny Randall's playing third base for the Mariners. A ball is bunted, and Lenny gets down on his hands and knees and tries to blow it foul as it's just trickling along the line. The

Kingdome's flat on the base paths, and Lenny knew it wouldn't go foul on its own, so he decided to help it. Of course, the umpires didn't allow it, but it's as bizarre as Lenny's humor and, frankly, some of our Mariner teams.

—*Ken Wilson*

I don't see how people can knock Seattle as a baseball town, because, as I've often said, "Hey, you fans don't owe the Mariners anything; the Mariners owe you a team." When you consider that only twice have we finished above .500 and have still drawn two million, there's nothing wrong with baseball in this town.

People say, How in the world can you stay in Seattle? Well, I've had other opportunities to go to bigger markets, much more money, but you have to live here to understand what it really means to a kid from the Midwest who appreciates the aesthetics of the game. I make more money than I ever dreamed of making, so why be miserable in New York or Los Angeles or Chicago? Plus, I want to be here when baseball turns around. I figure it's a matter of time after, what, 10 managers?

We've finally signed a cable deal out here: 100 TV games over three years. They're not getting a lot of money out of it, but it's a start, and Mariners' baseball will be shown in areas it's never been into, Idaho, Montana, Utah, up into Alaska, northern Oregon, and California. The exposure matters more even than the money. Now, all we need is the team.

—*Dave Niehaus*

The game that meant most to me as a broadcaster—and the Padres in their history—was Game Four of the 1984 playoffs against the Cubs. It was best-of-five then, and the Padres had to win to force a fifth game. They did, 7-5, as Steve Garvey drove in five runs—the last two on a ninth-inning homer. [The call: "Pitch is on the way to Garvey. Hit high to right-center field! Way back! Going! Going! It is gone! The Padres win it! . . . In a game that defies description, Steve Garvey, in the ninth inning, hit one over the 370-mark, and the Padres beat the Cubs, 7 to 5! Oh, Doctor, you can hang a star on that baby!"] Baseball's funny. You wait a lifetime to see a game like Garvey's, and when it happens the details never leave. "Oh, Doctor!" is right. I can taste its medicine even now.

—*Jerry Coleman*

Teams get lucky; even bad trips can have a happy ending. In 1986, the A's were a last-place team going nowhere—actually, to Kansas City. That series, Dave Kingman was unhappy with a female beat writer named Susan Fornoff and, in one of the most mindless stunts a human being could pull on someone, sent a gift-wrapped box to the press box for her during a game, and in it was a rat. It typified where that team and Kingman's persona were headed. The A's lost a game in that series when the tying run, Ricky Peters, was picked off third for the final out of the ball game—I've never seen it again. The A's leave Kansas City after those incidents and fired manager Jackie Moore. Oh, yeah, about ten days later, they hired a guy named Tony La Russa.

—Ted Robinson

I grew up in Illinois. Going back to Chicago [to do the 1985-89 Cubs] was like a second youth. Midwest fans are knowing, courteous, appreciate the opposition, yet partisan and hands-on. It's funny. Cub fans are so frustrated, you think they'd be fed up, but what a great place Wrigley Field is to go. So, despite losing, baseball matters so much that fans stay intoxicated. I remember 1989. The Cubs had a great start, then hit a slump, which prompted a fellow named Ken Foxx to send me a letter. Enclosed was a verse ballad based on *Macbeth* that he'd composed to ban the Cubs' hex. I read it and think, hey, this is kind of interesting.

> Anson, Chance, and Wilson, Hartnett, Hornsby, Brown, and
> Grimm
> Hex the Mets, the Birds, and Expos
> Stand behind the Cubs and Zim. Double, double, toil, and
> trouble
> Fire burn and Cubbies bubble. Eye of newt and raven beak
> Presto, it's a winning streak. So heed this curse from Bill
> Veeck's vines. Our Cubs are the champs of '89.

One game, the Cubs get way behind, and I read this on the air, and they come back to win. Enormous reaction: People calling in, wow, this really works. I said, Wait, temper your reaction 'cause you don't want to abuse its powers. After the Cubs, I broadcast in New York—it's everything and nothing at once due to vastness. A great baseball heritage, but tough to put a personality on it because there are so *many*. Knowledgeable, not shy, love opining—you know, "Who's better, Williams or DiMaggio?"—but not as family style as Chicago. Even now, Spike O'Dell of WGN Radio calls and asks me to read the Cubs' poem. I still carry it in my wallet.

—*Dewayne Staats*

The whole first year of 1993 was special for the expansion Colorado Rockies. [Manager] Don Baylor was a good friend of former Commissioner Fay Vincent. Don always said that if he ever became a manager, he wanted Fay to be there. The Rockies opened Monday, April 5, in New York City, and back from Europe flies Fay, at Don's request, to throw out the first ball. The Rockies lost twice to the Mets and then came home to open on Friday at Mile High Stadium, before an Opening Day record of 80,227 fans.

I've covered Opening Ceremonies at the Seoul and Barcelona Olympic Games, and the '86 World Cup soccer finals in Mexico City—144,000 in Azteca Stadium. The Rockies' first-ever opener was as big as those combined, yet different. For 30 years, the Rocky Mountain region had been baseball's bridesmaid, and now the big leagues were here and it's an ode to joy. Eric Young was the Rockies' lead-off batter in the bottom of the first, and, on a 3-2 pitch, he got their first hit in Mile High Stadium. And that first hit was a home run. You could hear the roar in California.

Eric got kidded because he didn't hit many home runs. I'll say. That was his last until the final home game of the year, when he hit a pair back-to-back! Some bookends: his first on Opening Day, the other two on Closing Day. No more amazing than the entire opener—crisp, the sun out, and a region in love.

—*Charlie Jones*

The Florida Marlins learned early what expansion means. Let me tell ya' about the first road trip we took, spring training 1993. We were to play an exhibition game at Homestead, Florida, with all proceeds to benefit the victims of Hurricane Andrew. It had hit a year earlier. The Cleveland Indians then deserted Homestead as a spring training site because of the damage. So this exhibition is a big deal, we're *playing* the Indians, and we don't even mind that it's a four-hour bus ride.

We got up early and split into two buses: one with manager Rene Lachemann and his coaching staff and some players and media, the other filled with players. We take off and about three miles into the trip hear a loud explosion. So we pull over, find one of the tires obliterated, limp into a convenience store, and try to get a tow truck. We're sitting there—here's the problem—as the other bus keeps going. Lachemann wanted both buses to arrive at the same time in Homestead, so they get on cellular phones and after about 25 minutes contact the other bus. You talk misery loving company: The bus makes a U-turn and comes back to this convenience store to join us! We're watching, waiting, and finding this impossible to believe.

Our traveling secretary had arranged for sandwiches on the buses, so the guys start eating them. But there were no soft drinks, and he'd forgot to arrange for condiments in those boxes. No mayonnaise, mustard, nothing to put on. We got bread and meat; everything's dry. It takes an hour for the tow truck to find us. The tire gets fixed, and off we go. Four hours later, we reach the park, play the game, then check into a local hotel to stay overnight. We look around and see a humungous convention of, yes, *bagpipers* staying at the hotel for the next couple days. Up and down the hallways, these guys run around in long boots and short checkered skirts, all playing bagpipes, blowing at 3 in the morning. None of us got any sleep. A night to forget.

I think we knew then what our first year might be like.

—Joe Angel

CHAPTER ELEVEN

STARGAZER

MICKEY MANTLE

If you couldn't fantasize about being Mickey Mantle in Ike and JFK's America, forget it, man, you were squaresville, freaked out, a nerd, out of it (but good). "I wish I was half the player he was," Al Kaline said of the orb who won the 1956 Triple Crown and led the league in slugging, runs, and total bases. Added Casey Stengel of the 1956, '57, '62 Most Valuable Player: "Mantle was better on one leg than anybody else on two."

Like Babe Ruth, No. 7 shunned moderation. On April 17, 1953, in the City of Presidents, Mick wafted the first "tape-measure" home run. His 1956 season—52 homers, 130 RBI, and .353 average—may be the best baseball year of post-World War II America. In 1963, Mantle crashed an extra-inning blow that almost became the first ball hit out of Yankee Stadium. A year later, he cut the Cards with a ninth-inning, Game Three winning poke, breaking Ruth's record for World Series home runs. Among his Classic marks: Most runs [42], homers [18], and RBI [40].

When Teresa Brewer sang "We Love Mickey," she spoke for Baby Boomers everywhere. No one could run faster, hit farther, or was hurt more often. Once, Mike Garcia was asked how to pitch Mantle in a close game. The Indians' righty said, "You don't." Sunny-dark superstar—Achilles Okie in New York—he was, and is, a mythy rural legend before his time.

I once broadcast in the Class C Western League, where meal money was $1 a day. That's how it was—anything to save bucks. The bucks went to the big club, and the Yankees did things first-class. They supplied the players and a Greyhound cruiser. No short-cuts for them. They caressed the talent, especially the Joplin shortstop in 1950, who went the next year to the majors. Mickey Mantle hit 26 homers in a Class C League—the greatest mismatch I've ever seen. He hit balls out of sight. Only 18, but already ready for Triple-A. Tremendous arm and speed. Those parks had rocks, not dirt. Mantle'd send them flying. He hit the ball so hard it got to infielders fast. Didn't help 'em. A bobble, and Mick's standing on first base.

Harry Craft managed that Joplin club and said all along, "This kid's a center fielder, not shortstop." The problem was that DiMaggio was already there. Next year, they switched spring training sites: The Giants went to St. Petersburg; the Yankees, to Arizona. In that rarefied air, Mantle hit balls into the next county and made the club in center. With DiMag about to retire, Craft got his way. Colleges are producing a lot of players now, but the minors make everything tick. Just as they did when I first saw Mantle.

—*Merle Harmon*

Healthy, Mantle was the best I ever saw. Who else could run to first base in 3.1 seconds and hit a 600-foot homer? He just got hurt so often. He tore up his knee in the wire fence they had in Baltimore. He'd already hurt one knee, so to strengthen both he played bandaged from ankle to thigh. One World Series, Mantle was hurt and pinch-hit a home run. Another Series [1961], he played despite an abcess. Jiminy Crickett, you saw *blood* oozing through his uniform. Between games of a double-header, they'd unwrap the bandages and massage his legs. The circulation came back, and Mickey'd amaze everybody by coming back on the field.

No one equaled Mantle's threshold of pain. It's one reason his teammates—[Tony] Kubek's an example—idolized him. His father and grandfather had osteomyelitis, a degenerative bone disease, and Mickey really thought he was going to have it, too. I remember after he got to be 'bout 30 years old. The myth started that it was all catching up to him. Staying out with [teammates] Whitey Ford and Billy Martin, night after night, cost Mantle years off his career.

I never bought it. Sure, they had a good time, beat curfew, that sort of thing. But Mantle's injuries didn't have a thing to do with booze or, you know, some house detective. They came from how on the field he pushed himself so damned hard.

—*Mel Allen*

For many years I thought I was goofy about something that happened in the '57 World Series. I made a pitch to Mantle on a clear day in Milwaukee. Mick swung and ticked the ball back against the screen. Later, I told our players, "I thought I smelled wood burning." They said, "Oh, give me a break." For a long time I felt I was the only guy who smelled it. People probably thought I was nuts!

I kept asking sluggers, "Ever swing at a ball and smell wood burning?" Finally, Bob Watson said, "Sure. Didn't you ever look at a bat and see a little brown spot? That comes from the friction of the ball against the bat. It's a burn mark." Redemption! Another stranger-than-fiction tale came from Mr. Watson. He told me that he'd heard that Jim Rice checked a swing in a ball game, didn't hit the ball but still cracked the bat.

Do you believe it? Have you ever seen Bob Watson? Or Mickey, who started me on this crusade? Just look at their forearms. Think I'm gonna' disagree?

—Ernie Johnson

Some sports are like Chinese dinners. *Baseball* stays with you. I'll never forget April 1953. Turn-of-the-century guys like Ty Cobb would tell me that they never saw another Mantle. At five his father taught him in Commerce, Oklahoma, how to bat both ways. [Washington's] Griffith Stadium had a scoreboard that topped the bleachers in left-center field, and, this day, Mantle hit a shot that clipped its top. Red Patterson was Yankee public relations director and went out beyond the outfield, and I got to wonderin' why. The answer is that somehow Red got a tape and found the ball in somebody's backyard. It was supposed to have traveled 565 feet, and this was *after* being slowed by the scoreboard. If there's ever been a reason for "How about that!"—man, it was now: The first "tape-measure" home run.

—Mel Allen

As Senators' Voice I seemed to be continuously calling record events— most records set against them. The 565-foot homer, for example. Mantle's swat left the park so fast, and its trajectory was so low that the crowd's reaction was more shock than screams. "Did you see that?" was more of a reaction than "Wow!"

National Bohemian, the sponsor, had an "X" painted on the sign so that fans could point to where the shot hit its ad above the bleachers before leaving the park. But the "X" didn't stay long. Mr. [Clark] Griffith, the Senators' owner, used white paint to have the "X" removed. "I didn't want that reminder intimidating our pitchers," he said. Actually, it didn't take a sign. Chuck Stobbs gave up that historic homer. He later showed he had versatility. Not only did Chuck give up the longest drive going out of the ball park, he notched the longest wild pitch in the other direction. His errant throw sailed all the way up to a concession stand, spattering mustard over a fan about to enjoy a hot dog. A new way to relish the occasion.

This wasn't the longest Mantle home run I broadcast. At Yankee Stadium, batting lefty, he launched a [1956] missile against Pete Ramos which cleared the first, second, and third decks in right field and was still ascending into outer space when it hit the perforations of the light tower—just a foot from being the first ball to leave the park. The soaring time of this round-tripper left ample opportunity to describe its flight with all the splendor it deserved—voice rising to a crescendo, backed by the roar of the crowd. I remember thinking at the time: Mantle would make any broadcaster look good.

—*Bob Wolff*

There's never been a fair ball hit out of Yankee Stadium, but I was there when it almost happened [May 22, 1963, 11th inning *vs.* Kansas City, off Bill Fischer, to give the Yankees an 8-7 victory]. This was before the Stadium was refurbished, and the only reason it didn't clear was that the ball hit the overhang. It was like a plane taking off, and the *New York Times* saw fit to diagram, by triangulation, the ball from home plate. They said if it hadn't hit the triple-tiered facade, the ball might have reached the Bronx County Courthouse two blocks up the street. OK, so I exaggerate. But not by much.

I don't know much algebra or trigonometry. I know there was only one Mick. Ralph Houk was Yankees' manager in 1963. Of the home run, he said, "How'd you like to have that one chopped into singles for the year?" Well, how *would* you?

—*Mel Allen*

I was doing the A's broadcast that night and still remember how many people call it the mightiest ball ever hit at Yankee Stadium. [1932-68 Yankees' player and coach] Frank Crosetti, for one, said he'd never seen a longer shot. It was still rising when it missed by, say, 18 inches, of going out. George

Alusik was playing right field for the A's, and when Mickey connected, Alusik never moved a muscle. The next morning, I have breakfast with George and Bill Fischer. Fischer said, "Man, George, you showed me up on that ball Mantle hit. Why in the world didn't you turn around or do something, act like you had a chance to catch it?" Alusik said, "Listen, I wasn't concerned about catching that ball or trying to pretend. I was worried that the ball was hit so hard it'd hit the concrete, knock blocks off, and come down and kill me." I guess that team loyalty will carry you so far.

—*Monte Moore*

I was watching on TV when Mantle took Fischer into orbit. By the time the camera spotted the ball, it had struck the facade and dropped onto the field. It got out so fast. A guy from Harvard's Physics Department figured it would have traveled 620 feet if it hadn't struck the upper deck—then, 374 feet away and 108 feet high. Nobody could do that but Mantle, just like nobody was as famous for a two-strike drag bunt with the infield back.

As we later learned, and as he admits, Mickey wasn't a role model, but he was a hero. I was eight in the 1960 Series. In Game Two, Mickey homered over the dead center-field fence at Forbes Field—457 feet—so far they actually put the batting practice cage on the field. No righty had ever cleared it. The Yankees won games by 16-3, 10-0, and 12-0. Outscored the Pirates, 55-27. Outhit 'em a ton [.338-.256]. But lost the close games, including the seventh with Bill Mazeroski's homer. Afterward, Mantle cried like a baby in the clubhouse. He played in 12 Series—winning seven—and says it's the only time that he truly felt the Yankees were by far the better team.

A few years ago, I came back from the studio after a prime-time NBA game and around midnight walked into a restaurant of the Manhattan hotel where I was staying. I stuck my head in there, and it looked abandoned until in a corner I saw two people sitting: Mickey Mantle and Billy Crystal. They waved me over, and it turns out that Crystal grew up on Long Island, as I did, and was three or four years older. He was a Yankee fan like me, idolized Mantle, and so for the next four hours we sat there recalling specifics of games that Mantle played in.

The whole time Mickey's saying, "Shoot, I don't remember that. Damn. Did that really happen? Holy sh. . . ." Ya' know, he *did* it; Billy and I *remembered* it. Tells you something right there.

—*Bob Costas*

Mantle is an American icon. People may be shocked at his innocence when it comes to idolatry. Mickey's not stuck on himself—his idol is Ted Williams—and he never brags. He likes nothing better than to revel in the warmth of just being around other players. That's why I get a kick out of a story Mickey told me once in Manhattan. Seems he and a friend had just come back from a Binghamton Card Show.

Now, Binghamton's in upstate New York, oh, an hour and a half from Cooperstown, and Mickey, as a baseball fan, wanted to visit the Hall of Fame on his own. Naturally, being Mickey Mantle, you might imagine people would request his autograph and pictures throughout his visit. Mickey certainly did. So while his friend drove, he decides that he'll sign about 200 autographed pictures, put them in his coat pocket, and hand them out to folks. That would let him enjoy the Hall of Fame and not be bothered by people who are there to visit.

Mickey pays his way in for his friend and himself, and they're in the Hall of Fame all day—about six hours—with 200 autographed pictures of himself in his pocket. Only problem is that not one person recognizes him! After a while, he takes off his sunglasses—it upsets him so—and still nobody salutes our hero as he goes through the Hall of Fame. That night, he and his friend eat at the Otesaga Hotel. Mickey says the closest he got to someone recognizing him—imagine, *Mickey Mantle!*—was when the busboy brought up his car after dinner and said, "Aren't you, no, you couldn't be."

—*Tim McCarver*

For years I had Mantle's '58 All-Star card in my wallet. Then, somehow it got misplaced. Tony Kubek made a big deal out of it on "Game of the Week," said I'd lost an heirloom, and I got about 50 of them in the mail from sympathetic viewers. The fact is I've never *not* carried a Mantle card! In my wallet is a 1966 that I've had a long time. It's falling apart from people asking to see it, so it's going back in.

I've never considered baseball cards for their financial value. Their value is emotional, kind of a marker in your life. You saved your Mantles and Hank Aarons and put Hector Lopez on the spoke of your bike to make that cool sound when you're driving down the street. It's OK to flip and trade them and try to keep them in mint condition—but an investment, no. Other than your investment of the heart. Which in a way sort of defines Mantle.

—*Bob Costas*

CHAPTER TWELVE

FINE AND DANDY

NATIONAL LEAGUE

*S*ome National League franchises evoke a name. Say Pittsburgh, and you recall Roberto Clemente; Cincinnati, Pete Rose; St. Louis, the Man (Stan), whom Ford Frick, dedicating his statue, called "Baseball's perfect warrior, baseball's perfect knight." Pitching at Shibe Park equaled Robin Roberts; all of Wrigley Field, Ernie Banks; second base at Ebbets Field, Jackie Robinson; center field on any planet, the "Say-Hey Kid."

The saw declares that "Anyone can play baseball." Exempli gratia: Ozzie Smith, "The Wizard,"a palatine at shortstop. Fernando Valenzuela, putting batters and pounds away. Marvelous Marv Throneberry, of whom Ralph Kiner said, "Marv never made the same mistake twice. He always made different ones." (See Chapter 13 for that "other" league.)

Icon or reverse Midas snatching defeat from the jaws of victory, big leaguers are best at what they do. Even there, a sense of humor helps. At Crosley Field, a terrace graced deep left field. "The Reds taught you how to go up the incline," said converted catcher Ernie Lombardi upon tumbling. "They just didn't teach you how to come down."

N o nicknames beat baseball's. Everybody knows "The Babe." Then there's "The Man"—and there *was*. Stan wasn't a leader like guys now are supposed to be—screaming, yelling. Musial led by example. [3,630 hits; 7 batting titles; 1943, '46, and '48 MVP; and Hall of Fame '69. Said Warren Spahn of the 1942-63 Cardinal: "Once he timed your fastball, your infielders were in jeopardy."]

In 1958, Stan had 2,999 hits, the Cardinals open a series next day in St. Louis, and [manager] Fred Hutchinson sat him down because he wanted Musial to get the coveted 3,000th hit at home. But in the ninth, the Cardinals are losing, 2-1, two out, two on base, and Hutch says, "You want to go up?" Stan says, "Hell, let's win the game." He pinch-hits and lines a rocket down the left-field line. The tying and winning runs score, and he's got his 3,000th hit. Sure, he'd rather got it in St. Louis, but with Musial it's win the game first, forget about when you do it.

Stan's as beloved as when he played. When I hear things that happen today, with players not signing autographs for kids, I can't believe it. I've seen Musial play a July afternoon double-header in St. Louis—it gets so hot then—and about 150 people wait across the street from old Sportsman's Park for him to come out. He does, and after two games you'd think he'd get in his car and go home. Instead, Stan waited an hour and a half and signs every damn autograph that these kids had for him. That's a gentleman.

I could wear you out about Stan The Man. Even more than his prowess on the field was his greatness off it. Today, players get these unbelievable salaries. Musial didn't make a fraction of their pay. Doesn't matter. You can't buy class.

—*Harry Caray*

I came up to the Cardinals in the 1940s. And I started as an assistant groundskeeper, not catcher. Part of my job—this is the truth—was washing the sanitary hose of the players. One of the guys on our team was [Stan] Musial. I broke into baseball washing Musial's socks. I kid him because I say, "Yeah, Stan, you were a good hitter, but we used to always put on your socks 'TGIF': Toes Go In First." Anything to help The Man.

—*Joe Garagiola*

Musial is the Norman Rockwell ballplayer, both hero and role model, among the most genuinely nice and happy people I've known. A couple years ago, Stan sat in a round-table discussion, and the moderator was saying ballplayers aren't as good today. He said, "Stan, .331 lifetime, what do you think you'd hit today, watered-down pitching, expansion, the whole thing?" Stan said, "Oh, .285, .290." The guy said, "Stan, you're a modest guy, but what are you talking about, .285, .290?" Stan said, "What the hell, I'm 71 years old."

—*Bob Costas*

My dad had a political background [U.S. Senator William Jennings Randolph, Democrat, West Virginia]. I grew up in Washington, D.C., and hung around Griffith Stadium. Indirectly, it led to my first baseball job—and to a baseball hero. In 1958 I was helping my dad in his campaign for a Senate seat and met a man who owned a radio station. I wanted then to be a pro golfer; my dad wanted me to be a politician. I'm asked, "How come you didn't get into politics?" I tell people they don't know anything about the broadcast business if they don't think it's political. Anyway, my career started with Babe Ruth baseball on WHAR Radio in Clarksburg, West Virginia, a 250-watt station.

By 1968, I was doing doing KMOX pre- and post-game shows when Anheuser-Busch asked me to do a special on Stan Musial's [1969] induction at Cooperstown. I spent two months researching and going back to Pennsylvania and meeting hundreds of people who'd known or played with Stan. We became close friends and still are. I'll never forget a segment that we taped: a golf course, where we intended to play one hole and have Stan talk about anything he wanted to as we strolled along. In typical Musial fashion, he hit a great drive, a wonderful second shot, and made a six-foot putt for a birdie on a very tough, 444-yard par 4. Birdied the hole on a one-take, smiling all the way.

A lot of people thought we'd staged it, but they don't know The Man. That's just the way Stan is, extraordinary for combining talent with humility. He'll do anything he can to help people out—and *without* a political bone.

—*Jay Randolph*

Ever hear of a guy by the name of Pee Wee? He probably made more pals and kept them than any other player. I see him occasionally, or I used to, the last time at the World Series. A friendship never dies with Pee Wee Reese. He represents something very dear: a romance of the time we spent in the baseball world, an era Brooklyn fans recall with a sigh, as if to say, "Those were the good old days." Know something, ya' heah? They were.

Isn't it amazing the way that nickname stuck? He's not even listed as Pee Wee, just Harold Reese, Ekron, Kentucky, July 23, 1918. I always felt that Lou Boudreau had the greatest instinct at shortstop, but Pee Wee's with him. He'd come up with balls that you swore were already in center field. In his 16 years, the Dodgers won seven pennants. Most of all, he proved Leo Durocher wrong. This nice guy never finished last. Go to Cooperstown [Reese's induction, 1984]. Better, ask anyone who remembers Brooklyn's heartthrob of a team.

—*Jimmy Dudley*

Warren Spahn was my Braves' teammate and one of the greatest pitchers of all time. [Two no-hitters, 13 20-game years, lifetime 3.08 ERA, and 363 victories. Eight times Spahn led the N.L. in wins, and tops it lifetime for victories, shutouts, and innings pitched.] It's said he'd walk a player intentionally in a close game and then pick him off. Spahnie's pick-off move to first base is the best I've ever seen. One night, I saw him pick off the base runner, umpire, and first baseman at the same time. None of 'em saw the ball coming!

You know, lefties are a special breed. If there's nine players on the field and one of them has his hat on crooked, chances are he's a southpaw. Warren was often the butt of jokes; he'd be upset if you didn't kid him. We used to say that two things helped pick guys off. One, Warren's big nose: "When you move your head, your nose hypnotizes the runner." Two, he'd have his hat pulled on crooked, and they didn't know if he was looking at home or looking at first. There was a story on the banquet circuit that I can't verify, but, knowing Spahn's great move, I don't doubt is true: One night he picked a runner off first base, and the batter swung.

—*Ernie Johnson*

In the old days, I'd ride in the back of the players' bus and sit with the guys on trains and, later, planes. You sorta' felt like part of the ball club. The Braves had some of the biggest agitators in the National League, and you had to know how to take verbal jabs, or you'd get a lot more. Yet it was close-knit; they wouldn't take outside guff. Our games were heard in my hometown, Chicago. My mother said she could always tell when Spahn was pitching by my voice—more excited. Spahnie was my favorite among a lot of favorites on that club. ["The night Warren won his 300th game," Ernie Johnson said of August 1, 1961, "almost brought tears to Earl's eyes. Spahnie was a clown off the field, and serious as a safe-cracker on it."] He'd tip me off on the strengths and weaknesses of rival hitters, and how he'd pitch them. It was great in the booth because I knew, say, what Spahnie was trying to do to a hitter like Mays or Ernie Banks. No wonder he won more games than any lefty in history.

—*Earl Gillespie*

Great at bat, Willie Mays was acrobatic in the field. When a final out was made at Candlestick Park, Willie would sprint into the Giants' dugout and then the clubhouse. One night there were two outs and two runners on as a pop fly was hit to shallow right. Felipe Alou was running in as Chuck Hiller at second base ran back, each looking up and searching for the ball. Mays sprinted between them, caught it off his shoe tops—the third out—and kept on going into the dugout. What makes it amazing is that Alou and Hiller hadn't seen Mays, didn't know he caught the ball. They're both looking for it in right field, and Mays is already in the shower! Willie was always ahead of the game.

—*Lon Simmons*

With the [1965-69] Astros, I saw the greatest individual play I've ever witnessed by—who else?—Mays. Denny Lemaster and Juan Marichal were locked in a scoreless game at Candlestick in the eighth inning. Mays was at first base with one out when Jim Ray Hart singled in the hole to left field. Usually, on a hard-hit ball to left, the runner stops at second, right? Mays just kept going when he saw left-fielder Dick Simpson, not to be confused with ['50s outfielder] Harry Simpson. Harry was known as "Suitcase." They called Dick "Briefcase," and on this ball he kinda' lollygagged after it.

Bob Aspromonte was third baseman and cut-off man. He took Simpson's throw and glared at him as if to say, "How can you let this guy go to third base on a hit to left field?" As Bob is glaring, Mays keeps going. He finally throws home, and Willie beats it—safe! Mays wasn't running on the pitch, there was no error on the play, the ball was a single hit to left field, and he still scored from first base. It was the only run of the game as Marichal won, 1-0—that, and the most incredible base running feat I have ever seen.

—*Harry Kalas*

I'm often asked, "Who's the greatest player you've ever seen?" My answer is always, "Willie Mays." He hit for average, had great power, was a superb runner and base stealer—and his fielding was even better! Terrific speed led to catches I'd never imagined, let alone seen.

Mays was a rookie in 1951. One day, the Giants were playing at Forbes Field when Rocky Nelson hit a line drive to left-center. Mays got his usual quick jump, but saw he couldn't reach the ball with his glove hand. So he reached out his *bare* hand and, racing at full speed, grabbed it. The best catch I've ever seen. The Pirates were retired. Mays headed for the dugout. He got there and met silence. His teammates were giving him the cold-shoulder treatment. Finally, Willie couldn't stand it.

Mays walked from one end of the dugout to the other. "Skipper," he said to manager Leo Durocher, "didn't you see that catch? I just made a great catch."

"You did?" said Leo, faking ignorance. "I didn't see it. Go out and do it again next inning." Which Willie did for the next 22 years.

—Ernie Harwell

I'm in the bullpen in the '50s in the old St. Louis park, and a ball is hit toward us, over Hank Aaron's head, toward the right-field concrete wall. It'd rained, and the grass was slick as Hank races back, reaches the warning track, and slams on the brakes because he's gonna' hit the wall. He puts down the gloved hand to brace himself and his meat-hand over his head, then slips as the ball hits his bare hand. But he holds it, turns, and flips it to the infield. The greatest catch I've ever seen. He went back to his position, kneeled over, and heard us going crazy from the bullpen. He looks over and winks, as if to say, "Routine, guys, routine." Today, guys spike the ball, prance like idiots. Not Hank. You couldn't tell whether he went 4 or *0* for 4.

Later, I did mostly TV during Henry's [1966-74] career in Atlanta. My radio play-by-play was limited to two innings, the third and seventh. The irony is that Hank seemed to pick those innings to hit his big home runs. Number 500 came in the third or seventh, so I got to call it. Ditto for 600 and 700. Even 714 came when I was on radio. I thought it was very unusual. I used to thank Henry. Marconi would have loved him.

—Ernie Johnson

I'm at Wrigley Field the day after Ernie Banks got hit in the nose by a Vernon Law fastball and was carried off the field on a stretcher. Hank Sauer was Ernie's teammate [also, 1952 National League MVP and "Mayor of Wrigley Field"]. It was like a good-natured changing of the guard as Hank's Cubs became Ernie's. [Plucked from the Kansas City Monarchs for $20,000, Mr. Cub hit a record-tying five 1955 grand slams, whacked 48 homers in 1956, won the 1958-59 MVP Awards, and in 1970 hit home run No. 500.] Sauer says, "Ernie, how can you be so dumb as to get hit in the nose?" Banks was no slouch in the head or with a bat [retiring in 1971 with 512 home runs]. He eyes Sauer, whose proboscis was rather prominent, and says, "Hank, if that ball hits you in the nose, it carries for a home run."

—Vince Lloyd

Juan Marichal was one of the greatest pitchers I ever saw [high-kicking like Gwen Verdon by way of Gower Champion to hurl a 1963 no-hitter, twice lead the N.L. in complete games and shutouts, make 10 All-Star teams, and six times win 20 games. In August 1965, Juan clubbed Dodgers' catcher John Roseboro over the head with a bat and was suspended. He was also 243-132 with a 2.89 ERA]. Juan grew up in the Dominican Republic at a time when it was a dictatorship. I remember one game in particular. A brother of the dictator [General Rafael Trujillo] was running the air force—in effect, National—team, which Juan beat, 1-0. Two days later, a knock came on the door. Juan was drafted into the air force to pitch for its team. A short time later, he lost a game, 1-0, and was thrown in the air force brig for losing. Truly, Juan was wise before his time.

—Lon Simmons

Jim Pendleton may be the only guy in baseball history acquired for a franchise. Jim was an original Colt .45's outfielder who came to Houston [1962] because of Bobby Maduro. Maduro was a businessman who wanted to move a Triple-A team into the Colt .45's official minor-league territory—here, Jacksonville. But he couldn't buy their rights since his money was in a Cuban bank account and unobtainable. The silver lining was Maduro's ownership of other minor-leaguers like Pendleton. So Houston management said, "Give us Pendleton, and we'll give you our rights to Jacksonville."

One day, Jim was on first when Al Spangler hit to right-center field. By the time he reached third, it was clear there was something wrong. He'd slowed up, then stopped, then got going again. I thought maybe he was hurt. Yet the ball was hit so deep that Jim slid into home safely. There he laid, and the catcher and umpire start laughing. Later we found that Pendleton had lost his cup. It fell out when he rounded third, rolled down his pantleg, and was hanging down around his knee about the time he hit home plate. What ballplayers can overcome.

—Gene Elston

My first World Series was 1964, Cardinals-Yankees. The middle games [3-5] were at Yankee Stadium, and it's as terrific as baseball gets. In Game Three, Mickey Mantle hit a home run on the first pitch off Barney Schultz to open the bottom of the ninth inning and win, 2-1. Oh, what a blast! I still see it orbiting. But it's the next day that's imprinted on my memory. We had to win to tie the Series, and marvelous relief pitching by Roger Craig and Ron Taylor helped do it [4-3]. But what stands out in my mind is Kenny Boyer's Grand Slam homer in the sixth inning. We lost Kenny in the 1980s [to cancer, at 51]. He was quite a warrior. I still see him nearing third base and his brother, Clete, getting in the baseline and almost intentionally forcing him to run behind him as Kenny whacked him on the ass. It was like Clete telling Kenny that there's more to life than a Series. I guess blood is thicker than homers.

—*Tim McCarver*

Robert "Bo" Belinski had a good arm—could have been one of the great pitchers—but was more intent on being a playboy. Maybe Bo's priorities weren't straight, but they were always sure!

One night, we were in Los Angeles, and Belinski invited me to go to a party of Hollywoodites, starlets, and would-be starlets. It was a Friday night, and he was scheduled to pitch the next day, a day game at Dodger Stadium. We got back from the party just in time to catch the team bus to the park. All I have to do is broadcast, but I'm wondering how in the world Bo can possibly pitch. All he does is throw nine innings of shutout ball. Houston didn't score either, so he wasn't involved in the decision, but when Jim Wynn homered in the tenth to finally break the tie, everybody thought, "There but for the grace of Bo."

His teammates knew that Bo was in another world that day. About the fifth inning, someone took his left-handed glove, which he sat at his side when he was in the dugout, and replaced it with a right-hand glove. It's a long walk from the dugout to the mound at Dodger Stadium, and out ambles Bo to the mound not realizing he has a righty's glove. He gets there and still doesn't know. He starts his warm-ups, and finally the light goes on. Better late than never for the unsinkable, unfathomable Bo.

—*Harry Kalas*

Doug Rader played for the [1967-75] Astros and became known for antics around the world. Doug would use our locker room as a driving range, teeing up a golf ball while guys dove for cover in lockers, behind trunks, and under the whirlpool. Then he'd ricochet it around the room as players prayed it hit someone else. Someone asked Larry Dierker once, "How come nobody took Rader's golf clubs away?" He answered, "'Cause they wanted to live." Doug was that kind of guy. In one TV interview, Rader advised Little Leaguers to eat bubble gum cards. Digest the card information, and become good ballplayers. Another time, he said eat the bases and home plate, and they'd be better. Amazin'.

—*Gene Elston*

Rader was an amazing character. Having played a few rounds, I remember him more for golf than baseball. One time, Doug, Joe Morgan, my dad who was a minister, and I were playing golf down in Florida, and Rader wasn't having a good round. He was throwing out four-letter words during the afternoon, and my dad didn't say anything. Finally, we're on the sixteenth hole, and Joe said, "Dougie, ease off on the language. Don't you know that Harry's dad is a minister?" Dougie immediately went up to my dad and said, "Jesus Christ, Mr. Kalas, I didn't know you were a minister!" Only Dougie.

Once we played another round, and he had a terrible day. Dougie had a temper, and clubs had a tendency to snap in half or fly to the top of trees. By the time we finished, he had one club left. Another time, we're in Florida as Dougie hit a ball into the water. I'm riding in his cart, and he's driving as fast as that cart can go toward the water. I thought, well, you know, he'll peel off at the last minute. Yeah? We go into the drink, and see an alligator. The cart is submerging, the alligator's after us, and we almost lose our lives. A reason: Dougie was busy rescuing our clubs. We did, and completed our round.

—*Harry Kalas*

In 1966, the Braves moved from Milwaukee to Atlanta and opened at home against the Pirates. The year before, Tony Cloninger had won 24 games for Milwaukee. He was from Lincoln, North Carolina, and popped with pride when skipper Bobby Bragan named him Opening Night pitcher. This was the first game played in the Deep South, and to Tony no cost was too great to win. Maybe the cost was a great career.

Right out of spring training, Tony pitched 13 innings as the Pirates won, 3-2. Many felt his arm was never the same. Nor his bat, but in a different way! Later in '66, Tony pitches at Candlestick against the Giants. His first at-bat, he hits a grand slam homer; next time up, another slam. Eight RBI, then got a ninth, an all-time record for any pitcher in a game. On the one hand, his career fades because he pitches a 13-inning complete game. On the other, he makes the record books as the Braves score 17 runs, but isn't around at the end because the Giants hit him hard. Anyone who says they know base-ball is hallucinating at both ends.

—*Milo Hamilton*

Bob Gibson was very influential in my career. He's a very dear friend to this day, one of my top five friends in life. I remember my first spring training in 1960. Bob and I got on a bus following a road game in spring training, and we started to leave St. Petersburg. We were perspiring because we'd both played in the game, and I was sipping an orange drink. We were different—Bob a black man from Omaha and me a white kid from Memphis—and he was testing me. He said, "Could I have a sip of your drink?" and I looked at him and looked at my drink, and I said, "I'll save you some. Bob and I have talked about that for the last 35 years.

Gibbie liked to work real quickly on the mound [to real *effect*. He was 251-174 lifetime with a 2.91 ERA and an MVP and two Cy Young Awards]. Johnny Keane was the [1961-64] Cardinals' manager who used to want me to go out and slow Bob down. I told Johnny that Bob was a fast worker and didn't want any interference when he was pitching. Finally, I worked up enough courage to approach the mound and tell Bob to slow down a bit. *Big* mistake. Bob looked at me and snarled, "What are you doing here? Go back behind the plate. The only thing you know about pitching is that it's hard to hit." I love that story. Still, Johnny persisted. "Damnit," he said, "go out and slow him down." And I replied, "But he *likes* to work fast." Eventually, in 1963, I decided to appease both Gibson and Keane. I'd go half way to the mound, shout at Bob, then beat it back to the plate. Pretty diplomatic, huh?

—*Tim McCarver*

When Barney Schultz became Cardinals' pitching coach, Gibson kidded him unmercifully. "What can *you* teach me about pitching?" he'd roar. "You were a knuckleball pitcher, and I throw fast balls. If I threw a knuckler, you could help me." The upshot was that when Barney came out to the mound, it was torture. He'd look around, down at his shoes, look from Missouri to Montana, and still no escape! Just Bob saying, "Barney, what are you *doing* here?" It got to the point where Barney was scared to death to go to the mound and talk to Gibson.

One day in 1973, it was the first game of a double-header, and Bob was getting hit hard. It was unusual to see him shelled that way; in about 2 and 1/3 innings, he gave up 8 runs. You guessed it. Finally, here comes Barney. It takes forever to get to the mound. I was at first base, [Joe] Torre at third, Ted Simmons behind the plate, and we looked at each other as though to say, "Uh, oh, here comes Barney." Barney gets about four feet from the pitching rubber, and Gibson said, "Where you been?" Schultz looks as if to say he can't believe this greeting. Bob said, "I've had line drives hit off me all night, and you're in the dugout. Get me *out* of here." And Barney said, "Yeah, Bob, that's why I came out." Talk about a rare meeting of the minds.

—Tim McCarver

I think back to my first year at Cincinnati in 1974 and how many players bent over backward to help. There'll never be another Big Red Machine. Early that season, the Reds were playing a Saturday game at Jarry Park. It was cold, raw, as Montreal often is. We get to the park. Johnny Bench comes up and says, "Look, when the game's over and we get back to the hotel, I want you to go out with me." I was astounded. The game couldn't get over soon enough. We go back to the hotel, I meet him in the lobby at 7, and we're off to a nightspot. It's a lively place, and we have a great time. The only problem is that we didn't go out and eat dinner first, and throughout the night we're imbibing.

It didn't take long to realize that I was going to be sick. Around one o'clock in the morning, I'm absolutely green. Johnny grabs my arm and says, "You've had enough. I'm taking you back to the hotel." I wake up Sunday morning without a hangover, feel wide-eyed and bushy-tailed, and go to the park for the final game of the series. I can't wait to get to [manager] Sparky Anderson's office to tell him what a sensational night I'd had. I was surprised with Sparky's sarcastic look, but he didn't interrupt till I'd completed the story. "Is that right?" he said. "Exactly," I answered.

With that, he bolted from the office, and I'm wondering what is going on, so I follow him as he walks into the training room. There on the table is Bench, and he's not feeling well. Sparky said, "I understand you took Marty out last night and had a big time." Johnny said, "Yeah, we went out, but that doesn't have anything to do with the way I feel." Sparky said, "Let me tell you something. I don't care if today's game goes 25 innings; you're catching every inning until its end."

Johnny knew that nightclubbing wasn't why he felt punk—he had a fever of about 102—but tell that to Sparky! Bench put on the catching gear, went out and played, and—typical of his flair for the dramatic—hit a three-run homer in extra innings to win the game. All while being sick as a dog. Lesson one for a rookie radio announcer: What you did the night before, especially with a player, you don't tell the manager. I learned the hard way. Bench has since forgiven me.

—*Marty Brennaman*

Phil Niekro is a dear friend of mine. We were together for so many years with the Braves. It's funny, but Phil always seemed to pitch the last game of the year, and it always seemed to be in Cincinnati. That wasn't good, since in those days we were very bad and the Reds were the Big Red Machine. Dave Parker must have hit .600 against Niekro. I'm sure Phil would tell you Parker gave him more trouble than any hitter he ever pitched against.

Phil and I went out the night before, and he said, "How the hell do I get Parker out?" I said, "You've tried everything else, why don't you throw that little blooper ball and see what happens?" The first two times up Phil doesn't listen, throws his knuckler, and Parker lines out and singles. The third time around, Niekro throws a knuckleball for a strike. Then he looks at the booth, waves at me, and I start laughing 'cause I knew what's coming. Phil lobs up a blooper, and Parker hit it about 400 feet to the warning track in centerfield, and it was caught. Next time, same thing: Parker hit it about 390 for an out.

That's baseball: Niekro takes my advice, Parker bombs two balls almost 800 feet, and I can still say, "I told you so."

—*Skip Caray*

One day in the late 1970s, Mike Shannon and I were doing a Cardinal game in Chicago. The day before, there'd been runners at first—Lou Brock—and third and one out. A fly ball was hit to right field, Bobby Murcer caught it, the runner at third tagged, Murcer threw to the plate, and the runner was out. Meanwhile, Lou stayed at first.

Mike says to me on the air, "Bob, that's not good base running. Lou's got to make something happen here. He either goes to second base, starts to go and gets thrown out and lets the runner score, or gets to second in scoring position if the runner is thrown out at the plate. This way, it doesn't help you." Problem: Lou hears about this, and, the next day, after batting practice, Mike and I are upstairs with our producer, Tom Barton, when the phone rings before the game.

Tom says, "Mike, it's Brock for you." They have this conversation—I'm paraphrasing—and Mike says, "Yeah, no, that's not right, Lou, no, Lou, we were teammates, I love you." He said, "You're the greatest base stealer in the history of the game, but you're a horseshit base runner, you've always been a horseshit base runner, and you'll always be a horseshit base runner." Boom, end of conversation.

—*Bob Starr*

I've broadcast the Pirates since 1976. To me, the Captain is still Willie Stargell—as Bob Prince said, "Willie the Starge." I remember September 1979, a double-header in San Francisco. First game, Pirates lead, 5-3, in the bottom of the ninth. Willie's already homered twice. Two out, right hander Kent Tekulve on, Jack Clark beats out a bunt. The next batter was lefty Darrell Evans, then righty Mike Ivie. [1977-85 Pirates' manager] Chuck Tanner went to the mound, and I remember saying, "I can't believe he'd take Teek out of the ball game with Ivie on-deck." He didn't, but wouldn't let him pitch to Evans.

Teek went to left field, and Grant Jackson came in to face Evans. If Darrell reached, Kent would pitch to Ivie. As Teek went to left, Omar Moreno in center picked up blades of grass to show which way the wind was blowing—a little humor. Meanwhile, Tanner said to keep the ball away, which Jackson did, and on the second pitch Evans flied—where else—to left field! Tekulve made the catch and afterward met Stargell. These were the years the Pirates wore those double-rimmed Cap Anson caps, and Willie gave away stars for outstanding plays. Kent took the whole business seriously, actually sewed 'em on. He put stars for wins on the top rim, and saves on the bottom. This star went on his button.

The Pirates swept the four-game series and eventually won it all. Every time I think back on '79, Stargell was winning a game for us—and every big hit was a home run—including, as I recall, a winning two-run shot in Game Seven of the World Series against Baltimore. [Stargell's first-pitch, sixth-inning blast helped the Pirates win, 4-1, and cap their rally from a 3-1 game deficit.] No wonder he was the league's co-MVP.

—*Lanny Frattare*

Baseball is made up of strong personalities. Steve Carlton was no exception. He told me that since he was young he read theory and philosophy. A lot of people referred to him as eccentric. I found that Lefty was the type of guy who put his eccentricities to work on the mound. He'd take batting practice, come in, and enter a trance-like state before a game. At the time, I thought he was resting. Not till I retired did I learn he was ahead of his time. Steve felt that the more you visualized the outside two and inside two inches of the plate, the more you'd stay away from the middle. You may think that's foolishness, but Steve rarely threw fat pitches, so maybe there's something to it. *He* thought there was—and that was enough.

One day in the late '70s, Steve was throwing a lot of high fast balls and I was catching him and lost my temper. I'd been yelling, "Come on, Steve, bend your back, bend your back"—*ad nauseam*, I might add. I felt I was yelling too much and next day said so in so many words. I went up and said, "Lefty, you know, in last night's game, I felt I went too far, and I want to apologize to you." He looked down at me in that stare of his and said, "That's OK, I wasn't paying any attention to ya', anyway."

—*Tim McCarver*

One day J.R. Richard had just pitched a game in which he got into early trouble, straightened out, and won the ball game. Now, there are a lot of players who go on your pre-game show and, without asking, mention the help of God. J.R. was one of them, liked to talk about religion. In this interview, my partner Loel Passe asked what his problem was in the early going. And J.R. said, "Loel, I'll tell ya'. I was having trouble out there, and all of a sudden I felt something on my shoulder, and I looked up, and here was this little bird."

Loel looked a little startled. J.R. goes on, "And this bird was evidently sent down by God, and he told me to straighten up and go out and win this game, and that's why I turned things around." Then, Loel says, "What kind of pitches were you using about that time to make the change?" And J.R. said, "Shit, Loel, I'll tell ya'." A little much for me.

—*Gene Elston*

The Giants are in spring training in the mid-'80s, and Mike Krukow is pitching. As he releases the ball, he comes up yelping and holding his back, and [manager] Roger Craig goes out to have a look. Finally, the umpire comes out and tells Mike to throw a couple to see if he can continue. So Mike throws his first pitch on the screen back of home plate, draws a few "oohs" and "aahs." Now comes the second pitch, and it's like Krukow spikes it. Goes 'bout three feet. By now, everyone's aghast, especially the batter—I believe, Mike Brumley, a Cub rookie. His eyes got big as baseballs: Standing in, a big part of him's already in the first-base dugout. So Krukow throws a pitch, and this kid reaches as far as he can and weakly pops to first. Mike walks off the mound into the dugout and says, "I've always wanted to do that." He faked the whole thing, and now he's my broadcast partner.

—*Hank Greenwald*

I was released by the Yankees in 1980, joined the Cardinals the same year, and saw them take the 1982 World Series—their first in 15 years. We were a team nobody thought could win, but we had Whitey Herzog as manager—a teammate in the late '50s—and shortstop Ozzie Smith, only the best to ever play the game. Plus, Bruce Sutter, a great reliever who taught ya' heart.

One day, we fall behind the Mets in New York and start chipping away. We score two in the ninth to lead, 6-5, and now it's Sutter Time! He comes in, gets two out, but on an 0-2 pitch Frank Taveras dinks a single. Mookie Wilson belts a split-finger for a homer, and the Mets win. It was a quiet plane trip to Chicago. I say, "Amishman"—Bruce's nickname, 'cause he's quiet—"hang in there." Sutter says, "Just give me the ball again with a one-run lead." Next day, Joaquin Andujar goes eight innings and hands Bruce a one-run lead. Man, the Cubs never had a chance, 1-2-3. Sort of what the Cardinal franchise is all about. Don't talk a lot, just rely on guts.

—*Jim Kaat*

P ete Rose understands more about baseball than anybody on the planet. My favorite athlete to cover because whether it was March 10 in an exhibition against the Pirates, or October 10 in the World Series' seventh game, Pete didn't know how to play any way but all out. I've never seen any athlete with the intensity level that never ebbed an iota. Never met a brain that just kept thinking baseball, baseball—it's all he talked about. To this day, I hear Pete's voice in my ear when situations come up. Pete Rose gave me my Ph.D. in Baseball.

—*Al Michaels*

People ask me about Rose. I answer, Ben Johnson. It's discovered he used drugs, and they erase his records as if he'd never run a race. What's this, Red China? There is a great picture with Chairman Mao standing in the middle at a parade. Twenty years later, he's been erased from the picture. Wait a minute, what happened to Chairman Mao? Who? That's what's occurring to Pete. If Pete's are Hall of Fame numbers, he should be in the Hall of Fame. But what's happened is complicated. The Hall of Fame is a very select fraternity of the greatest players, and a lot of them feel the evidence says that Pete bet on baseball. That's the cardinal sin. What I think is that players have told the people at the Hall, "If Pete Rose comes here, we're never coming again" to the induction ceremonies. As of now, they reconvene each year. What will happen in the future, I don't know. I do know that Pete belongs in Cooperstown.

—*Jon Miller*

The hardest season that I've spent with the Reds was 1989, when allegations began in the spring concerning Pete's gambling and betting that ultimately caused his banishment from baseball. We'd developed a close relationship in the '70s when he was a star of the Big Red Machine and befriended me as a young broadcaster. To endure what he went through hurt me because we could see what was going to happen down the road.

As a player or manager, Pete was the ultimate in dealing with the media. Didn't matter whether you were from a major or small-town paper or radio or TV station. An incident from spring '89 points out how aware Pete was of the press. I did a daily radio show with Pete as manager—called, unoriginally, "The Rose Report"—and I'll never forget the day the story broke that baseball was starting an investigation into Pete's alleged gambling. The club was scheduled to play an exhibition game in St. Petersburg. By then, the Reds were based in Plant City, but I stayed in Tampa from earlier days when they trained there.

The trip is brief from Tampa to St. Pete, so it didn't take long to find a media circus. When the Reds arrive, Pete's not there. I say to coach Tommy Helms, "When's Pete coming?" He said, "Pete said to tell you that he'll be here in plenty of time for the show." I stand with the multitude waiting for the arrival. Pete gets there an hour before the game—a half-hour before our show's on the air—and, as he nears the infield, the mob descends. He raises his hand and tells the media, "Fellas, can't talk now, I've got to do a radio show." And he points to me and said, "Let's go into the clubhouse," so we do.

The only people there are Rose and myself. Before I turn the tape on, I said, "Pete, we can't avoid talking about this gambling. Not every day. But sometimes things are going to crop up that need to be discussed." He couldn't have been more gracious. "Look," Pete said, "we'll talk about it any time you want. When things come up you have to ask, ask. I'll answer the best I can." Here's a guy the world was starting to fall on, but he understood my job and was willing to do anything to make it easier. And he kept his word, because we discussed the situation off and on all summer. It was tougher on him than me. But not one time did he say, "I'm not going to talk." Frailties? Pete was, is now, and forever will be an amazing human being.

—*Marty Brennaman*

I don't think the National League was ever better than in the 1950s and '60s. Since then, both leagues have changed—dramatically, and for the worse. During my 11 [1953-63] years in Milwaukee, players read *The Sporting News* in the locker room. Today, it's *The Wall Street Journal.* Forget loyalty to the team, the city and fans, club owners, and even teammates. The players union so controls the game that baseball's existence that most of us old-timers knew is in jeopardy.

How long can the richest owner afford the ridiculous money demanded by 10-game winners? God, I wonder if there *could* be enough money to pay N.L. stars of that era like Henry Aaron, Willie Mays, Stan Musial, Jackie Robinson, and Duke Snider if they were active now. Today, guys collect long-term ransoms after batting .235. Can you *imagine* what a perennial 20-game winner like Warren Spahn would demand? What would you pay Juan Marichal? I'm thankful that I got my shot at broadcasting the National League when I did.

—*Earl Gillespie*

CHAPTER THIRTEEN

BOTH SIDES NOW

AMERICAN LEAGUE

*B*aseball is cyclical. The 1950s American League gave us Carlos Paula, Wayne Terwilliger, Reno Bertoia, Eli Grba. (Many tried to give them back.) Boston's early-'60s Dick Stuart, Don Buddin, and Pumpsie Green became sport's riposte to Larry Fine, Moe Howard, and SuperStooge Curly. Later, even Brooks, Frank, Powell, and Palmer—baseball's Round Table—couldn't keep the National League from ruling Camelot.

Enter the 1990s, where fact dubs the A.L. superior. Think of Frank Thomas, baseball's Strong-arm Kid, and Paul Molitor, its Andy Hardy parable. Cecil Fielder swinging like something out of Big Klu by way of Steve Bilko from the planet Krypton. Carlton Fisk, Nolan Ryan, and George Brett retire. Welcome Carlos Baerga, Juan Gonzalez, and Albert Belle.

Jackie Gleason as Ralph Kramden often vowed to send wife Alice "to the moon." Today, some insist that's where Ken Griffey, Jr.'s orbits land. Early Wynn said he'd knock his grandmother down to win. Following are American Leaguers who made memory cry "uncle."

M y best memory as a kid was our once-a-year trip from Charlottesville, Virginia, to Washington, D.C., to see the Senators play baseball. A family of 13 kids can be expensive, but my father worked for the Southern Railroad, so we rode free. The trolley line went right from Union Station to Griffith Stadium. Peanuts were a nickel a bag; and hot dogs with mustard, onion, and chili, only a dime. Had ever a king lived so well?

My father thought the baseball world ended with Walter Johnson. [It did for many hitters. The Big Train struck out 3,508, tossed 110 shutouts, and won 416 games for the 1907-27 Senators.] He was a giant Viking with broad shoulders and graceful bearing. My father used Walter as a standard of behavior. When a youngster, especially his, got out of hand, Pop said, "Walter Johnson would never do a thing like that." Whatever it was, you never did it again.

Pop loved to tell how Johnson got mad at a ball park policeman. There was a shy little black boy named Snowball who used to hang around the clubhouse doing any jobs to be around his heroes. One day, a cop collared Snowball and, believe it or not, was going to toss him out of the park. Quickly, Johnson shoved the policeman to the wall and shouted, "Don't ever lay hands on this boy again!" The officer started to answer, but Walter shouted, "Dadgum your soul, I mean it!" Remember that Washington was segregated and that "dadgum" was the strongest language anyone heard Johnson use.

I think of Walter when I see pitchers look to the bench after five or six innings. Once, Johnson pitched three shutouts against the Yankees in four days. They say you never outgrow your first hero. I never outgrew my pop's.

—*Jimmy Dudley*

Everything in life has peaks and valleys. Lou Gehrig had a disappointing 1938 season [29 home runs, 114 RBIs, and .295 average—his worst since 1926]. I'd go out to Yankee Stadium and see him, and I figured he was just in a slump. But in spring training of '39, Lou was still having trouble swinging the bat. Most everybody said he'll get over it.

It's late April, a Sunday, and one day there's a ball hit between first base and the mound. Lou came over to field it and was all thumbs—no coordination. That was the last game of a home stand. Monday was off. The Yankees would open in Detroit on Tuesday. Lou lived in Westchester County, near New Rochelle, and spent the day thinking how this might be beyond a slump, something terribly wrong. [It was amyotrophic lateral sclerosis, a hardening and collapsing of the spinal cord. "Lou Gehrig's Disease" took his life in 1941, at 37.]

By this time, Lou had played in 2,130 consecutive games, an amazing record not to trifle with. He was also Yankee captain, so he studied a long time. When they got to Detroit, he went to manager Joe McCarthy and said, "Joe, don't put my name in the lineup today." Joe was a great manager who realized Lou seemed to be coming apart, knew Gehrig was hurting the team by playing, but couldn't bear to bench him. To Joe, he was a son. On May 2, Lou solved the problem by telling McCarthy, "I can't go on like this. Take me out of the lineup." Joe's heart was breaking—this gruff volcano. "C'mon, Lou," he said, "you'll get over it." But Lou insisted, and, inside, Joe was grateful.

They called a press conference. Lou as captain took the lineup to home plate, and, unbeknown to him, the P.A. announcer read a statement once that happened. "Ladies and gentlemen, this is the first time Lou Gehrig's name will not appear in the Yankee lineup in 2,130 consecutive games." There was a thunderous gasp. Then Lou turned and walked back and sat in the corner of the dugout. I can still see Lefty Gomez, his pal, get up, walk over, and sit down beside him. Tears were coming down Lou's face.

It was a very difficult moment, this catastrophe building, wrenching his insides. Imagine Lou finally realizing that everything is coming to an end: his streak, whole career, his life. Lefty put his arm around him and said, "C'mon, Lou, cut it out. It took 'em 15 years to get you out of the lineup. When I pitch, a lot of times it only takes the other team 15 minutes."

—Mel Allen

Even the bat boy looked like a tree top [on Phil's rookie club, the 1941 Yankees]. Red Ruffing, [Bill] Dickey, [Joe] DiMaggio looked like a forest. Nobody paid attention to me, and I figured it was part of the initiation. But finally I began to worry that I'd done something wrong to deserve the ice treatment. Lefty Gomez looked like a nice guy, so I told him I was worried. Lefty told me, "Relax. They're not snubbing you. They just haven't seen you yet."

—Phil Rizzuto

I live by words, but I don't know where to start with Babe Ruth. In 1939, he was at "Lou Gehrig Day" when the Yankees retired Lou's number, the first so honored. By 1947, Babe had been in and out of the hospital with cancer of the larynx. He was dying, so the Yankees held "Babe Ruth Day," where Babe wore his trademark camel hair coat and matching cap on the field.

The late Eminence Cardinal Spellman was there, and I remember the ovation as I presented Ruth. Nor can I forget his hoarse whisper due to the cancer. I was worried because the situation demanded something, so I put my lips to his ears and yelled through the noise, "Babe, do you want to try to say something?" He put his lips to *my* ear and in a frog-like whisper said,

"Yeah, I *must*." Then he got to the mike, and whatever was left of his voice amplified on the P.A. system. The Yankees forgot then to retire Ruth's Number 3, so on June 13 of 1948 his number was retired. When he got to the dugout, Cardinal Spellman said, "Babe, anytime you want me to come to your house for Holy Communion, I'd be glad to do it." Babe said, "Thank you, Your Eminence, but I'd rather come to *your* place."

When he died two months later, the Babe drew his usual sell-out crowd. They poured into the streets outside St. Patrick's Cathedral and packed the church. Waite Hoyt, the great ex-pitcher, was in the front row, and seated next to him was a third baseman from Babe's era named Jumpin' Joe Dugan. It was a brutal day, and as Babe's casket came down the aisle, Dugan turned to Hoyt and quietly said, "Boy, it's so hot in here I'd love to have a beer."

Hoyt looked at the casket and turned to Dugan. "Yeah," he said, "so would the Babe." Ballplayers are like that—bizarre sense of humor. But there was never anyone like the Babe.

—Mel Allen

One of my favorite people in baseball was Satchel Paige. Satch was old [42] when he came up to the majors in 1948, but still fun. Everybody was a friend in our Cleveland clubhouse. Same thing on the road. Satch had a little girlfriend in Boston, and I mean "little," came up to his waist. One day at the station, we're waiting for the train to come, and this little girl was sashaying up and down the platform. Satch just looked at her and finally said, "Hey, baby, when you walk you shake that thing just like a caboose." She turned and looked at Satch. "Look here, big boy," she said, "you ain't seen nothing. You ought to see me when I got a passenger."

I don't know what I loved more, Satchel Paige's smile or his fastball. It started above his head, gathered speed as he went past his knee, and almost hit the ground as he delivered. One day we're in New York. Satch came in to pitch the last inning and threw a pitch to Tommy Henrich, who hit it into the right-field seats for a homer to win the game. On the train to wherever we were going that night, Satch was having dinner. Joe Gordon was our second baseman and yelled at him, "Hey, Satch, what was that pitch you gave to Henrich today?" Satch stopped eating, got his teeth straightened up, looked at Joe and said, "Mr. Gordon, I don't rightfully know, but he ain't gonna' see it no more."

—Jimmy Dudley

I found baseball's heart in the early 1970s when I spent 25 minutes in New Hampshire with Satchel Paige. He came to a dinner in Manchester, and we sat and talked about the old days, control, and throwing only the fastball. I still laugh at how Satchel mimicked what he told hitters: "If you think I'm gonna' throw anyplace but your letters, shame on ya'!" For me it was a wonderful trip back to a fellow I read about as a kid, saw pitch as a St. Louis Brown, relieve when I was living in Washington near Griffith Stadium—his hesitation pitch was *still* getting people out—and broadcast his last game in the major leagues.

It was in the old ball park in Kansas City [Municipal Stadium] in 1965. Satchel pitched three innings of scoreless ball against Boston—the only hit, an off-field double by Carl Yastrzemski. Stood them on their ears. He was who knows how old and gave up zero walks. A story and legend left the game in his last big-league appearance. When he told me, "I could go two innings now," you believed him, even then. Satch never was embittered about the black-white situation, or his making the Hall of Fame belatedly [1971]. All he was, as Paige once said, was the world's greatest pitcher who loved its greatest game. Bless his heart wherever he is—probably still hitting corners for the Guy who makes the final call.

—Ned Martin

T he most memorable game I ever called didn't involve a star but [1956-59 Senators' utility infielder] Herb Plews, a man of spirit and character. Every player has a game when things go bad. One day everything hit to Herb went off his chest, legs, arm, head, and he couldn't put an end to it. Finally the other team went ahead, and [1955-57 Washington manager] Chuck Dressen comes out of the dugout. For Herb Plews, this is the biggest moment in his entire life.

Chuck called Herb to the mound and spoke to him, and there was complete silence in the park. If Dressen took Herb out, it might cost him his confidence. On the other hand, if Chuck kept Herb in, it might cost the Senators the game. Chuck made the only choice he could with a man of Herb's stature: "Stay in!" If there'd been a crowd, it would have roared. The next ball went to Herb, and he bobbled it, picked it up, and made the throw for an out. But the Senators were still losing in the bottom of the ninth. Two outs, two men on, and Herb hits a triple to win the game. It was a scene that I still get emotional about. His wife was crying, the players sobbing. We didn't win many games when I did the 1947-60 Senators. But that didn't mean we didn't have heroes.

Herbie Plews. Tell me there weren't giants in the land.

—Bob Wolff

I don't know what it was, but DiMaggio had an eye-catching grace. When I made the Yankees, he was at the tail end of his career but still handled himself like a king in America's court. Once, DiMag was asked, "God, you're beating the Browns something like 22-1. Why are you out there running around like a lunatic?" He said, "Because maybe there's somebody here who never saw me play." What a way to look at life. Sometimes it's hard to bear down when you're way ahead, the ninth inning, your last at bat. Why care? Pride. The great ones never give a thing away.

—Jerry Coleman

One of the first things I noticed about Brooks Robinson was [when I was] trying to interview him; funny, I found out that he was interviewing *me*. When fans ask Brooks for an autograph, he complies while finding out how many kids you have, what your dad does, where you live, how old you are, and if you have a dog. He truly likes people. His only failing is that when the game ended, if Brooks belonged to its story—usually he did—you better leave the booth at the end of the eighth inning because he'd beat you to the clubhouse. By the time the press got there, Brooks was in the parking lot signing autographs on his way home.

Brooks played a very simple game. Hit it to him, and he'll catch it—on grass, artificial surface, a brickyard, concrete pavement, marsh, a swamp. Throw it to him, and he'll hit it.

One of my great memories is about Brooks' bat, not glove. We were playing Cleveland. Saturday night, rainy, cold. Brooks' career about over. He came into the game late as a pinch-hitter. And, oh, there weren't many people in the ball park—maybe 7,000. He hit a home run to win the game. And what followed was among the craziest acceptances of a homer I've ever seen.

The spectators ran down to the railing trying to get as close to the field as they could. Maybe they sensed it was Brooks' last home run [No. 268]. Whatever, this tiny crowd made as much noise as I've heard at a World Series. If there's a third baseman as good as Brooks, I hope I live long enough to see him. Every night that No. 5 played made the beer so cold.

—Chuck Thompson

Jimmy Piersall [1950s Boston center fielder] was a tragic case. He made three of the five greatest catches I saw in baseball. I'll never forget him disappearing into the bullpen one day and coming up with the ball. Casey Stengel called him "the best outfielder I've ever seen." Then the Red Sox put him at shortstop, and he started to bend under the pressure. They sent him down to Birmingham. That's when it really got bad.

I was in [Sox' owner] Tom Yawkey's room one night when the Birmingham general manager called. "Mr. Yawkey, you better come get this kid," he said. "I think he's sick." Yawkey said, "What's the matter?" He said, "Well, he's been squirting water pistols at home plate, and goes out and hangs numbers on the scoreboard and runs the bases backwards. There's something wrong with him. The fans love it, but I don't. You wouldn't either if you saw it."

They brought Piersall back up, and the prognosis was manic depression. They sent him to a hospital in Massachusetts, and he had shock treatments. Came out in bad shape but made it back. Great courage. I'd kid Williams. "In right," I said, "we had Jackie Jensen who was afraid to fly"—hired a hypnotist for road trips. "In left," I told Ted, "you're not the sanest guy who ever lived." Add Piersall, and we got the kookiest outfield that ever played in the major leagues. "I agree with you," he'd say. Some outfield! Piersall wasn't much of a hitter, but what a genius with a glove.

—*Curl Gowdy*

I got a thrill out of at-bats Ted Williams had at Tiger Stadium late in his career and seeing in person Mickey Mantle and Nolan Ryan, Andre Dawson, a Ken Griffey, Jr. But the player that will always mean the most to me is Al Kaline. One thing I've learned as I get older is how much greater my baseball impressions are as a youngster than adult.

Maybe because I've seen so much baseball, it doesn't have the impact [it had] when I was young. I saw Kaline as a kid, and his impact will never leave—his grace, terrific all-around talent, a good citizen—a player of whom parents said, "Hey, I'd like my son to be like him." Sure, Mantle and Mays, Musial, Brooks Robinson are great, but how could there be a better all-around ballplayer and person? I'll go to my grave thinking that baseball is Number Six at bat, two outs, ninth inning, delivering a line-drive single to left-center or scaling the wall in right, throwing a guy out—making all the plays.

This is true for kids of different players. To me, Kaline *was* my youth. That's probably why watching the 1968 World Series was so enormous: the Tigers finally in it and Al playing brilliantly [.379, 11 hits, 8 RBI, Game-Five winning single] and the entire country seeing one of the greatest ballplayers and, I truly think, gentlemen of all time.

—*Ken Wilson*

No one was bigger than Harmon Killebrew, a humble man with giant talent. [Hitting 573 home runs, No. 3 whacked over 40 eight times, tied or led the American League six years, and ranks third in all-time frequency.] He came from Payette, Idaho, and I remember the first time he saw a big-league game. The Senators were in Chicago, and he was 16 or 17. I was writing a weekly column and had Harmon write his first-day impressions.

Harmon was so modest it was hard to imagine his power. I loved to kid him, and one day came up with a great scheme. "Harmon, I'll bring you to a father-and-son game and put you into the game as Mr. Smith, a pinch-hitter. After you hit the ball 10 miles, we'll say, 'That's Harmon Killebrew, the American League home-run king [tying Rocky Colavito with 42 in 1959].' It'll knock people over." I was on P.A. and announce a "pinch-hitter." Harmon's in street clothes. People didn't recognize him out of uniform. I give the imaginary name, but I'm sure they'll know him the first time he swings. Here comes the soft pitch, and Harmon misses with two mighty swings. I figure Harmon's taunting them. On the third pitch, he dribbles one to the pitcher. I say, "Folks, the catcher tipped the bat. Let's do that again." Harmon gets up again and this time barely taps the ball.

Now I'm sweating. What do I say: "Folks, you've just watched Harmon Killebrew come up and not hit the ball to the infield"? Never. "Harmon Killebrew is the batter, but he has a great heart," I explained. "He doesn't want to lose the only softball you've got. But just to show his power, he'll fungo it out of here, and we'll retrieve and bring it back." They set up, and Harmon can't get *this* ball out of the infield. "Folks," I say, "let's get back to the game. It's getting late."

In the car back to Washington, the two of us sat in silence. "Harmon," I said, "Don't worry about it. You're gonna' be a Hall of Fame baseball player in hardball. Just skip the softer stuff." He did, and in 1984 made the Hall of Fame.

—*Bob Wolff*

In the 1960s, Harmon was as feared as any home-run hitter. One day, we were playing an exhibition game against the Dodgers at Tinker Field in Orlando. The center-field fence was about, oh, 400 feet away, and beyond it was a dark green screen, giving the hitter a good backdrop.

Don Drysdale was pitching that day. Even then, people referred to him as a headhunter. Some guys move a batter back from the plate. Drysdale'd knock him down by throwing at his ear. Believe it or not, in this *exhibition* game, he decked Harmon, and Killebrew hit the dirt, feet up in the air, bat flying, never said a word. He got back up, dusted himself off, and took that great stance he had before a pitch was delivered.

Most batters wave that bat and take little practice swings. Not Killebrew. He held that bat high frozen in position. I'm not sure if it was the next pitch, but he hit a fastball as hard as I've ever seen a ball hit. Harmon never even gave Drysdale the benefit of a dirty look, just trotted around the bases and touched home plate. It's funny how often the quiet guys have the most class of all.

—Ray Scott

I've seen a lot of players start their career, but none like July 23, 1964, at Minnesota's Metropolitan Stadium. The A's regular shortstop was Wayne Causey, who the night before broke his collarbone. They didn't have another infielder, so the A's called their Double-A farm club in Birmingham and asked for a guy who spoke so little English that in his plane itinerary they included an envelope with a message. He was to show it if he got lost; it explained who he was and how to catch the next plane. He got to the park next day about 30 minutes before the game and was put into the batting order in the second spot. Right after him was a guy named Rocky Colavito.

This guy weighed every bit of 135-140 pounds—was 5-foot-9—so, yeah, his first at-bat in the majors, he hit a home run. In those days, sports tickers linked big-league broadcast booths; they'd report home runs and pitching changes. Out goes the fact on Western Union, and we start getting calls. "Who is this guy, Campaneris?" they'd say. Didn't even say "Bert"; the wire used his full name, "Dagoberto Campaneris." I told 'em what I knew, which wasn't much, then sat back to watch Bert single, reach on a fielder's choice, and get a stolen base. Campaneris comes up a fourth time, and danged if he doesn't hit a two-run homer. All off Jim Kaat, not a bad country pitcher. Bert helped win this game, 4-3, in 11 innings.

You know the rest. Campy had a couple years with over 20 homers, was a dazzling shortstop, and led the American League in stolen bases six times. If you saw him play, you never forget him. I'll never forget his debut.

—Monte Moore

Perhaps the best trade the Twins ever made came after the 1964 season, when they swapped pitcher Jerry Arrigo to Cincinnati for utility man Cesar Tovar. Tovar became a terrific lead-off batter, could hit for average, steal bases, and play any position. In one game, he played an inning at each position, and the inning he pitched he struck out Oakland's Reggie Jackson.

Cesar's one weakness was an inability to remember signs. First-base coach Vern Morgan and manager Bill Rigney went through hell trying to get Tovar to remember them. Finally, Vern said, "I've got one more idea. If you want Tovar to steal and I'm giving him the sign, why don't I call out his last name three or four times, and when I do it'll be the signal for him to go to second on the next pitch." Rig said, "We've tried about everything else. Let's give it a shot."

A couple nights later, Tovar's on first base, Morgan is coaching, and Rigney puts on the steal sign. Vern says, "All right, Tovar, look alive. C'mon, Tovar, find your position. Atta' boy, Tovar, let's get these guys." With that, Cesar asks the first-base umpire for time. He walks over to Morgan and says, "Hey, Vern, I've been with this club for five years. How come you don't call me by my first name?"

—Herb Carneal

For years I hoped to do a World Series as the Red Sox' announcer. Then, in 1966 I go to NBC, and a year later the Sox win a great race to take the pennant, and I do it in my new *network* role. Carl Yastrzemski [.326, 44 homers, and 121 RBIs, MVP and Triple Crown] became a New England god. It took me back to the first time I saw him. He'd led the Carolina League his first year as a pro in batting, and was leading the American Association. We go to Minneapolis in 1960 for an exhibition game. I'm standing around and ask a guy, "Which guy is Yastrzemski?" He pointed to a figure swinging a couple of bats, and I said, "That little guy?" Not little, really, but I expected a giant after seeing Williams in left for so long.

At bat Yaz held the bat like he was about to kill a snake. He came up in 1961—talk about pressure, trying to replace Ted—and he didn't hit that much [.266]. But boy, could he field. Joe Cronin always said that Al Simmons was the best defensive left fielder in the game's history, and he rated Yastrzemski equal. Yaz had been an infielder in the minors, and that's how he played the outfield. Charging grounders. Flinging strikes to the bases. Led the league many years in assists and had a great arm. Any ball hit down the line—it's a single, believe me.

Yaz's power came later. He made himself into a complete player. He's got all kinds of longevity records [for example, Yaz's 3,308 games, the A.L. best-ever]. Some guys say the work ethic's dead. They should have told No. 8.

—Curt Gowdy

Sam McDowell [1961-71 Indians' pitcher] was a wonderful guy, big, 6-6 and 240, best stuff I ever saw. Could kill you with four pitches: slider, fastball, curve, and change. He could also rationalize more than any guy I knew. One night we're playing the Tigers, I'm in right field, and it's 0-0 in the seventh. Aurelio Rodriguez hits a low fastball over the head of left fielder Roy Foster. Foster wasn't a good fielder, but here it didn't matter. It's way beyond his reach—Secretariat couldn't have got it—and the Tigers score as Foster charges back, hits the inner fence, and topples over. After the game, I go into the clubhouse and light up a cigarette. Sam tells me, "Hawk, I got to get my behind out of here. I've been here ten years and never had an outfielder could catch worth a damn."

—Ken Harrelson

One night the Indians are in Oakland: Sam McDowell against Catfish [Hunter], a terrific game. I hit a two-run homer in the 10th, and we take a 3-1 lead. In the bottom of the inning, a guy gets on with one out, Eddie Leon makes an error, Sam walks the next guy, strikes out the next—his 15th—and Leon makes another error. Bases loaded, two outs. [Manager] Alvin Dark comes to the mound. Tommy Davis is sent up to pinch-hit. I'm playing first base, and we meet at the mound. Dark says to Sam, "I don't want you to screw around. Just blow Davis away with fastballs." What happens? Sam throws a high straight change, Davis hits it off the left-center-field fence, and we lose 4-3.

Afterward we go back to the hotel. I'm thoroughly pissed. I see Sam sitting alone at the bar, go over, order a couple beers, and say, "I'm not gonna' second-guess you, but why'd you throw him that change?" Sam says, "Hawk, you know, I thought about what Alvin said. Tommy Davis knows that I know that he knows that I know that he can't hit my fastball. But he was looking for it, so I decided to trick him and throw the change." I've been looking for a translator ever since.

—*Ken Harrelson*

I enjoyed my Twins' years and then, in 1973, join the White Sox. Here I meet Dick Allen, a true character. We called him "Moses": he led the Sox out of the wilderness. Dick played all-out, then loved to hit the race track. He'd come to the clubhouse: "You pitching, old-timer? I'll be out in two hours." Allen knew I worked quickly. One night in Cleveland, the bases were loaded, no one out, and Dick messed up a double play. The Indians led, 3-0, and he approached me on the bench. "Old-timer, sorry about that," he said. "I'll get those back for you." He goes out and belts two two-run homers. Sox win, 7-3.

Another night a gale's blowing out at Comiskey Park. Not a man alive could hit one out. Bill Singer throws, Dick hits it to left-center field—upper deck. If we chewed tobacco, we'd have swallowed it. He was all baseball. One evening, Dick's sitting in the clubhouse before the game when our P.R. guy brings the actor Elliott Gould by for a visit; at this time, Gould was in the movie "*M*A*S*H*." He leaves, and Dick says, "Hey, old-timer, who is that?" I tell him. Dick says, "Yeah, but can he hit a slider?"

—*Jim Kaat*

I'm tempted to say that Joe DiMaggio is the best all-around player I ever saw, but I'm going to surprise you by naming Frank Robinson. He was great in right field, fine arm, took the extra base every time he had to. If the club needed 25 stolen bases, Frank'd be safe on 24. Robinson looked like a guy who'd run over his grandmother if he had to. He was.

—*George Kell*

Call the mid-1970s through '80s the post–Willie Mays, Hank Aaron, Mickey Mantle, Frank Robinson, Roberto Clemente age. Its dominant player wasn't the best player, but Reggie Jackson knew what to do on center stage and sometimes would create it. Like a "Game of the Week" I did in 1984 in Detroit.

Tiger Stadium has an intimate broadcast arrangement. You're so close that you can overhear conversations at home plate; I've yelled down between innings to umpires to clarify things, and we talk. Reggie comes up in the first and homers into the lumber yard behind right field—one of the few balls ever hit over the roof. Next time up, he leads off after we get back from commercial. Suddenly, I hear a whistle where you put two fingers in your mouth and can be heard half-way across the state. I look down, see Reggie in the on-deck circle, and he starts to pantomime tying his shoe. At first I didn't get it. Then I do.

Reggie was always media savvy. Used to work network playoff games if his team didn't make post-season. So it hits me that when the inning starts and we're back on the air, he's gonna' enter the batter's box, call time-out to pretend to tie his shoe, and give us a chance to discuss what he did last time up and show his replay. We return. Reggie strides as slow as you please to the box, kicks the dirt, gets in his stance. Just as the pitcher's about to rock into motion, he asks for time with the regal flourish of "Casey at the Bat."

Reggie steps out, readjusts himself. Meanwhile, we're showing the replay and telling his story. Puts his cap back on and kinda' touches the top of his helmet, looks up at me, then singles to center. He gets to first base and points to the booth. "Hey," as if to say, "it's all a great show."

—*Bob Costas*

O ne night, I was having dinner with Ted Williams in Newton, Massachusetts, and I asked, "If you were paying your way today, who would you pay to see?" Without hesitation, he said, "Reggie." This was when Jackson was still playing. The following year out in Anaheim, I went over to Reggie's locker and told him. Jackson said, "You mean to tell me that the man said that about me?" He was like a kid at Christmas, completely thrilled.

Once I asked Reggie to do a public service announcement for a radio-thon we were doing for the Jimmy Fund, the official charity of the Red Sox for cancer research and the care of kids who have it. He was glad do to it, and when we finished I thanked him and started out of the room, and Reggie said, "Wait a minute, Ken." He reached into his locker and pulled down his wallet and gave a considerable amount. "I know what the Jimmy Fund is about," he said, "and I just want to put my money where my mouth is." Just one reason I've always liked No. 44.

—*Ken Coleman*

I broadcast 1980-81 for Texas, and Gaylord Perry's pitching for the Rangers in the Kingdome. Before the game, photographers are at work, when Gaylord thinks he'll have a little fun, so he reaches over and clicked off maybe five shots on one guy's camera. The photographer didn't think it's funny, which pleased Gaylord, who reached over and tried to click off *more*. They have to be separated, and the game's begun when word reaches us that the photographer had pressed assault charges, the police are here, and they're going to arrest Perry upon the final out!

The Rangers sneak Gaylord out through the center-field fence, then put him in a cab, rush to the airport, stash him on the truck loading food, and got him on the plane. Anything to avoid arrest. Meanwhile, pity coach Fred Koenig, bald [like Gaylord] and Gaylord's height. After the game, cops try to arrest Perry as we left the clubhouse for the airport. But Gaylord's not there, only Fred, and so they get handcuffs out. We finally convince 'em they've got the wrong man, get to the airport, and there's Gaylord—feet up, no cares, nursing his second or third beer.

Dan O'Brien, Mariner general manager, smoothed things over so that the next time we hit Seattle the King of the Spitter didn't wind up in the Slammer. The irony is that a year or so later Gaylord Perry wound up playing for the Mariners in the Kingdome—and winning his 300th game.

—*Mel Proctor*

M ickey Hatcher was a member of the 1980s Twins, and he loved to have a good time. So one spring training he decides that to celebrate St. Patrick's Day he'll show up at the ball park with parts of his body painted green. He appears, the players come on the field before an exhibition game, and there's Mr. Hatcher in full uniform, his face, neck, arms, hands painted green. And everybody's having a wonderful look at Hatcher. What a crazy guy, he's celebrating St. Patrick's Day. Boy, is he a package or not?

Mickey's taking fly balls when he realizes that his skin has begun to burn and he can't stop it—no matter what he does. He forgot that skin has to breathe and that the real paint he'd put on was killing oxygen. Hatcher had to run off the field. The trainer called an ambulance. They took him to a hospital to medically remove the paint to avoid severe skin burn. Mickey missed the game, was very uncomfortable for several days, but was soon back with the club. You'll be pleased to know that he has not been painting since.

—*Joe Angel*

I grew up in Michigan, went to Central Michigan University, and visited Tiger Stadium many times as a kid. That's what made the second of Nolan Ryan's no-hitters so special. It happened in 1973 [July 15], and I was behind the mike with Don Drysdale for the Angels as Nolan scorched the Tigers.

Ryan pitched his most powerful game—18 strikeouts in the first seven innings—and the symbol of Tiger frustration was a former American League batting champion [.361 in 1961]. In his third at-bat, Norm Cash got in the box wielding a leg from a clubhouse chair as a substitute for his Louisville Slugger. Not until he saw strike one did the umpire notice that he was improperly equipped. Cash told me later that when ordered to go to the dugout and fetch a bat, he said, "Why? It ain't gonna' make any difference. I'm not gonna' hit Ryan anyway."

This was a time when the Angels provided few moments of greatness. To paraphrase an old Braves' pitching credo, it was Frank Tanana and Ryan and three days of cryin'. Today was different. I was in the park of my youth, and in a visitors' broadcast booth so close to the field that you could feel and, yes, hear, a legend at his omnipotent best. Oh, my!

—*Dick Enberg*

I called Nolan's 5,000th career strikeout—August 22, 1989, at Arlington Stadium—on Rangers' TV. Ryan entered the game with 4,994 strikeouts. We knew that if he stayed in the game that he'd top 5,000; and he did, in the fifth inning, when he struck out Ricky Henderson, and the crowd went bananas. Then I used something that I learned from [producer] Don Ohlmeyer at NBC: a shut-up. If the event warrants, be quiet and let the crowd and TV director take over to capture the emotion. Our director had close-ups of the crowd, Henderson, players mobbing Ryan. This went on three minutes, and I didn't say a word. People ask my greatest moment: It's this. To even get 5,000 [Ryan retired with 5,714], a pitcher would have to average 250 strikeouts a year for 20 years—and it ain't gonna' happen. I had laser prints made of my score sheets, and had every player and umpire in the game sign it. Some history *won't* repeat itself.

—*Merle Harmon*

Wonder why the universe respects Mr. Ryan? It's his work ethic and sincerity, the courtesy he shows to people lining up for autographs while other players blow it off. Take the night Nolan needed six strikeouts for

5,000. When he threw the first pitch, I've never seen so many flashes, or heard such a gasp. It was like fans were saying, "Nolan, this is your night, we love you, and no one's going to stop you."

After the game, I stayed in the booth an hour and a half and did interviews with radio stations that wanted to know the atmosphere, how it happened, etc. I finally leave through the Ranger locker room. Virtually empty. Then I see No. 34 smack dab in the middle of the locker room riding the stationary bicycle. I say, "Nolan, I can't believe you're not out celebrating! This is a magic night. What are you doing?" He said, "Mark, I'm in my forties, and if I don't ride this bicycle, I won't get ready for my next start. I got to ride a bike for 45 minutes after everybody else leaves the day I pitch so that I can get ready to stay in the five-man rotation."

Here is Nolan Ryan at the absolute pinnacle of a career that spanned 27 years, riding a bicycle in the middle of the room, alone, in his sweat clothes. And I was there to witness it. I thought, Boy, anybody who writes good things about Nolan Ryan is telling the truth. No one meant to baseball what he did, and forever will. He worked like he did for himself and for pride. It was a moment where I understood what Nolan Ryan was all about.

—Mark Holtz

Growing up, I saw a lot of guys play their whole career in one city. With today's money, they don't need to. When baseball history is written, one of the last one-town players will be [Brewers' 1974-93] Robin Yount. Maybe he wasn't an Aaron or Mantle in talent, but no guy meant more to his city. Milwaukee is a blue-collar town, and here you had a guy who liked motorcycles and racing cars. Busted his ass for you day after day. Loved baseball in a place which eats and sleeps it.

Yount was a two-time MVP as a shortstop and then outfielder after a career-threatening injury. Musial and Kiner are the only guys who made that switch and won the award. Like them, he didn't say much, didn't need to, had the sense to retire when his skills started fading. I think of Robin when I drive to County Stadium off the interstate into that huge parking lot. People grilling bratwurst. Tailgates everywhere. Weddings with guys in tuxedos. It's what baseball today lacks—a sense of community—and Robin helped build it.

—Bob Uecker

Objectively, records are made to be broken. In business, you try to top the prior year. Still, knowing the circumstances of his leaving the game and his untimely passing—and thinking of Lou [Gehrig] himself—a big part of me has wanted his consecutive games streak to stand. Yet God bless Cal Ripken. Everybody asks him the same question about the streak. You sympathize for the guy and only hope he won't come up short due to injury. That's life, doing better than someone else did. You hate to see a guy get that close to something and not make it. It's like Babe Ruth's record broken by Hank Aaron. You could admire Babe but get excited when Hank did it, and it didn't detract from Ruth. He's still the top guy in baseball history. Same with Gehrig.

All this adds to a game, and, for an announcer, it's wonderful. Gives you stuff to talk about: what happened, what's going on now, and how it relates to the past. One more thing. Knowing Lou, if the Good Lord let him be on this earth, he'd be the first person to congratulate Cal.

—Mel Allen

I worked with Bob Wolff in 1960 when he was Voice of the original Senators, and, before that, Arch McDonald from 1956 through his '60 death. Arch had a world of stories. [The late writer Morris Siegel called him "probably the most popular announcer Washington ever had."] A lot were about Walter Johnson. In the '30s Bob Feller was up from Iowa and striking out everybody. Arch asked Walter, "Is Feller as fast as you are?" And Johnson, always modest, said, "I think I threw a little faster."

I broadcast lousy teams, but had a treat neither Bob nor Arch enjoyed. In 1965, [manager Gil] Hodges obtained some former Dodgers to bolster the roster—notably, Frank Howard, Ken McMullen, Pete Richert, and Dick Nen. Of all the expansion players from 1961 until Bob Short moved the Senators to Texas for the '72 season, Howard was far and away most popular. Big and friendly, his home runs were majestic. I'll always recall Frank hitting 10 homers in 20 at-bats in early 1968; one cleared the roof in the left field at Tiger Stadium.

Hondo's blasts went so far that management painted the upper-deck seats in RFK [stadium] white to mark where they landed. It's sad. They're among the few things left to remind us there was ever baseball in Washington.

—Dan Daniels

CHAPTER FOURTEEN

OPEN YOUR EYES

UMPIRES

Fiorella La Guardia said, "When I make a mistake, it's a beaut." Umpires are trained not to make them. In baseball's bible, only God eclipses the men in blue.

Think of 1905–40 National League umpire Bill Klem, aka "The Old Arbitrator," who sired arm signals to coincide with balls and strikes. "I never made a wrong call," he said—pause to dust home plate—"at least in my heart." Doubt is denied entreé to the umpire's table of reminiscence.

Bill McGowan swaggered like a thespian. Al Barlick had a voice that shattered glass. Cal Hubbard meant imposing size. Jocko Conlan: polka-dot ties. Tom Connolly—a British accent and reserve—he went 10 straight years without kicking out a player. Each knew hard scrabble, endless bus rides, and cries of "Kill the ump!"—no funhouse of daily peals.

The adage says, "That umpire is best who is noticed least." Another byword is equally true: Nothing is real in baseball until the umpire calls it so.

To me, umpires are special. I can't think of anyone who loves baseball more. Jocko Conlan was an outfielder when one day he pinch-hit behind the plate in 1935 as Red Ormsby was overcome by heat. He must have enjoyed it, because umpiring became his career.

Jocko couldn't stand whiners. In one game, Phillies' outfielder Richie Ashburn kept complaining about pitches. "All right," Jocko said, finally. "You umpire. I'm letting you call the next pitch." Ashburn was astounded: "You're kidding." Jocko said, "Nope, you call the next one." The next pitch was a foot outside. Ashburn said, "Strike."

Conlan called time, and went out to dust the plate. He looked up and said, "Richie, I gave you the only chance a hitter ever had in history to bat and umpire at the same time. You blew it. That's the last pitch you'll ever call. You're not gonna' louse up my profession."

—*Ernie Harwell*

Jocko was a great umpire who for some reason wouldn't call Willie Mays safe. Willie never tried a steal if Conlan was umpiring at second base. The tables turned one night in the Los Angeles Coliseum, where the lights were terrible. Johnny Roseboro hit a drive into center field where they had an interior fence, and the ball cleared it for a homer. The problem was that umpiring at second, Jocko ran out and couldn't see the ball. So he turns to Mays. "Did that ball go over the fence?" Mays said, "No, it went through a hole in the fence." There *was* no hole, but Jocko gave Roseboro a ground rule double anyway.

—*Lon Simmons*

I'm asked, "What about weird baseball moments?" The weirdest was 1959 at Wrigley Field, Cubs-Cardinals. The Cubs' pitcher was Bobby Anderson. Catcher, Sammy Taylor. At second base, Tony Taylor; shortstop, Ernie Banks; third base, Alvin Dark. The batter was Stan Musial; and the plate umpire, Vic Delmore. On a 3-2 pitch, the ball went past everybody to the screen. The umpire said "ball four" as the Cubs hollered their heads off, saying that Musial had fouled the ball off.

The bat boy picked up the ball and gave it to Pat Pieper, the P.A. announcer who sat behind the plate with a bag with baseballs in it. All this as Sammy Taylor held out his mitt and Delmore put a ball in it—both out of habit. An argument rages while Dark, a thinking man's third baseman, raced in and reached into that bag and, we'll assume, got the ball that the batboy had given to Pat. Meanwhile, the Cubs haven't called time out, so Anderson grabs the other ball from Taylor's hand just as Musial runs past first, hears the Cardinal bench yell, "Take second, go to second," and slides into there with his back to the infield.

Whackier is that Dark and Anderson both throw to second at once! Anderson's throw went into right-center. Alvin's throw, to the third-base side of second, goes to Ernie Banks. But Ernie wasn't visible to the sliding Stan. So Musial saw Anderson's ball hit the outfield and, thinking it's the only ball in play, starts for third and goes two steps before Ernie says, "Look what I got," and tagged Stan. What a mess, a United Nations on the field. They finally rule that the game ball is the one Dark used to throw to Banks and that Stan was out. Solly Hemus, the Cardinal manager, was ready to protest the game to the seven seas. As it turned out, the Cardinals won, so a protest wasn't needed. I'd have loved to have been in President Warren Giles' office that next day when they tried to explain.

The next day, I confronted Delmore and said, "Vic, you know I'm not the kind of guy who hammers umpires, but I wouldn't be much of a reporter if I didn't ask why you put that second ball in the game." He said, "Jack, I've been lying in my hotel room, looking at the ceiling all night, asking myself the same question, and I don't know." Not a great punch line, but a great story: two balls in the game at once.

—*Jack Brickhouse*

That day was incredible. Sammy Taylor didn't have a good arm, and it was a hell of a hot day. So when the pitch went back to the screen, Taylor didn't take off, just turned to Delmore, and Vic gave him the ball. At the same time, Dark beats Pat Pieper to the real ball. Then, the real ball is thrown from the plate to get Musial. I remember saying, "I can't believe this"; nobody could. The umpires segregated to decide what to do. They had a rule book, I didn't, but it didn't help them or us. After a time, the crowd begins to laugh.

Interesting that the symbols of each franchise were involved. Musial was as nice a guy as you'd ever want to see, and when he sat in the dugout or restaurant, no one was more gregarious. But on the air, he was difficult, shy; you had to drag stuff out of him. When he first came up [1953], Banks was worse. I was asked to get a Cub to speak at a hotel for elderly Jewish people near Wrigley Field. I asked Ernie, and he said, "Yes," but didn't like it.

It was his first public appearance, and afterward he said, "Gee, that was kind of fun," as long as people asked questions. Today nobody has to ask; Ernie enjoys just talking. Looking back, nobody enjoyed themselves that day at Wrigley Field. Especially Vic Delmore. In the off-season, he was fired.

—*Vince Lloyd*

I like umpires. Ask a question, get an honest answer. The Yankees had a catcher who liked umpires, too. One of his favorites was Cal Hubbard. They used to fight like cats and dogs, but were great friends. Cal was a big man [nearly 6-3 and 265 pounds]. Yogi Berra came up to Hubbard's belly-button. They had fun arguing on every strike, until, one day, Cal called time. He looked down at Yogi and said, "Stand up," and Yogi turned around and looked up at him. Cal said, "You're the catcher. Go back and work like one. I'm the umpire, and no more arguin' with me or I'll bite your head off." At first Yogi was stunned. He turned back to catch, then all of a sudden said, "You try, Cal Hubbard, and you're gonna' have more brains in your stomach than you got in your head."

—*Jimmy Dudley*

I'm sure that you remember the great umpire Bill Klem. Bill used to boast that he never made a wrong call in his life—as he said, "at least in my heart"—it was a famous saying. So in 1965 I'm working a Pacific Coast League with a fellow named Lyle Nelson in our booth at the old Honolulu stadium, which had four telephones. The first was to call cities around the league to get updates on other games. Back then, forget satellite transmissions, and the press box didn't have a ticker. The second phone went to the dugout for information on injuries; the third, a direct line to the radio station. Four was an extra telephone for our use only. Nobody knew the number; the phone never rang. If it did, it was a wrong number because no one knew how to reach us.

We're doing the game when suddenly phone Number 4 rings that hasn't rung all year. Lyle picks it up as I'm describing the game: "Here's the pitch, and it's low. Ball two." Lyle looks over, and I look at him and say on the air, "Who is it, anyone we know?" knowing full well that it has to be a wrong number. He says, "Do you know anybody named Clem?" I said, "No, well, only Bill Klem. Maybe it's him." He's sort of pondering, scratching his chin, and says, "No, it couldn't be Bill Klem. He never made a wrong call in his life."

Well, at this point I became totally paralyzed, I can't talk. I'm bent over in laughter. I don't know how I finished the inning—must have been five minutes before I could talk. It's easily the funniest thing that has ever happened to me in any phase of broadcasting. Anytime I get a wrong number, I hope the caller forgives me when I start laughing into the phone.

—*Hank Greenwald*

There was a time in the 1970s when some people with unusual attitudes took it upon themselves to do a little streaking. One night in Baltimore, we got into a rain delay before 27,000. We hadn't yet had a streaker. A guy determined to change that got out of his clothes, jumped over the railing, and ran to second base. Like [the Orioles' Rick] Dempsey, he slid on the tarp into second base, then third. Then he slid into home plate. By that time, the security folks were waiting. He didn't resist—wasn't trying to hurt anybody—just smiled and laughed.

They led him to the first-base dugout, where, waiting for the rain to stop, was one of my all-time favorite umpires, Nester Chylak. He was crew chief that night, and he's sitting watching this fella'. [P.A. announcer] Rex Barney and I are up in the press box as this gentleman is escorted off the field into the dugout. The minute he goes in there, Nester jumped out and whistled. Barney and I looked his way. And Chylak stood there in front of 27,000 people and raised his right hand up and separated the thumb and the index finger by about one inch.

Every person in the park roared.

—*Chuck Thompson*

The A's were in Kansas City before moving to Oakland in 1968. The next year, the Royals replaced them. What a great rivalry. All sorts of strong feelings. One night in the 1970s, they're playing at Royals Stadium, and the first four Oakland hitters hit bullets. Boom—it's 3-0, nobody out, guys on base. I look out, and [Royals' manager] Whitey Herzog is strolling toward the home plate umpire, and everybody's puzzled. Nothing up to now had warranted an argument. They talk several minutes, and the crowd's wondering what the hell is going on. Meanwhile, I'm thinking, Man, they got good swings; and a light went on. Does Whitey think they're stealing signs and know what pitches are coming?

I shouldn't have done this—no proof—but I say on the air that Whitey may think they've got his signs. I recounted the ways you could flash a sign to the hitter, one being binoculars in the bullpen. You'd have a pitcher there who puts a towel over his right leg for a fastball. Little towel: a breaking ball. That simple. Suddenly, everybody turns and looks out toward the bullpen. And as they start for there, I feel like the guy with a huge fish on his line. I'll be damned if Whitey and the umps don't walk out to the left-field bullpen, go through the big screened-in gate, and start going down the line. They get to the end of the bench, and Whitey leans over and picks up binoculars. I'm watching with *my* binoculars, and suddenly a heady feeling hits me: In all of this, Whitey and I may have been the only two people in Royals Stadium who were on to the A's ruse.

It's not always true, but on this hot summer night, I knew exactly what was going on. For one game, call me a player. I was as much a part of it as anyone on the field.

—*Denny Matthews*

In 1988, my first year with the Red Sox, they trail Kansas City, 9-8, in the seventh or eighth inning. Rich Gedman lofts a fly down the right-field line that hits the foul pole and goes into the stands. I called it a home run, and the first-base umpire called it foul. The replay showed that it hit the foul pole and it was clear that the umpire, Dale Scott, missed it. But as the Red Sox argued and we showed the replay over and over again on television, the umpires wouldn't yield.

Now, the Red Sox were in the third-base dugout, and their hollering hit Dale Ford, the third-base umpire, who gave it right back. I said, "Well, Dale Scott made this call, not Dale Ford, but Ford did a Red Sox' game several weeks ago and ejected a couple players, and it's obvious that the Sox have some bad feelings." Boston loses the game, and next day I go down to the clubhouse. [Manager] John McNamara's door is closed, and I say, "What's going on?" I'm told, "Dale Ford's in there." And I say, "Wow, they must have looked at the tape of the game, and he saw they missed it, and he's going to apologize."

Finally, the door opens, and John and Dale are chatting when McNamara points at me and says, "That's Sean right there," whereupon Ford starts to lambaste me. "I heard what you said last night. Friends in Boston called and told me you said I have a running feud with the Red Sox and I don't like John McNamara. Nothing could be further from the truth." I said, "Wait a minute, that's not what I said." He said, "Yes, it is, friends told me." I said, "Dale, here's what I said," and offered to take him to the [production] truck and show him a tape of last night's game so that he could see for himself.

Dale Ford said, "Oh, no, I don't need to do that. I know what you said." So I answered, "Hey, if this is how you handle disputes on the field, no wonder you have so many problems." From then on, Dale's been less than pleasant when we meet. I don't let that affect what I say on the air, but most people I know in the American League agree that he's its worst umpire.

—*Sean McDonough*

In early morning [April 5, 1993] of the Florida Marlins' first regular-season game, a huge storm hit south Florida. Thunder and lightning and all kinds of rain. I doubted the game could be played. But by about 10 o'clock, the skies cleared. We figured it was Carl Barger up there looking out for us, the former club president who died without seeing the Marlins play a game.

I was on the field for the Opening Day pre-game ceremonies. Sellout crowd. Joe Robbie Stadium renovated to look like a baseball park. I introduce Bryan Harvey as a man with almost as many saves as John the Baptist. Some scene. Charlie Hough was pitching against the Dodgers of Tommy Lasorda, who at one time was Charlie's minor league manager. Tommy'd once told him that Charlie needed a new pitch to stay in the majors, and that pitch turned out to be the knuckleball. Just a lot of ironies.

To me, one of baseball's best umpires captured the whole day. The first pitch showed that if Charlie threw a knuckleball within a couple of feet of the plate, Frank Pulli'd call it a strike. Jose Offerman leads off, and Charlie throws a knuckleball a foot outside, and Frank goes up with the right arm. The crowd went nuts. The season's started on a called strike. Offerman can't believe it. The second pitch—big dancing knuckler—had to be *two* feet outside, and again up goes the arm, and the crowd is wild! In disbelief, Jose digs in again and waits; he knows what's coming. Another knuckleball, again nowhere near the plate, and Frank orchestrated the crowd: Strike three! Bedlam!

Charlie got 'em 1-2-3 in the first inning. He goes on to win. Jeff Conine gets four hits. Harvey gets the save. Picture-perfect. Joe DiMaggio is in his 70s and had thrown out the first ball during pre-game festivities. Hough was 45, and his knuckleball doesn't crack the speed of sound. After the game, Charlie summed up the wonder. "Here I win the game, and DiMaggio throws harder than I do."

—Joe Angel

Umpires deserve a little credit, because they unfairly take a lot of heat. Sure, they miss one here and there; and it frustrates you if it's against your team. I don't root for the Padres—none of this, "Oh, boy, let's go"—but obviously I want them to do well. Even if they don't, it's silly to blame the ump.

In Atlanta, Gene Richards hit a ball, and the Braves' left fielder caught it, ran maybe 10 steps, and came to a three-foot fence dividing the field from the bullpen. As he leaped the fence, the ball dropped on the playing field, and umpire Ed Vargo ruled it in play. Gene toured the bases and got a so-called inside-the-park homer as Braves' broadcasters began tearing Ed apart. I always thought that if you caught the ball and took a couple steps, it's a legal catch. Vargo was the only one who knew the rule: If you don't release the ball *voluntarily*, you haven't released it. Some umpires are slow in calling balls and strikes—others, too dramatic—but they know the game.

Once, the Pittsburgh manager put Willie Stargell's name in the line-up in the fourth *and* sixth spots in the official scorebook. Alvin Dark was [Padres'] manager and caught it right away but didn't say a thing. Stargell gets a double, and up comes the second Mr. Stargell, who happened to be somebody else. Doug Harvey was the plate umpire, and Dark runs up and says, "Lookit, there's a problem! We got two Wilver Stargells in the game at one time!" Harvey looked at his scorecard, at Stargell, and at the hitter. "Well, Mr. Dark, I know who Wilver Stargell is, and I know he's not at home plate now. Therefore, no matter what the line-up card says, Stargell's hitting fourth, and this man up for the second time is hitting sixth, and I don't care *who* he is!"

Next day, I said, "Doug, give me that ruling. How can you arbitrarily make an opinion on something so nuts?" Doug said, "Check rule," whatever it was. I did. It says when something happens on the field and no rule applies, the umpire can do what he wants to make the game proceed. Doug was right. The next time a guy bats out of order, don't ask a broadcaster. Only a rocket scientist could figure this stuff out. Leave it to baseball's wizards—the umpires—and sit back and relax.

—*Jerry Coleman*

CHAPTER FIFTEEN

I SING THE SONGS

VARIETY BEHIND AND BEYOND THE MIKE

*H*eywood Broun once wrote of radio, "Graham McNamee took a medium of expression, and [gave] it a sense of movement and of feeling. Of such is the kingdom of art."

Jimmy Dudley shaped art via poetry; Lindsey Nelson, by his vividness of language; Bob Prince, through a speaking style mixing Bellevue and Las Vegas. Vin Scully gives the score like clockwork. Dizzy Dean treated it, to paraphrase Ring Lardner, like a side dish he had not ordered. It also helped that their vocal cords turned heads.

Mel Allen and Red Barber were often likened, but their contrasts more entice. The Ol' Redhead was white wine, crepes Suzette, and bluegrass music; Mel, beer, hot dogs, and the United States Marine Band. Barber sat back from the microphone and chatted. "Never raise your voice," he said. "When the crowd yells, shut up." Engaged, Allen filibustered, often brilliantly, for hours. "When the crowd shouted, so did you."

You will never confuse, say, Milo Hamilton with Harry Caray, on- or off-air. Announcers can be high rollers, fast livers, deacons, dirt bags, butchers, bakers, beggermen, and/or thieves. "Baseball Voices differ behind a microphone," says Harry Kalas, "and also away from it." From pew to bar to library to lobby, baseball mikemen loved diversity before diversity was cool.

*A*fter I got out of high school I went to Coffeyville, Kansas, to play in the semi-pro Ban Johnson League with a friend of mine, Casey Black, who was ending his freshman year at the University of Tulsa. A Boston Braves' scout—yes, there was such a thing—wants to know where we are. Our folks tell him, and he says, "I'd like to see them out in Winfield, Kansas"—a far piece west of Coffeyville—on a certain weekend in July. "We're having a try-out camp. If it works, I'd like to sign them."

Casey and I pack our suitcases and start hitchhiking. A fellow takes us three miles, then drops us. We're in the middle of nowhere when I see coming down the road a big truck with high steel sideboards and what seems to be a winch and pulley system. Being raised in rural Oklahoma, I know I've seen this kind of truck but for the life of me can't remember what it was. The truck stops to pick us up, but those high steel sideboards keep us from seeing through. The guy leans out and says, "Little en', you get in the front—big en', in the back." I was "big en'," so Casey sat in the front seat, and I had to climb over the sideboards. I look in there and see a dead horse, and it hits me: This is a dead animal truck and this horse has been expired for some time and his aroma is somewhat pungent and there are little things crawling on it that don't look too neat.

This guy takes off. I turn my suitcase on its side so I can stand next to it and hang over the edge to get fresh air as he drives along. The man took us about 40 miles. Casey saw through the back window what'd happened to "big en'" and was laughing up a storm. It's terribly presumptuous to think about writing my memoirs. But I've often said that if I did, the title would be *Forty Miles on a Dead Horse* or *Dead Horse Scrolls*.

—*Bob Starr*

Baseball's a small town. Names come around and tie together. In 1954, I was a Cardinal broadcaster and saw Stan Musial hit five homers—and drive in 11 runs—in a double-header against the Giants at Busch Stadium. The oddity was that the ball he hit farthest was caught by Willie Mays. If you remember, the old park in St. Louis was 430 to center, and Mays raced back and caught it. Stan pulls it a bit, and he's got six home runs.

As it was, his five set a record for a double-header. Fast-forward to 1972. I'm doing the Braves against the Padres—another twin-bill—and Nate Colbert ties Stan's record with five home runs and drives in 13! Back then we didn't do a "Star of the Game" show after the game, so the next night Nate's my lead-off show guest. I mention I'd been there when Musial hit five and Colbert ties him, whereupon Nate says I'm not alone: We're probably the only two people who saw both events happen!

Nate Colbert grew up in St. Louis and that day in 1954 was in the knot-hole section of Busch Stadium's right-field pavilion. Years later, the little kid turns slugger and ties The Man. Unbelievable how the past dovetails with today.

—*Milo Hamilton*

In the early '50s, Bill Veeck bought the Browns. He is one of the most intriguing people I ever met: bright, creative, his mind on fast-forward. Bill was the establishment but wore the cloak of the common man with his self-imposed dress code—no ties—and ability to wow blue-collar guys. He loved being the man who drank anybody under the table, told great stories, and regularly bought the house a round. We spent hours together, many traveling to some community in Missouri or southern Illinois, spreading the Browns' gospel. It's there that the idea sprang which made history, in the wee hours of the morning returning from Herrin, Illinois, to St. Louis after a banquet and as always a visit to the town's most popular tavern. Bill said, "Ya' know, wouldn't it be nice to just once get our leadoff man on base in the first inning?" He dropped the subject, then later says, "Getting that man on in the first would be some event."

Eventually, I'm summoned to Bill's office and, entering, saw this little man barely able to see over the desk. "Bud," Bill said, "meet the Browns' new lead-off man, Eddie Gaedel." Eddie in his squeaky voice says, "You know, I'm a good player and bet I could hit anybody that they pitch against me." Veeck says, "If you make one move with that bat at home plate, it'll be your *last* move." So the plot was set, and only Zack Taylor, the manager, Rudy Schaffer, the general manager, and myself knew it. On Sunday [August 19, 1951, before 20,299] at Sportsman's Park, I knew what was goin' to happen but couldn't pre-warn the audience, and who'd have believed me—a *midget* in the big leagues?!

Ed Hurley was the plate umpire; Bob Swift, the Tiger catcher; and Bob Cain, the pitcher. In the bottom of the first, up comes this tiny figure with miniature bat, and imagine what those listening thought when yours truly said, "Leading off for the Browns at 3-foot-9, 62 pounds, 26-year old Eddie Gaedel." Probably that I should go home to bed. Hurley exploded as Gaedel neared the plate—thought it was a farce—and summoned Taylor, who quieted things by showing the signed league contract. The crowd's scream-ing, Gaedel is announced over the P.A., and enters the batter's box, doffs his hat, knocks dirt from his spikes and takes his deep crouch—about a six-inch strike zone!

Catcher Swift just shook his head and sat down behind home plate to give Cain a target. Bob pitched almost from a kneeling position and, instead of being irritated, just couldn't keep from laughing. It didn't last very long, but it was a wild scene that I'm confident will long linger in the memory file. After walking on four pitches, it took Gaedel about five minutes to travel the 90 feet to first, the Browns having finally got their lead-off man on base.

—*Bud Blattner*

It doesn't get better than 1951. In August the Giants were 13 and 1/2 games behind Brooklyn. The Dodgers won 24 of their last 44 games, but the Giants won 37. That caused a best-of-three playoff for the pennant. The Giants won the first game; Brooklyn, the second; and on October 3 I drove from my home to the Polo Grounds and pinched myself. For Game Three I'd be on coast-to-coast television [NBC]. My Giants' partner, Russ Hodges, would have to settle for local radio. How could things go wrong? Easily, as it happened!

At lunch Russ asked, "Ernie, isn't it my time today on TV?" I knew better. "No, yesterday I did the middle three innings on TV. Today I've got the first three and last three." Russ knew I was right. So I was coast-to-coast when Bobby Thomson hit his homer in the ninth inning to win the game; beat the Dodgers, 5-4; and win the pennant. What did radio bring Russ? Immortality. What did coast-to-coast bring me? Nothing. It's fair to say that TV was still not a household fact.

Proof of my anonymity is how people to this day ask, "What'd you say when Thomson hit his homer?" Nobody asks what Mr. Hodges said. I say that as soon as Bobby hit the ball I said, "It's gone." Then I started worrying. I looked out and saw Andy Pafko waiting against the left-field wall. "Uh, oh," I thought, "suppose he catches it!" He didn't, and, as Russ said, "The Giants win the pennant!"

Mrs. Harwell doesn't know anything about baseball, so she can't second-guess me. She *does* know life. When I got home, I was still in shock. Everybody was. Lulu saw me and said, "Ernie, I've seen that dazed look on your face twice in my life. When our first child was born and the day we got married."

—*Ernie Harwell*

Two same-year stories about baseball when you're young; here, eight. In September 1960, we moved to California from New York. It took five days to drive with a U-Haul from Long Island to Los Angeles. As we drove cross-country, a great joy was to pick up Waite Hoyt in Cincinnati on the car radio and Jack Buck and Harry Caray doing Cardinal games and Earl Gillespie with the Milwaukee Braves. Finally, someplace in Nevada, we picked up the Dodger network, and we heard Vin Scully's voice. My father said to me, "We can hear the Dodgers. We're almost there."

We get to California, and I refuse to go to third grade during World Series mid-week games, then all-afternoon. "You can send me to school," I told my parents, "but you'll never see me again because I'll run away from home." A wise decision: I wouldn't remember details in the classroom, but I recall like today the details of each game. Game Seven was Thursday. The Yankees fell behind, 4-0; went ahead, 7-4; then trailed, 9-7, after Bill Virdon's double play ball came up and hit Tony Kubek in the throat. It still irritates him. Once I brought it up on "Game of the Week," and Tony put his hand on my thigh to stop me. I relented so that circulation would resume. The bad hop let an obscure catcher named Hal Smith hit a three-run homer to give the Pirates a 9-7 lead. The Yankees tied it in the ninth before Ralph Terry in the bottom half gave up Bill Mazeroski's home run.

I recall then going to my room and taking a vow of silence. My initial vow was not to speak until Opening Day of the 1961 season. That impracticality, even for an eight-year old, dawned on me quickly. But I did keep mute for 24 hours, my way of protesting the cosmic injustice that my Yankees had lost the Series.

—*Bob Costas*

People ask, "What was your biggest thrill?" I've been the lead announcer for 50 years. I've seen great ballplayers, broadcast or listened to so many great games. Yet my greatest thrill is that this poor little orphan boy from St. Louis was one of three generations doing major league baseball at the same time. My son Skip Caray [Voice of the Braves], his son, who's my grandson, Chip [of the Mariners], and me. Now if I'd only had sense enough before I was born to nickname myself Flip, we'd a' had Flip, Chip, and Skip. What an act *that* would have been.

—*Harry Caray*

It happened by accident. We had a March meeting where WGN decided we'd go to the Sox' game. [On April 10, 1961, John F. Kennedy became the first American president to be interviewed at a baseball game, on WGN-TV's "Lead-Off Man Show," prior to throwing out the first ball at the White Sox' opener at Griffith Stadium.]

Jack Brickhouse would do the play-by-play and me the pre-game. A few minutes later, I said, "Hey, why not try for the President?" Jack said, "Nothing ventured, nothing gained," and laughed.

We contact Frank Darling, president of the Electrical Workers' Union, and a strong Democrat. Frank called the White House, and so did Mayor [Richard] Daley, a big White Sox' fan. JFK wouldn't have been President without his help in '60. We get the word—Kennedy will do it—but I had no chance to talk with anyone before getting to the ball park. I arrived and tried to get near the President's box, and there's a mixup. The Secret Service didn't know about it; they want to kick me out. Then, salvation. The presidential party appears, and there's [Senator] Everett Dirksen, whom I'd known since I worked in Peoria.

Well, instead of a few moments, we interviewed JFK for 15 minutes. Dave Powers [1979-94 Kennedy Library director] was his personal aide and huge baseball fan, and he'd chip in when the President didn't know an answer. One thing said a lot to me about JFK as a man. I asked where Mrs. Kennedy was. He smiled and said, "Well, it's Monday. She's home doing the wash."

—Vince Lloyd

Our early-'60s expansion Senators didn't have a lot of delights. One was Danny O'Connell. Danny came up the National League and played with the Pirates and Giants. Had the knack of making a sort of Eddie Stanky or Leo Durocher type play from time-to-time. His problem in the Senators' years was a bad back. It troubled him in more ways than one. I recall one of his teammates accused Danny of malingering: "Nothing at all's wrong with you." Angered, Danny said, "Listen, I'd like to see you try to get laid with my back."

—Dan Daniels

When your first year of major league broadcasting ends with a historic homer, it's kinda' special. On October 1, 1961, at Yankee Stadium the Red Sox' Tracy Stallard pitched his best game of the season, losing 1-0. The one run was Roger Maris' 61st homer. As Maris toured the bases, Stallard followed every footstep. Curt Gowdy was off doing football, our game wasn't on TV, so Art Gleeson and I were calling it alone on radio. And the inning Maris smashed the mark was the fourth, mine.

Personally, I didn't want to see Babe Ruth's record broken, because I was a kid when he was still playing. Still, as an announcer, you'd love if it happened on your watch. Before the game, I did something announcers aren't supposed to, interviewed Tracy in the dugout about how he felt about No. 61. "Well, I got one good fastball. I don't want to walk him, and I'll throw him the fastball. More power to him if he hits it."

Most people have only heard Phil Rizzuto's call of Maris' homer. It's in the Hall of Fame. They don't know the other call is mine, like Ernie Harwell's lost TV call of Bobby Thomson's home run. But this 37-year-old rookie broadcaster was glad I was there to do it. In 1961, we had a 19-day road trip to six cities, something you'd never hear of now. Jackie Jensen, who didn't like to fly, jumped the club and went home. Bill Monbouquette set a league record for strikeouts in a night game. But the topper was the Maris homer. Mercy! What a year.

—*Ned Martin*

I've broadcast eight radio/TV no-hitters, all different. The craziest came in 1962. Early Wynn started the season at age 42 for the White Sox with 292 wins. He thought this'd be his last year because his career was waning, and by the All-Star break he had 299. A breeze to 300, right? Several weeks later he still hasn't won another game for a White Sox team that didn't score for him. No problem. The Sox put a beautiful program together with memorabilia of his career for the fans. They plan to give it away the night we play the Red Sox at Comiskey Park. We'd beaten Boston about every time we played. So White Sox' management said, "Like death and taxes, he'll win tonight." They gave souvenirs—a big button with "300"—to fans coming into the park. It was a fast game, 'bout two hours, and Early pitched like a kid. Slight problem. A fella' nearly half his age, Bill Monbouquette, pitched a no-hitter to beat Chicago. That's a difference I'd rather *not* have seen.

—*Milo Hamilton*

I think I set a record by televising eight no-hit games: six of them Cubs, one against 'em, and one for the White Sox. The first was 1955, Sam Jones against the Pirates. In the ninth inning of a 4-0 game, Jones walked the bases full before Cubs' manager Stan Hack came out. Sam stays in and proceeds to strike out the side! Later, I asked Stan, "What'd you say to him when you were out there?" He replied, "Get that blankety blank ball over the blankety blank plate, or your tail is out of here."

Kenny Holtzman had two no-hitters. His first [1969] was at Wrigley Field. Late in the game, Hank Aaron hit one that everybody said, "It's gone— and so is the no-hitter!" Yet there's a little recess in the wall in left field, and Billy Williams backed up to those vines as the ball seemed to hit an invisible shield and stayed inside the park. Catch made, and Holtzman makes history: a no-hitter where he strikes out nobody. Another no-hitter was Don Cardwell's in 1960 against the Cardinals, the first time he'd ever worn a Cub uniform. What a way to start. Too bad it was downhill from there.

In 1972, Milt Pappas became the only guy I ever saw throw a no-hitter to leave angry! The count was 2-2 with two out in the ninth. Milt has a perfect game, and he throws a pitch that he thought hit the outside corner, until umpire Bruce Froemming said "ball three." Pappas gave him that Greek glare; boy, was he upset. The next pitch hits the same spot, and it's called "ball four" and forget the perfecto. Pappas got the next batter to pop up for the no-hitter, but he's still burned about blowing one of baseball's few-ever perfect games.

Pappas told me that next day he faced Froemming. "Bruce, why didn't you call one of those a strike, because that's what they were, and you'd have made history by calling a perfect game." Froemming said, "Milt, if I did that, I wouldn't a' been able to live with myself." Pappas said, "So how do you live with yourself on all the other lousy calls you make?" You can imagine how *that* was received. Just another easy day at the ball park.

—*Jack Brickhouse*

Nineteen sixty-eight was The Year of the Pitcher, especially the night the Mets and Houston played and it was 0-0 going into the last half of the

24th inning. The Astros won when Al Spangler hit a ground ball between Al Weis' legs, I believe, and Norm Miller scored. Two things about the game. It was the longest ever played to a conclusion in the big leagues. Second, John Wayne was in town to make a movie. Our radio booth was next to the Astrodome Club, where people ate, and had a bar, and that's where I first spotted Wayne, enjoying the game. We go extra innings, and he moved up not far from me. The last time I saw John Wayne was in about the 23rd inning; he'd moved into an empty radio booth and was absolutely sloshed. They had to carry him out of there. That's my biggest remembrance of the Duke.

—*Gene Elston*

I retired as a player in 1971 to go into pro golf. I kept at it for three and a half years, took instruction, but my game was deteriorating. So eventually, the 12th of February 1975, I decided to give it up. Golf's not cutting it for my wife and me. That night at 3 A.M. I wake up sweatin', wondering, What am I gonna' do? That very morning, Mary Trank, a secretary to Tom Yawkey and [Red Sox' G.M.] Dick O'Connell, called. She said, "Richard said come up and broadcast our games."

A year earlier, O'Connell had asked if I wanted to do color. Now to renew the offer when he didn't even know I was kissing golf off— unbelievable. I took the audition, got the job, and went to spring training for my first game with the Sox. I was uptight, but we get through the first few innings. Everything seems fine. The Expos pinch-hit and bring up Tim Foli. Stockton [Dick, Sox' TV Voice] says, "Foli is a pepper pot." I say, "Yeah, he's a feisty little guy. Got a lot of balls."

My jaw dropped. Dick's jaw dropped. I think I'm fired. I'm disconsolate. My wife comes up after the game and says, "How'd it go?" I tell her, and suddenly even golf looks good. But the damndest thing happened. Ninety-eight percent of the letters understood that it was a rookie mistake; 'course, they also added, "Please don't do it again." Never again have I referred to a guy's gonads. Hey, the Hawk learns fast.

—*Ken Harrelson*

In 1968, the Athletics moved from Kansas City and became the Oakland A's. On May 8, their pitcher was a 22-year-old right-hander from North Carolina. It was a cold night at the Oakland Coliseum, but Jim "Catfish"

Hunter was as hot as it gets. Back then, Minnesota was a Murderers Row: Cesar Tovar, Rod Carew, Harmon Killebrew, Tony Oliva. What Hunter did that night against them was something not seen for 47 years in the American League: He pitched a perfect game.

In the first seven innings, Catfish struck out nine. His only scare was going 3-0 on Oliva in the eighth. The ending: strictly Hollywood. Hunter's perfect, two out in the ninth, as Rich Reese comes to bat. The count went to 3-2; then Rich starts fouling off pitches, maybe six. It seemed a lifetime. Then, strike 3, and it's over. In '68, local TV stations covered games, got clips early, and rushed back to the station to play them on the 11 o'clock news. This game wasn't televised; not a single station was there to record the last outs, no camera, *nothing*. My good luck was the perfect game; the bad, my draw. Al Helfer was my A's radio/TV partner, and we'd alternate innings. One day I'd do the first 4 1/2 innings; Al, the last 4 1/2. Next day, we switch. This time, I did the first half. Imagine my adrenaline in the later innings. And I couldn't say a word!

Al was from the old school of ignoring a no-hitter in progress. It was a superstition. You didn't jinx the pitcher. So if anybody only tuned in the last few innings, they had to try to figure out what's going on. I'd have said "no-hitter" and "it's a perfect game" from the start, but Al didn't acknowledge it until the final out. Then he said, "My goodness, the boy has pitched a no-hitter." Maybe he didn't realize it was a perfect game. Only 6,298 fans were there that night; baseball hadn't caught on yet in the Bay. What those of little faith missed.

—*Monte Moore*

We're at Busch Stadium one night for a Monday game, and ABC-TV is sending it to the nation. My wife, who seldom comes to the ball park, happened to be there. Prior to the game a young KMOX sports reporter named Nancy Drew came up to the booth and decides to sit with my wife, Brenda. A little later, one of the ABC people is sitting with Jim Toomey, then the Cardinals' public relations director. He sees the two women and says, "Who are those two good-looking gals in the KMOX booth?" Jim says, "You won't believe this, but that's Nancy Drew and Brenda Starr." The guy says, "You're kidding me." Stranger than truth—and true.

—*Bob Starr*

I broadcast World Series for NBC-Radio and TV the three years—1972 through '74—that the A's were in it. At that time, it featured announcers for the competing teams. The home-team guy did TV; and the visiting Voice, radio. In 1972, the A's played the Reds, which meant that my path crossed with Al Michaels'. I also witnessed something that hasn't occurred in a World Series before or since—or any game I've ever seen.

The A's led the Series, three games to one, when in the fifth inning of Game Five, Rollie Fingers came on—unusual, since he was a late-inning closer. Clearly, manager Dick Williams is going for the kill. We're in Oakland, so I'm on TV, and the A's lead, 4-3, two out, Bobby Tolan on base, and Johnny Bench up. Tolan steals second, opening first base, and the count goes to 2-2. Williams then asked time to go to the mound, called catcher Gene Tenace and third baseman Sal Bando over, talked, and walked back to the dugout. He was nodding, as were Fingers and Tenace—heads bobbing all around. As Dick left the mound he points to first base and says, "OK, put him on," an intentional walk.

Bench got in there, Fingers came down to a set position and looked at second base, and Tenace stood up as you always do when giving somebody a free ticket. As Fingers kicked his leg in the air, Tenace squatted back down behind the plate. Then Fingers broke off one of the best sliders of his life, just nailed a bit of the outside part of the plate and caught Bench without a swing. Johnny Bench was shocked—struck out on an intentional walk? Not something that happens, or is forgotten, every day.

—Monte Moore

O nce, in the Rangers' clubhouse, a teammate pulled a knife on another teammate, Jim Norris. The eight-inch blade startled me. Guns and rifles in the clubhouse I'd seen, but a knife seemed out of place, especially since it was pointed at Norris' stomach. During the tense ten seconds the teammate held it, Norris appeared remarkably calm. After the guy retracted the knife, I asked Norris how he managed to stay so unruffled. He said that he wasn't worried because he knew by the way the teammate was holding the knife that he didn't know how to use it. I can't wait to get mugged on a New York City street so I can tell the assailant that I'm not giving him a dime because he's holding the knife at a 135 degree angle.

—Billy Sample

During my time in St. Louis, Jack Buck, the players, and the Cardinals' club were very active in the charity for cystic fibrosis. If you don't believe in divine providence, this story might convince you. One night a youngster with cystic fibrosis came to the ball park with his dad, mother, and sister. At Busch Stadium, we had a double-level booth with a little three-step stairway down to the broadcasters. As you look out at the field, the mother and daughter were to my left; behind me to my right, the young man, who was very frail, and his father. Obviously, they wanted whatever time he had left to be nice, and Jack had been instrumental in getting them into our booth.

This young man said, "Boy, to get a foul ball would really make the evening." We nodded but knew that foul balls tended to land below or above us; not many entered the booth. A guy wire that helped hold up the backstop ran into our booth above where I sat and hooked to a large standard behind us. And behind me—but in front of the father—was a box, maybe 10 inches high, wide, and deep, we used to store stuff and now was empty. I'm explaining this because during the game, lo and behold, a foul ball came back up and hit that guy wire; ricocheted down and hit the box, which deadened the ball's velocity; then landed on the counter and rolled right to that little boy.

A couple weeks later he passed away. I've often wondered whether the Big Guy used us to give this little boy one of his last joys on earth.

—*Bob Starr*

The 1975 World Series is maybe the most exciting ever, and Game Six everything that makes baseball great. [At 12:34 A.M., October 22, Boston's Carlton Fisk lanced a 12th-inning drive off the left-field foul pole to beat the Reds, 7-6, and tie the Series at three sets each.] I'm asked how it felt to sit in the booth at Fenway Park and watch Fisk's homer. Beats me. This was the last year that networks used local-team announcers on the Series, and I was chosen by the Reds. At Fenway, I was on NBC-Radio as the visiting-team Voice. Which leads to why I saw this historic finish on a TV in the visitors' clubhouse.

When the Reds built a 6-3 lead in the eighth, NBC had me go to the team clubhouse and get ready for the celebration. You know the rest. After I left the booth, Bernie Carbo hit a blow to center that got the Red Sox even [6-6]. By that time, I was down in the clubhouse and feeling drained like everybody else. NBC made the decision to keep me there in the event the

Reds won. When Fisk homered, I saw it on TV, just like people all over the world watching in homes or bars.

This was the type of loss that would have devastated most clubs. [Reds' manager] Sparky Anderson was up most of the night with [advance scout] Ray Shore, rehashing what'd happened. I think Sparky felt that if there is fate, those gods were dictating that the Red Sox win that Series. Obviously, fate took a powder. Tony Perez hit a sixth-inning Game Seven homer [off Bill Lee's blooper pitch, to cut Boston's lead to 3-2]. Then Joe Morgan got the ninth-inning hit that broke the 3-3 tie and gave the Reds the win. I don't think there's been a Series to equal it. It's just that I would have liked to see Fisk swing.

—*Marty Brennaman*

In the attaché case that a baseball broadcaster carts around is your team's history, the history of baseball, all the old and current stats—your entire lifeblood in the game.

One night at Yankee Stadium, I'm sitting on the left, and my attaché case is on my right. My partner, Eric Nadel, is to the right of the booth, and his case is on the left. My lid was closed. Eric has a case where the lid opens to the sky usually closed, but tonight for some reason open. In the third inning, 16 delicious ounces of Coca-Cola arrive. I put it on the floor so not to spill it. As Eric reaches for his drink, he drops all 16 ounces into the open attaché case that contained Texas Ranger and baseball records of the last 15 years.

The look on Eric's face was the scariest on any face I have ever seen: horror and bewilderment as his entire career seemed consumed by foam. To this day, there are times when Eric will go into that same attaché case and pick out a piece of paper. It's rather folded and moldy, and recalls a nightmare that I hope no other announcer at any time during any game will endure.

—*Mark Holtz*

One day, former Oriole pitcher Pat Dobson filled in on a telecast, and we thought we'd have some fun with Oriole pitching coach Ray Miller. So we set up two chairs in front of the dugout. The Dobber would conduct a mock interview with Ray, but it wouldn't go on the air; we weren't even going to tape it. They sit down, and Ray thinks the cameras are on as Pat says, "We're with Ray Miller, the Oriole pitching coach. Ray, how does it feel to be the only homosexual pitching coach in the American League?"

By this time, Ray realized that we're funnin', so he chooses to play along and begins a great detailed description of the Orioles' entire staff. Everybody's laughing as I look up toward the press box and dining area at Anaheim Stadium and see people running out of there like someone had set off a fire alarm. Ron Fairly, one of the Angel broadcasters, came sprinting down to us on the field in a panic: "What in the hell are you *doing*?" We didn't know that the audio of that interview was being piped into the executive and press dining room.

Imagine these executives in their coats and ties sitting there having lunch, and all of a sudden their ears filled with this interview between Dobson and Miller with four-letter words and obscene descriptions. I could just picture them choking on their food and spitting it up. At that moment, I identified!

—*Mel Proctor*

In pre-game warmups, it's my habit to go down to the Oriole press box and check out the lineup with our P.A. announcer, Rex Barney. One night, our attention was drawn to behind the Oriole dugout. A fan—we found out later—had had a heart attack. As this happened, the Texas Rangers were out on the outfield running—among them, the pitcher Doc Medich. Rex looked at me, and I looked at him, and we thought the same thing. So Rex turned on the P.A. mike and said, "If there's a doctor in the house, would he be kind enough to report behind the Oriole dugout?"

Now Medich is in uniform. He's running. He doesn't have to heed the P.A. announcer. But Medich saw fit to stop running, race toward the dugout, and climb into the seats. With help from a Baltimore policeman, he worked on this gentleman and stabilized him, got him to where they could put him in an ambulance and take him to a hospital. The beauty of the story is that the next time the Rangers came to the ball park, that gentleman who was stricken with a heart attack threw out the first ball. Who did he throw it to? The Rangers' pitcher who helped save his life.

—*Chuck Thompson*

One game shows why baseball is the greatest of sports: Game Five of the 1986 American League playoff. [October 12, Red Sox at Angels: Final score in 11 innings, Boston 7-6.] The Angels were a strike away from winning the game—and the pennant. People focus on Dave Henderson's ninth-inning homer, which was the quintessential moment: two outs, two strikes, the cops and horses and dogs are on the field, and everybody ready to run out of the stands. Henderson homers to give the Red Sox the lead. Then, in the bottom of the ninth, the Angels came back to tie the game, load the bases, and have Bobby Grich and Doug DeCinces coming up with one out, and couldn't score.

Just the highlights last till morning. But what I liked from this game is that the more you knew baseball, the more there was to savor. The Red Sox pitcher in the ninth is a nondescript middle reliever, Steve Crawford, who'd never been in a pressure situation. Ninth guy on a 10-guy staff—mops up, gets a save now and then—trying to save a pennant. After the game, he tells a reporter, "If there was a bathroom on the mound, I'd have used it." Baseball provides the unlikeliest heroes. One day: Steve Crawford's moment in the sun.

—*Al Michaels*

If you polled a group of ex-baseball players and asked what they miss in retirement, almost all will say the loss of that special camaraderie athletes share. It doesn't always mean meeting your buddies after the game for a drink, but other things you might not think of. I mean, there is no profession in which I could see Oscar Gamble hit a batting practice pitch 450 feet and ask, "Oscar, did you get all of it?"

"Did you see it land?" he said.

"Yes."

"Then I didn't get it all."

—*Billy Sample*

In 1988, perennial All-Star Wade Boggs admitted to an extramarital affair after Margo Adams told and showed all in *Penthouse*.] My feeling was not to talk about it on the air unless it affected Wade's play or the Red Sox'. Then came a bad weekend for the Sox in Baltimore, Margo was now big news, and after a long wait for a plane to Cleveland and drinking on it, a fight broke out on the team bus. We get to the hotel, and it spilled into the lobby. The media was there, and people pointed to this affair as the cause.

The next night, I broached Wade and Margo on the air, and Boggs didn't like it. The papers pictured me as the only one willing to even mention this—I did it only because it was hurting the team. At that time Wade hadn't admitted the affair, and there were rumors that players and players' wives would be depositioned. On the air, my partner Bob Montgomery said that many fighting teams had been successful like the A's and Yankees in the '70s. I agreed—tension's inevitable when a team's together seven months a year—but I said what bothered me was this was a commercial flight and a public hotel. Representing the club, they had an obligation to represent the organization.

I don't know how those comments reached Dwight Evans, but next day he told some writers if I didn't like traveling with the team I should travel on my own. It's a big deal, and I'm still in the first couple months of my first season. I went home off that trip and walked into Fenway's press room, and Mrs. Yawkey [owner Jean] called me over. She was very reclusive, and I'd never had a lengthy talk with her, and as I walked toward her, I'm thinking, "I'm barely here and I'm already in trouble." Instead, she took me by the hand and said, "I just want you to know there might be one or two players who don't think you're doing a good job, but their opinion doesn't really matter much. Mine is the one that matters. Just keep up the great work."

I went skipping out, and problems with players went away as we got to know each other.

—*Sean McDonough*

One of the most terrifying experiences I've ever had was during the 1989 A's-Giants World Series at 5:04 P.M. [Pacific Time, Oct. 17]. This was Game Three, and, already, weird things had happened. The previous game, a ball had rolled under the bench of the A's bullpen. In the regular season, that's a ground-rule double. But in the Series, that rule had changed. According to the commissioner's rulebook, the ball was playable. Fine. What wasn't was how we [ABC-TV's Al Michaels, Jim Palmer, and Tim McCarver] hadn't been apprised of the rule change.

That's why we'd criticized third-base umpire Eric Gregg for calling the ball playable. We were wrong, but only because we'd been kept in the dark. In the third game, our response was to issue an apology saying Eric was right—but still being fair to ourselves. So tempers were short as my wife, Anne, Al's wife, Linda, and Jim's wife-to-be, Joni, were in the very small booth at Candlestick Park. I was on the air, coming out of a replay of Dave Parker diving into second base, when the earthquake hit.

People ask about earthquakes. It felt like the 1984 playoff between the Padres and Cubs. I was at Wrigley Field, and the stands so shook from stomping that I feared they might collapse. Here, I felt the same without realizing that at Candlestick you have concrete and not wood. I'll never forget Al and I being knocked to the floor and Al saying, "We're having an earthquake"—before we had to go to the generator. Nor how we looked up at Palmer and Jim was frozen to the camera. Al and I'd been knocked off our stools, and Jim's looking at the camera like he was going on next. Professional that he was, he was ready for anything.

The Series resumed 10 days later, though many people don't know who won. [Oakland, in a four-game sweep.] Almost everyone knows where they were when the earth split wide.

—*Tim McCarver*

I think it was 1990, in one of Steve [aka "Psycho"] Lyons' last days with the White Sox, and we're at Tiger Stadium. Lyons hit a ground ball and dives in safely at first, and gets a lot of dirt under his belt. He jumps up, calls time, unbuckles his belt, drops his pants, brushes the dirt off, and then looks around like, "Oh, I pulled my pants down," pulled them back up, and everybody goes nuts. I'm doing play-by-play and say, "Steve Lyons has just pulled down his pants in front of everyone. It may be an overcast night, but the moon's shining brightly inside Tiger Stadium." And then all I could do was laugh. It has been my theory that Lyons did this because he was desperately trying to get on "The David Letterman Show" with a guest appearance. He says he didn't do it on purpose, so I guess we'll never know. In any event, a cultural highlight of my career.

—*John Rooney*

When Oriole Park at Camden Yards opened in 1992, one of the most popular features was Boog Powell's barbecue pit on Eutaw Street, beyond the right-field fence. Fans lined up around the block waiting to visit Boog and get autographs and sample his barbecue beef and special sauce. One night, Boog came into the booth and brought Jim Palmer and John Lowenstein and me barbecue sandwiches. We put him on the air and talked about his business, and I asked if there was some way that he specially treated his meat. Without batting an eye, Boog said, "Well, we thought about bringing in Pee Wee Herman to beat our meat, but he wasn't available." This was just after Pee Wee had been arrested for exposing himself in an adult theater. How do you follow a line like that? By switching the subject, which, believe me, I quickly did.

—*Mel Proctor*

Some guys can turn the fire off when they leave playing. Not me. Alvin Dark said in a book that "Ken Harrelson would do anything to win a baseball game." I carried that into the booth. As a player, I'd go 0 for 4 and if we won—great. Four for 4 and we lose—I felt like shit. I get into TV, and I'm broadcasting with Don Drysdale with the White Sox. One night we're ahead by three runs in Anaheim when the Angels score four in the ninth to beat us. Don says, "Hawk and I will be right back after this," but I'm still pissed as we return for the close. Drysdale says, "The relief didn't get it done"; hands me the mike; and I just looked at him, didn't say a word. Finally, he says, "OK," and we go to commercial. I just knew that if I said anything, it'd be so bad I'd probably get fired. Viewers probably thought it was laryngitis.

—*Ken Harrelson*

My biggest thrills have always been successes that my kids have had in Little League or school events. Professionally, it's easy: Frank Cabrera's playoff hit that scored Sid Bream with the winning run to [beat Pittsburgh, 4-3, in the ninth inning of Game Seven and] send the Braves to the '92 World Series. I have a tape of that inning, and I think it's the best work I ever did.

I was fortunate to have the radio call in the ninth inning. I'm sure other people could do better, but I don't think I could have done it better than I did. There were seven people in the booth: me; our engineer, Rick Shaw; partners Don Sutton, Pete Van Wieren, and Joe Simpson; our TV producer, Glenn Diamond; another producer named Ken Nolan. I am told that when Cabrera got the hit, they all began screaming and pounding me on the back. But I never knew it, didn't feel it. My concentration was so total that all I knew was Frank's hit meant the pennant.

Here I was, 52 years old—jaded, you'd think. But I literally never knew people were beating me to death! You get to a big moment and just keep broadcasting. When Cabrera swung, you could'a stuck a pin in me and I wouldn't know it. I'm asked if baseball grabs you. Hell, sometimes baseball *owns* you.

—*Skip Caray*

CHAPTER SIXTEEN

LOVE OR MONEY

SPONSORS

*E*ven the Cubs should grasp the Cardinal rule of business: Know what makes your product special and then sell like hell. Today, the bigs flack via terms like consumer presence, cross-licensing, property sales, and local, regional, and national products—yet sadly misread the core of their appeal.

Baseball is not outdoor NBA, summer roller derby, or jai-ali, but America's richest legacy. That, and you needn't be seven feet tall to hit a curve, 300 pounds to catch a fly ball, or Jack LaLane to complete a 6-4-3. As a child, I learned to hit to right, throw inside, and keep the runner close. I liked it better—well, better back then.

When Byrum Saam shilled for—what else?—Phillies cigars, Lindsey Nelson sketched Miss Rheingold, and Bob Elson hailed General Finance Co. and Friendly Bob Adams. When Jimmy Dudley chortled "Mabel, Black Label," Mel Allen urged me, at eight, to "grab yourself a Ballantine!"; and the Home of Champions Network flaunted Atlantic Refining Company's "Red Ball Service."

I can still warble its aria of a theme song, "Atlantic Keeps Your Car on the Go"—my riposte to Vin Scully and Farmer John sausage, Ernie Harwell and Stroh's, or Bob Prince guzzling the horrid Iron City. Perhaps Bob Wolff put it best.

> When the sponsor writes your name
> What he wants to hear
> Is not who won or lost the game
> But how you sold the beer.

Incredibly, New York was the last big-league city to allow games on radio. From 1934 through '38, its three teams—Dodgers, Giants, and Yankees—agreed not to broadcast on a daily basis. They thought, mistakenly, that if you aired games, people wouldn't pay to see 'em. It took General Mills and Wheaties to change their mind.

Wheaties sponsored baseball in almost every other big-league city. Come 1939, and the Dodgers hire Red Barber to air all games on WOR. So General Mills pressures New York to go on the air, by saying, "Here's $400,000 for the rights fee"—far less than what teams now get locally, but enough to convince the Yankees and Giants to let home games be brought to you by the Columbia Broadcasting System. Now, in life, timing *can* be life. I'm already at CBS, and now I start the [1939-42] Giants *and* Yankees; the league schedules made sure at least one team was on the road.

I'd alternate between the Stadium and the Polo Grounds, then re-create whatever road games fit into programming, and I'd make things up on the fly. The one constant was Wheaties. General Mills brought in announcers who'd done games elsewhere, to show us the style. A guy hits a homer, and they'd say, "It's into Wheatiesville for a homer!" He's trotting around the bases, and you talk over the cheering crowd about the wonderful things Wheaties did for you—Vitamins A through Z. He goes into the dugout; you're still at it. Man, "Wheaties, go get 'em!"

Each game, they'd sell three innings to a sponsor. One was White Owl Cigars; people don't smoke 'em now like then. And they'd give you a sheet of "ad-libs" tying players' exploits, you know, back to Wheaties. It got your mind working that way with other sponsors. Home runs became a "White Owl Wallop" [or, later, "Ballantine (Beer) Blast!"]. OK, so it was no "Breakfast of Champions." At least it was alliterative.

—*Mel Allen*

In Washington, I almost lost my job when I started out, because I had to pour the beer just right. Our sponsor was National Bohemian, and they insisted I have the right head on the beer. Simple? Stay with me. They sent me to spring training, and after a month of practice I could pour with either hand. I was the only ambidextrous beer pourer among big-league announcers, and never missed. All, mind you, while looking at the camera.

They wouldn't let me tilt the glass—had to be upright. No problem. I just sensed I had good hands for pouring. At last, it's Opening Day at Griffith Stadium, and I'm getting the notes of the presidential party. If I said, "the

Governor of North [Carolina]" instead of "[the Governor of] South Carolina," I'd lose a state, or "Admiral" rather than "Vice-Admiral," my ship was sunk. That's not what worried Norman Almony, director of marketing for National Brewing Company. A half-hour before the season starts, and he's concerned about the *beer*!

Norm says, "Let's have a final run." Keep in mind that all spring I've been perfect. He gives me a glass in the booth. I pour, and the beer goes over everything. "What's wrong, Bob?" Norm's panicking, but reassures me— "must be nerves." By now I know this game's gonna' be judged on nothing except my beer pour, so in the second inning I'm ready. "Boy, this National is one great beer." I'm pouring and can feel the beer all over me. Just a sopping mess. Naturally, I knew the minute the game ended—it didn't matter now who won or lost—there'd be a meeting and I'd face the sponsors. "What happened to the beer?" I felt like a spring phenom who folds when the club heads north.

Thankfully, my assistant, Joe DiMona, rescued me when he wisely remarked in the post-game crisis meeting, "Look, the beer Bob poured in spring training came from the refrigerator at the same temperature each day. Where'd this stuff come from?" The press room. "No wonder!" he said. "This is *hot* beer. Bob's used to pouring *cold*. Get a refrigerator, and he'll be perfect." We did, and I was. Thanks to Joe my career didn't go up in suds.

—Bob Wolff

Every announcer has sponsor stories. For years I'd been doing Cardinal radio for a St. Louis brewery, Griesedieck Brothers. You can imagine the jokes regarding *that* name. Well, in the early '50s, the team was in financial trouble, and Gussie [August A. Jr.] Busch bought 'em to keep the franchise in town.

Busch headed the big Anheuser-Busch Brewery, and everybody spread the word that he'll want a big-name announcer. They didn't know that the first trip the Cardinals made to Chicago, Gussie Busch and an aide latched their private car to the train. I'm playing gin rummy with some players when I get a message that Mr. Busch wants to see me. Everybody figured this is it: I'm gonna' find the club is worried every time I said "Budweiser," people'd think "Griesedieck." Gussie surprised 'em, says, "We want you to work with us." I shake hands and go back to my game.

The next season [1953], I'm their broadcaster but have been told I can't read any commercials because I'd been so associated with Griesedieck. This goes on a month, and I get a call. "Damn it," Gussie said, "what do you think we're paying you for? Why aren't you selling our product?" I said, "Your people said I wasn't supposed to say a word about it for a year." He said, "Forget that, starting tomorrow you're selling Budweiser." From then on I sold it 48 hours a day, and it's funny that it led to the only thing I'm ashamed of in my life. In late '69 the Cardinals fire me; after 25 years, I expect a gold watch and get a pink slip. I go to a place near my home and in a moment of petulance had the bartender go across the street and get a six-pack of Schlitz. I knew Schlitz was Anheuser's worst competitor, and Gussie hated 'em. So I had him bring the beer because I knew the TV station would come out as soon as they knew I was there.

Now, I love Budweiser. Once, I'd been sponsored by Falstaff—I had Bud in my refrigerator. I was sponsored by Meister Brau—had Bud in my refrigerator. I drank Budweiser for, number one, its taste. Number two, when I started working for Anheuser, I wasn't making much but bought about $5,000 worth of its stock. That stock has tripled 3 for 1 at least 15 times; 2 for 1, at least 10 times; 3 for 2 stock dividends, at least five. Anheuser-Busch made me rich with a lousy little $5,000 investment 40 years ago, and here I am drinking its competitor!

People think I'm a smart investor. Little do they know how dumb I am and how smart I am by being lucky. They do know that to this day I drink nothing—well, almost nothing—but Bud.

—*Harry Caray*

We were doing a Sunday "Game of the Week" from Cincinnati's old Crosley Field. During Dizzy's [Dean] turn at the microphone, our camera zoomed down on a little black boy looking through a hole in the center-field fence. Of course, Diz made a production out of it: "That's the way I used to do it," he said, "a Little Leaguer watching his heroes," and so forth. We return home, and early Tuesday morning I'm told by CBS and our ad agency—Diz, too—to come to New York immediately. Next day we learn the NAACP [National Association for the Advancement of Colored People] was threatening legal action because of something we'd said, so I thought and studied and couldn't think what it was.

Late Wednesday morning a large delegation of lawyers and executives representing the NAACP, Diz, myself, and the agency met in a CBS conference room to screen the game in question. They began playing the tape and finally reach the point where Diz is talking about the kid peering through the fence. Diz's comments are reviewed, the tape is slowed, and finally it becomes clear that Diz's pronunciation of Little Leaguer came out as "Little Legger" and then misinterpreted as "Little Nigger." Well, a sigh of relief emanated from CBS. The NAACP group huddled and seemed satisfied, and then converged upon Diz to apologize.

Diz was a good golfer and renowned hustler on the links. He stood up, met them face to face, and said, "Ya' cost me a lot of money, for I had two great golf games arranged, and I'll never forgive ya'." End of trauma in perhaps a less-than-gracious way.

—Bud Blattner

One problem I had in TV's early days was that I had to sell the product. This is before taped commercials; everything was live. Once, I got cigar-smoking lessons. Talk about a crisis. "Don't do it like Mel Allen," they began. "He puts it in the front of his mouth. Put it on the side." One night, I'm working that cigar and put it in the ashtray. "Stop!" this guy orders. "What happened?" I said. He says, "Cigarettes, you put into the ashtray. Cigars, you keep in your mouth." Finally, I get the technique right, and it helped my career. In the '60s, I became Voice of Madison Square Garden. The reason I got the job is the cigar sponsor, and others said to the Garden, "You got to hire this guy. He can sell anything—not well, but he tries."

My first night at Madison Square Garden, they let me ad-lib the cigar ads. The big commercial was the Robert Burns Imperial, which was in that glass tube. They told me to talk about its aroma—the smell of that fresh tobacco—and I'll never forget looking in the camera, the cigar under my nose, and saying, "Boy, this wonderful aroma makes you want to go out and buy it." I get through with the commercial and know I'm on the way to greatness. My career has been made. The phone calls are gonna' start.

The first call came from the head of the advertising industry. "Congratulations," he said. "Those words were great. Just one suggestion. The next time you're talking about that cigar and its wonderful aroma, please take it out of the glass tube first."

—Bob Wolff

My early-'60s White Sox pre-game TV shows were sponsored by a Chicago conditioner called Hair Arranger. One night my guest is outfielder Jim Rivera—"Jungle Jim"—a very colorful guy. At the end of the interview I thanked Jim "for this wonderful visit. And as a token of appreciation here's a bottle of Hair Arranger." With that Rivera took the bottle, held it up to the camera like he was applying for my job, and said, "Gee, thanks a lot, Vince. I use this every time I shave." He thought it was shaving lotion.

—Vince Lloyd

In 1961, my A's were in New York, and we'd had a long night game. Early next morning, the phone rang. A voice on the other end said, "Is this Merle Harmon?" I say, "Yes." He says, "This is Simmn. . ." To me it was garbled because I was half-asleep, but I heard him say, "Would you be interested in doing a national sports show for ABC television?" I thought a player was putting me on, because guys did things like that. So I said, "Excuse me," and he repeated himself. "Oh, sure," I said, acerbically, "if I can work it into my schedule. Just talk to my agent." Meanwhile, I'm trying to figure out who's putting me on; why can't I recognize the voice?

He asks, "Who's your agent?" I say, "He's tied up." He replies, "We'd be glad to contact him, but we'd like to see you because we're leaving for Chicago today to do the All-Star Game"; that's when the college All-Stars played the NFL champion. Suddenly, bells go off! "Excuse me, who are you?" I said. "Chet Simmons of Sports Programs, the sports production department for ABC-TV. We want to talk about a show we're planning; could we see you this morning?" Panic. I can't believe what I've done! "Oh, I'm so embarrassed. I thought you were a player putting me on. I must have sounded like a moron." Chet laughed and said, "Boy, it must be fun to travel with a baseball team."

At that time, Simmons' group produced ABC's sports. Later, the network acquired Sports Programs, and it became what we know as ABC Sports. I go to their office to talk about the show, something called "Saturday Night Sports Final." Living in Kansas City, I kept wondering why they would bring me to New York each weekend just to do a live sports roundup—but I didn't ask, and they didn't say. They just said, "We'll get back to ya'; you're a candidate." When I hit the street, I was on cloud nine, thinking, "Wow, if I could just get this deal!"

I did and commuted to New York every fall weekend for the show, which followed the Saturday fights. It led to "Wide World of Sports" to track meets to "College Football Scoreboard"—all sorts of ABC programs. Thank God Chet Simmons didn't blow me out of the tub when I wised off like an idiot.

—Merle Harmon

Before the FCC stepped in, we were allowed to drink beer on TV. You just had to watch it; the beer could mount up. So we hired a great announcer named Johnny Batchelder as the perfect choice to sell Old Georgetown beer. A ready smile, enthusiastic approach—he could make that beer sound good! The problem was that Johnny swallowed. Add to that a long double-header and the sun beating down: About the middle of game two, he was gone.

Johnny'd be saying, "Let me tell you about this great beer," and I'd tell him off-air, "Don't fall down doing this." I was worried, until I had a brainstorm. "Tell ya' what we'll do. You come out, say what a great beer it is, bring it to your mouth, make believe you're swallowing. Then when the red light goes off, spit it in this bucket. Nobody will know the difference, and you can last the whole game—extra innings, too."

Our next double-header, I bring the bucket. John says, "Great beer." The only problem is that the camera hadn't gone off when John completes his act. You see John say, "Boy, the beer is great," then spit it out. Just a little disconnect. That was the last suggestion I ever made about the beer.

—*Bob Wolff*

My second year with the Royals [1970], I'm working with Buddy Blattner. One of our sponsors was a food manufacturing outfit in Kansas City, Guy's Foods, that made snack food: pretzels, nuts, Doritos, potato chips. It was a Friday night, mid-summer, in Milwaukee, about the third inning, when our producer/engineer hands me a card. It said, "Guy's Foods," so I'm supposed to think of an appropriate one-liner. My wheels start spinning.

I'm thinking, "Friday is July 2nd—Sunday's the Fourth—a holiday weekend so everybody'll be outside." Al Fitzmorris throws a pitch for the Royals. I say, "For those of you planning a holiday picnic, take those good Guy's potato chips." A nice drop-in. Unfortunately, Fitzy took forever to pitch, so I have more dead air to fill. I think, "Boy, that came out good. I'll give 'em another plug." So, God help me, what came out of my mouth was, "And fans, while you're in the store, be sure and grab Guy's nuts."

I'm petrified, as I know what I've said. I look over at Bud, and his face's as white as a sheet. It said, "Heavens, what have my young men done now?" I get back to Kansas City and figure I'll be fired. Guy Caldwell was company president, and he'd already heard the story. The miracle is that my all-time blooper had made him howl! Here's to a sense of humor. It can save careers.

—*Denny Matthews*

In the early '70s, the Red Sox had just lost a double-header at Cleveland. I said, "We'll be back in a moment," to wrap up the second game. Just then our traveling secretary, Jack Rogers, came by and says, "Be on the bus in 40 minutes." It was cold, we'd lost a couple, I'm not in good humor, so I said, "Bullshit," not knowing the engineer's receiver was open. At the station, the guys were on the floor, but elsewhere the phone rang off the hook. I got a letter from [then-flagship] WHTH telling me to recap the incident, seal the letter, it may not have to be used, but we may have to fire you. I wrote it, but nothing happened. It was outrageous to happen then. Now, it'd be a nursery rhyme.

In 1991, more trouble. The Red Sox won a game at Fenway with two outs in the ninth, which should make you feel buff. But the way it happened was pathetic. Mike Greenwell hit a ball that went through the third baseman's legs—people stumbling around, Keystone Cops. I'm on cable TV and say, "I'll be back in a moment"—this was after a nearly four-hour game—then turn to [partner] Jerry Remy. "Boy," I say, "that sucks." With that he points to the mike, and I thought, "Uh, oh, that came out while the mike was on." There were complaints, and next day I got called to a meeting. The general manager said, "Don't worry, I just wanted to know if you said it." I said, "Yes, and at the time I meant it." He said, "I don't blame you. It did."

—Ned Martin

I got a close-up look at one of my heroes, Spuds Mackenzie, as the Bud Lite's party animal was making the rounds at a party sponsoring the Major League All-Star voting. Spuds may not drink and drive. But I worry about that listless far-out look in her eyes. Maybe she should be checked for narcotics.

—Billy Sample

Memos, we got memos. In August 1971, a station executive wrote me saying he'd been out of town last week but understood that on a TV post-game show I'd appeared without a necktie. He was right. In those days, I'd finish up on radio, then go to the dugout and get the star of the game for a post-game TV show. This day, it was about 95 degrees. I didn't have on a jacket, shirt, and necktie—what sane person would? In the first game of a double-header, my partner, Ken Coleman, gets a memo. It warns never again: Ken was to find a post-game substitute for me in the event that I was "not attired in accordance with company rules set forth above." I wore a tie after that and told Ken maybe the last day of the season I should show up in a tux. I still wouldn't look for me on the best-dressed list.

—Ned Martin

I get to ABC-TV after working for NBC, and ABC signed me only because then I had wavy hair and they were selling Vitalis. When they asked, "Got any good announcers?" the answer was "OK, bring him up, we need a guy with hair." I get there, and on my second show, a fellow sits in front who I'd never met and keeps eyeing me. When it's over, I said, "What was this guy doing?" It seems he was from the ad agency; there'd been a *complaint*. Remember Vitalis' slogan: "It does away with greasy kids' stuff"? This guy said my hair was greasy; he's worried I'm a mole for the competition. So for hours they start testing my hair—put water on it, then powder. My hair's the issue, but my job's at stake. Some people kept saying I didn't have the right hair for Vitalis. Finally, a guy—he might even have been Vitalis president—suggests, "Why don't you lower the lights?" That lessened the glare and subdued the grease. Vitalis endured, and so did I.

—Bob Wolff

Sponsors pay the bills, but one of the enduring banes of broadcasters is the pre-game show. There's not one of us who doesn't hate the idea of going to the ball park every day and sorting out, "Ah, who'm I gonna' get today?" Which leads to a very funny guy I used to work with named David Glass. One night we're out after a game in Montreal with our engineer, and sitting in this bar when a lady of the evening comes over. She says to David, "For $100 I'll do anything you want." He looks at her and says, "How about the pre-game show for a week?"

—Hank Greenwald

CHAPTER SEVENTEEN

SHOW ME

OWNERS

Nineteen forties' children learned that Lincoln, on his deathbed, said to Abner Doubleday, "General, save baseball. Protect it for the future." A decade later, staying to golf at his Augusta, Georgia retreat, Dwight Eisenhower was scored for forsaking Opening Day; as President, he never missed another.

I think it fair to say that America has not changed that much. How baseball is perceived has. Bill Veeck, William Wrigley, John Fetzer, and Tom Yawkey owned teams for tangible reasons, including love of baseball. Today, many owners rival bottom-lining Hessians more than protectors of The Game.

Add stupidity to avarice; a more woeful sum would be hard to find. The late Edward Bennett Williams owned the Orioles and football Redskins. "What's dumber than the dumbest football owner?" he liked to ask. "The smartest baseball owner." Like leprosy, will disgust at their myopia wear the big leagues' popularity to the nub?

In the 1940s, Joe Engel was owner and president of the Chattanooga Lookouts. One day a hold-out player wired Engel, "Double my salary or count me out." Joe answered by telegram: '1-2-3-4-5-6-7-8-9-10.'"

—Ernie Harwell

My first major league broadcasting assignment was with the 1950 St. Louis Browns. Bill and Charlie DeWitt were the owners, and, after I had signed my contract, they honed in on my running mate. Several days later, the DeWitts announce they're signing a man that had broadcast Washington games for 17 years. It didn't take long after he'd arrived on the scene to see that my partner was not exactly a wizened play-by-play announcer. This more or less disturbed Bill and Charlie, who upon further research found that he had been the Washington, *Pennsylvania,* announcer. That launched my big-league broadcaster career—and sort of ended his.

—*Bud Blattner*

In 1949-50, I was Mel Allen's assistant at Yankee Stadium. Then I got an offer from the Red Sox. I liked New York. I was doing basketball at Madison Square Garden. The Yankees were the greatest name in sports. But I wanted to be some club's top announcer, and I knew Mel would never leave New York. Plus, the Sox weren't Mickey Mouse. The more I thought, the more I liked—Ted Williams, Fenway, six states, great fans. Finally, I took it. My 15 years [1951-65] there were the happiest of my life. Looking back, I can't believe I was torn.

The first time I met the owner of the Red Sox was after my first two games with them in '51, both at Yankee Stadium. The Sox got shut out in one game, had one run in the other, and I started to get these telegrams—"Go back to New York, Yankee-lover"—blaming me for everything. Worse, I'd mispronounced some of the towns up there—Worcester, Swampscott—so they hired a fellow to coach me on places which had an English accent. I'm thinking, "Gee, I should have stayed in the Bronx."

I'm on the field when the telephone operator sends a message that Mr. Yawkey wants to see me. I was scared to death as I walked upstairs to his office. Yawkey was a multimillionaire, but here he looks like he doesn't have a dime: khaki pants and faded shirt. He got up and said, "Curt, I just want to welcome you to the Red Sox." Says he'd followed me in New York and liked it. Listening, the world left my shoulders. I say, "Mr. Yawkey, what kind of broadcast do you want?" He says, "Look, they've had major league baseball here since the 1876 Braves. The Red Sox came into the American League in 1901. New England knows baseball; just give 'em the game. I don't want line drives made into popups or excuses for errors."

Boy, was I relieved; that's how I'd always done it. A guy hits a two-hopper: It's two hops on radio. "No cheering," Yawkey says. "Tell it straight." The Celtics had the greatest homer that ever lived, Johnny Most, but people loved him. I'd get letters that said I didn't root enough! I always thought that was up to the fans. Barber was down-the-middle. Scully played it straight.

Yawkey let me do it that way, too. I got sick in '57 and missed a whole year with a back problem. T.A. told the neurosurgeon, "I don't care how long this kid misses, his job is always ready. One year, five years, he's got a permanent job here."

Tom Yawkey is the most marvelous man I ever knew.

—*Curt Gowdy*

For a long while it was a ritual to go to New York City for the annual Baseball Writers Dinner. [Orioles' owner] Jerry Hoffberger bought a table. I was working Washington Senators' baseball and went for the first three or four years and, you know, it didn't do very much for me.

About 10:30 at night at the banquet, I said to guys at the table, "Well, I'm going to cut out of here and get a little sleep. See you guys tomorrow."

"OK, kid," they say, and away I go.

I know that my pals from the Senators are over at Toots Shor's Restaurant. I get a cab, go to Toots, belly up to the bar with writers and club officials. And we're having a nice night. All of a sudden I feel a tap on my shoulder, look around, and there's Mr. Jerold C. Hoffberger. Mr. Hoffberger looks at me and said, "Kid, you got a hell of a bedroom."

—*Chuck Thompson*

The "Old Fox," Clark Griffith, was a fine pitcher in the early days of baseball [winning more than 20 games six straight years for the Chicago Cubs]. Then he became a manager, and 1912-56 owner of the Senators. Later, Clark had some difficulty with finances. Still, I was an admirer. He was a one-man gang.

Say, it was raining up a storm. Clark'd phone me in the booth and say, "We're goin' on, 'cause I want to see a game." Clark loved baseball. All day he'd be surrounded by people: family, folks who sold insurance, made ball park signs, dressed up the field. He'd work from 9 in the morning till 1 in the afternoon, then have lunch or play pinochle. Clark was brought up in the Old West. So, daily, come what may, at 4 o'clock he cleared everybody from his office. Not to muse about the night's game. In solitude he listened to "The Lone Ranger," on radio or, later, TV.

To Clark this brought back youthful memories. Once, to celebrate his birthday, I contacted Clayton Moore—the Lone Ranger—who made a congratulatory record especially for Griffith. Clark would look at a pitcher and say, "He's landing on his heel," "the motion's off," "the finger release is not quite right." Amazing perception. I don't know which I loved more, Clark's tales of Bat Masterson or guys at bat.

—Bob Wolff

If Bill Veeck were alive today, I'd hire him. Doesn't matter for what—he could do anything. We knew each other in Chicago before I came to Cleveland. He had the courage of a lion and showed it every time he whacked other owners. Bill thought most of 'em were idiots. He was right, and so honest it was painful.

Veeck was born to baseball, his dad having run the [1919-33] Cubs. His mother was an avid fan. From them he got the guts of a burglar. Once he threatened to trade Lou Boudreau, our shortstop and captain [also, 1948 MVP]. He invited fans to comment, and they said, "No trade." Only Veeck had the confidence to put his soul on display. And what a hustler. Ever hear 75,000 seats rattle in a ball park? One night, Veeck told fans that there was a big batch of food stamps under a certain seat. At a given signal, everybody turned their seats over to see if they'd won. I never heard so much noise in mid-Manhattan.

Once, Bill sent all the way to Hawaii to get orchids to give to the ladies at the park. Veeck had a leg blown off in World War II. He replaced it with a wooden leg that had an ashtray where he could empty his cigarette butts. Bill was baseball's greatest fan. Probably he's now telling the Good Lord how to increase *His* take at the gate.

—Jimmy Dudley

In 1952, I joined the NBC-TV Network and moved from Dallas to New York. The city then had three big-league teams, and baseball was the biggest thing around. The Giants played at the Polo Grounds and were owned by Horace Stoneham. He'd watch a game, then go to Toots Shor's restaurant and talk for hours with its owner. Both Horace and Toots were great fans. It is rumored that many deals involving Giant players started and were completed as Scotch ran fast and free.

Baseball people still talk about "Horace Stoneham" rainouts. The offices at the Polo Grounds were in deep center field, and Horace had an office beneath the scoreboard, with a window through which he watched the game. Here he spent many afternoons which extended into the evening and beyond.

It is said that Mr. Stoneham was awakened one morning by what he thought to be a heavy rainstorm. The water was pouring down so hard that he could barely see through the window. Problem: A game was scheduled that afternoon. No problem: Horace picked up the phone, called the proper employee, and said, "Game postponed because of rain." The employee murmured, "But. . .but, sir." He got no farther before Horace cut him off.

Mr. Stoneham said that, as the Giants' owner, he wanted today's game called off because of rain. He is then said to have gone back to sleep. That day was one of the most sunny you can imagine, so gorgeous that the crew had decided to wash the scoreboard. Anxious to do a good job, they sent gallons of water up against that structure. Some of it cascaded down to cover the window of Horace Stoneham's office.

—Lindsey Nelson

After the draft took place in late 1961 for the start of '62 expansion, Casey Stengel said, "The Mets is great. They give everybody a job just like the WPA." Paul Richards was general manager of the Colt .45's, and he wasn't as amused about our situation. In fact, the merchandise so depressed him that he wanted to give it back. Paul couldn't understand how the New Yorkers were satisfied with a draft so bad it later led to 120 losses. Richards was so appalled about the players *he* got in the the draft that he made a real offer to the Phillies to trade their entire rosters straight up.

Down the line, Richards and our owner, Judge [Roy] Hofheinz, were at odds, and Hofheinz fired him. At the press conference, Mickey Herskowitz, a writer for the *Houston Post* who's followed baseball and other sports for many years, said, "Well, you know Paul. There are times when the Judge is his own worst enemy." Richards said, "Not as long as I'm alive."

Judge Hofheinz was the closest person we had to an eccentric. He made the traveling party wear cowboy clothes on the road: blue western outfits with black cowboy boots gilded in orange, black cowboy hats, and a belt buckle embossed with a pistol with "Colt .45's" written on it, an orange tie, white shirts with red and blue baseball stitching. No wonder that when the club showed up at airports or hotels with their hats, coats, and cowboy boots, people hooted. Amazingly, the closest we came to casualties was when Bob Lillis hung out a bus window giving an autograph. The kid took Bob's hat and scrammed. The uniforms are still around. Mine's still hanging in the closet where it's been since Paul Richards got fed up, went to Hofheinz, and told him to give up this traveling uniform. I'm sure it hurt him, but the Judge agreed. Even owners can be wrong.

—Gene Elston

When I joined the Kansas City A's in 1962, it was traditional that when the Yankees came to town for a weekend series, Municipal Stadium was filled with people who arrived by bus, train, and car from Mid-America to see these great names. Charlie Finley was the owner and on the ball park grounds gave fans things to think about—anything beside the game, the A's being rather bad. He built a zoo of monkeys and other animals behind left-field, the "picnic area." But I like what Finley did in the area between the *right*-field home run fence and, behind it, the Brooklyn Avenue wall. It was a grassy incline, but not too steep for people to sit on. On Yankee days, folks spilled onto it. Charlie's problem was that it was too steep to be mowed.

So Charlie bought some sheep, in honor of the A's colors, dyed green and gold. During the week, they were turned loose to keep the grass eaten down. Charlie even had a guy dressed in an old shepherd cloak—the cap, a shepherd stick—who'd guide them during games when there were no people. Come the Yankees, and he removes the sheep, fences 'em in, and opens the area for folks to sit in the spillover. He forgot that sheep tend to leave reminders behind. We were in the booth before game-time when a guy came in, irate, and said he was looking for whoever was in charge. Seems he'd sat down where the sheep had left their droppings. Pants ruined, day at the park soiled—I want restitution, who cares about the Yankees?

I'm told that he was asked to bring his clothes into the A's office and they'd be cleaned and pressed. Charlie always tried to go the extra mile, and it always seemed to backfire. Like another escapade at the old park. Charlie felt a mechanical rabbit in the ground behind home plate could help the umpire. So he gave him a basket, put game balls in it, and had the rabbit rise from the earth. That way an umpire wouldn't have to stash baseballs in his pocket; he'd just point to a ballboy near the dugout, who would punch a button, and the rabbit came up, unloaded the balls, and returned underground. Charlie also invented a compressed air jet at home plate for the umpire's use. He'd step on a button, and the device would go "psss." Presto. No need to clean the plate—and still the dust was gone.

One day a guy comes to bat who hasn't seen this before, and first thing you know there's a little dust on home plate. The batter is bending over, pounding his bat, getting ready for the pitch, when the umpire presses the button, the airjet goes "psss," and the guy jumps straight up in the air and falls backward in the batter's box. Talk about lack of luck. No wonder Charlie moved to Oakland.

—Monte Moore

After the Cardinals told me *adios* [October 1969], I went to Oakland for a year. There was no mistaking that here was a club that soon'd be a world champion, the last real dynasty we've had [winning the 1972-3-4 World Series]. Sal Bando, Bert Campaneris, Dick Green were in their early 20s. Don Mincher and Mike Epstein were at first base. Gene Tenace behind the plate. Joe Rudi, Rick Monday, and Reggie Jackson in the outfield. They had pitchers like Vida Blue and Catfish Hunter and Blue Moon Odom and Kenny Holtzman. On and on. Plus Charlie Finley.

I always judge people by how they treat me. Charlie was a friend. He had a penthouse on a lake and let me use it, had a Cadillac and gave me the keys. I only wish his team had been in the Midwest where my roots were, but you didn't have to be a scientist to know they were going to be a great club. You know, Charlie didn't have anybody in his office. I think he had one scout, carried a briefcase, lived in Chicago, yet wound up with this world of talent. If free agency hadn't forced him to break up his club, he'd have won a ton of titles more.

—Harry Caray

Today, the Braves get huge crowds, but believe me, it wasn't always so. There were times in the '80s where we finished last and did anything to try to get people at the park—wild pre-game shows with, among other things, an ostrich race.

Ted Turner was and is the Braves' owner, and he'd be on the field racing ostriches. For those who've never seen it, you have a little wagon behind an ostrich and a broom in your hand. Put the broom to the ostrich's right eye, and he goes left; to his left, he goes right. Pete [Van Wieren], Skip [Caray], and I'd be in it. There were motorized races with bathtubs on wheels, even camel races. Ted was in 'em all. We had no pride when it came to creating interest.

One day, Turner competed against, I think, Tug McGraw. One rolled a baseball with his nose from home to first base; the other, from home to third. At the end, I said to Ted, "Gees, look at your nose." It was all skinned like it'd been in a meat grinder. He said, "Yeah, but I won"—and he did. Thank God, now it's different. Winning is the best promotion.

—Ernie Johnson

Lou Piniella was Yankees' general manager at a time when Dave Winfield got into a mess about a charitable foundation, and [owner] George Steinbrenner went to the papers about it being improperly funded. Steinbrenner called Lou into his office to talk about getting Kevin Bass of the Houston Astros in a deal just to get rid of Winfield and says, "Lou, I want you to go down and look at Bass. Now, I don't want you to go through the press entrance, don't go into the press room, don't use any credentials. Just go incognito and scout Bass." George said, "Number one, wear a raincoat. Number two, wear a hat and sunglasses and sit out on the bleachers so nobody notices you." Obviously, Lou goes crazy. "George, you're out of your damn mind. It's [the Astrodome] *indoors!* They'd put me in a padded cell if I went down there in that disguise." Whether Steinbrenner didn't think or realize the Astrodome is inside, who knows? Either way, Lou didn't go.

—Dave Niehaus

In 1980, George Steinbrenner released me from the Yankees. Two years later, my Cardinals won the World Series. In 1986, I broadcast the Yankees, and George doesn't renew my contract. I announce the Twins the next year, and *they* win the World Series. That leads to CBS, where in '91 I'm a field reporter for maybe the best Series of all time. [Three Twins-Braves' games went extra innings. Five were decided in the last inning; and four, the last at-bat.] That led to ESPN in 1994, and now Madison Square Garden. Looking back, I think George is a good-luck charm.

—Jim Kaat

You know how Steinbrenner likes to run things, even calling the manager to tell him when to move players to a certain position. Lou Piniella managed for him in the '80s, and one day finally had enough: "George, I know where your box is. If you want me to take the pitcher out when I walk to the mound, put your thumb up; if he stays in, put it down." Comes late innings, and Lou goes out to the mound, looks up to the box where Steinbrenner is. George has his back turned, and Piniella puts his hands out, palms up, waiting for George to leave the pitcher in or take him out. Steinbrenner never turned around and later came down to the office. "What the hell ya' doing?" says Piniella. "You want me to change the pitchers, I told you to put your thumb up; you don't, thumb down. Why'd you show me your back?" He says George said, "Well, I couldn't make up my mind."

—Dave Niehaus

CHAPTER EIGHTEEN

ANTICIPATION

PAST TO FUTURE TENSE

*E*ach decade blazes symbols of its special place and time. The Good War *flaunted the Andrews Sisters; the 1990s, Madonna and Roseanne. As a college student in the early 1970s, I brooked the Magi of Cocker, Cosell, and Crosby, Stills, and Nash. Other names span generations. The Gipper, scripted from early radio to a 1980s presidency. Johnny Carson, lauded for his hale commentary. Guy Lombardo, our rite of yearly passage. "I hear Guy says," a comic jibed, "that when he goes he's taking New Year's Eve with him." Father Christmas had nothing on his New Years yet to come.*

Despite their ministry, baseball has been personally beheld—at the park, in the paper, via radio/TV—by more people than any American institution. It is absurd to confine baseball to a single decade, or, as a writer said, "Putting a town into a piece about Curt Gowdy is like trying to establish residence for a migratory duck."

Think of baseball—resolutely middle-brow and middle-class; to many, still a civic Beulahland—as an Andy Hardy parable. Bart Giamatti was right in calling it a winnowing force for good. Baseball is subjective: What tastes chocolate to you may seem vanilla to me. Sadly, objective is today's reality: Millions regard the game as mythy anachronism—to their lives, less Main Street than detour.

In 1990, 61 percent of CBS-TV poll respondents said that they cared about baseball; in a similar 1994 national survey, 39 percent. Does the Strike of '94-95 mean baseball's strike three? Aborted season. Latent records. No World Series for the first time since 1903. Has baseball become the Flying Dutchman, spurning Port Common Sense? Too few young fans, household names, day ball, and network-TV continuity. Too many three-hour games, football fields, wild cards, and prostitute playoffs. Loving baseball, the Voices worry about it, too. This chapter sends an SOS before the sport is forever MIA.

Like Broadway, baseball is a peculiarly American institution. Embracing the game now demands a cockeyed optimist, high as the Fourth of July. Many yield because of baseball as it was, *as opposed to* is, *its Voices helping us to fly on wings. Recall Mel Allen or Ernie Harwell, bright and bromidic. Harry Caray, a life where time was never planned. Jon Miller, Al Michaels, or Bob Costas on enchanted evenings when moon-happy nights pour light on the dew. Each takes us miles beyond the moon or right there where you stand—whistling and crowing and soaring through our memory—their talent more precious far than gold.*

Since 1921, the Storytellers have left America stuck like a dope on a thing called hope. Not on any chart, we have found them in our heart. Their laughter still rings in our dreams.

No one has really defined baseball's charm. Maybe no one has to. I think it's enough to say that suddenly you catch a glimpse of the calendar—grab a whiff—and, to any fan, it's spring. It's been over 125 years, and only a few rules have changed; it's still always asking, What's next? Will the new season bring forth a new Babe Ruth, Nolan Ryan, another Mantle? I know no pitcher will ever recapture my most beautiful All-Star Game memory: July 10 of 1934, 48,000 fans at the Polo Grounds.

In the first inning, the American League got a couple guys on base off Carl Hubbell of the Giants. Catcher Gabby Hartnett calls time. "Settle down," he says at the mound, "throw the thing"—it being Hubbell's famous screwball. Next batter's the Bambino. King Carl threw the thing three times. Lou Gehrig got three screwballs—so long. Up came Jimmie Foxx, who always regarded left-handers like a fox looks at lamb chops. Three pitches, three strikes, the side is retired. In the second inning, Al Simmons went down swinging. Then Joe Cronin. Never like it before or since.

Unbelievable. Five of the greatest hitters the game had ever known came to bat against King Carl Hubbell; only Foxx even got a foul. Bill Dickey broke the spell with a single; then Hubbell struck out pitcher Lefty Gomez. That's how Lefty likes to remember it—six Ks in seven batters—makes him feel like a hitter. Everybody remembers Gomez. If he got a hit it was because a fielder fell down. Lefty Gomez or Carlton, here it comes, here it is, if it's summertime, it's baseball on the way. Adios, amigo, it's always with us. At least until the Strike of 1994.

—Jimmy Dudley

People know that I give the good with the bad. I don't go to the park to knock, but we're in an exposure age. Out of 162 games, the Cubs televise 150 on [Superstation] WGN, Channel 9. What should I say? "Bases loaded, the star at bat, a chance to win the game. Oops, he pops up—game's over—he really made a great play." What you say to build credibility is, "Hell, he popped up, screwed up, and we lose." There isn't a bad announcer in the majors, but too many do it because they get a lot of money when they'd really rather be playing golf. I don't play golf. Number one, I'm lousy. Number two, I wouldn't want to play the damn game. How can you hit a little ball not bothering anybody—just lying in the grass—with a big club as you try to hit the hell out of it? It's cruel. But anyway, I digress.

People know my style isn't phony. I only say what's in my heart. So I've had to be a better salesman for baseball and the team than other guys who protected their jobs by not making anybody mad. I'm glad I provoke argument. Because what bothers me isn't the gloom and doom you read about baseball ratings going down; they can be down today and up tomorrow. What worries me is announcers who statistic you to death. Who can't read from a library? "Ball one. Strike one. That man was hitting X at night, Y by day, and Z against lefties." Who cares? Tell me what the guy is doing—is he mad at the manager or isn't he?—things people are *interested* in.

You read stories about the days when nobody'll be at the ball park; they'll just have it televised. I pray that they're wrong. You gotta' have people caring and booing and yelling and approving and disapproving—and announcers who are like that! When folks no longer go to the ball park, baseball will be dead, and I hope I am too, and probably will be.

—*Harry Caray*

I'm asked why so many great announcers are southern. My facetious answer is we were too lazy to make a living! It's specious, too. I think it stems from the South's story-telling heritage. When I was growing up, we had no television, not much radio. We'd sit on the front porch and hear Mom and Dad and their friends talk about relatives and the local banker and the beauty parlor operator and who married whom. It's not a long jump from that to spinning tales. Anyone who's spent time in the South knows what I mean—and how its leisurely stories fit baseball. I hope baseball recalls how a never-changing nature can appeal to an ever-changing world.

—*Ernie Harwell*

Today's baseball has a play-by-play man and also usually a former player to analyze plays and add expertise. Back in the '50s not many teams had gone to the former player as a color man, excepting Joe Garagiola in St. Louis, the Cubs' Lou Boudreau, and for a short time Mel Ott with the New York Giants. At Cincinnati, former pitcher Waite Hoyt did play-by-play, but that was it—no ex-players doing color in Philadelphia, Pittsburgh, and Brooklyn in the east, nor Milwaukee in the west.

My [1953-63 Braves'] partners were Chris Schenkel, Blaine Walsh, and Tom Collins. The first couple Milwaukee years, I was on the road solo. Finally, Miller Brewing Company hired Chris to help me in the east. He was fighting then to break into sports broadcasting in the tough New York market. The kid from Indiana did Braves' color and commercials, then went on to play-by-play of the football Giants, college football, and bowling on ABC-TV. The Blainer had warmth, humor that Wisconsin loved, and worked hard to learn baseball. Tom Collins was a rabid Wisconsin sports fan who worked with me the last couple of years I did the Braves—fun-loving, even as our club's fun had passed.

You'll notice none of them were ex-athletes. Also note they were capable of doing the job. It's a lesson that somehow, somewhere, I hope baseball learns.

—*Earl Gillespie*

Now, a guy hits .245 and people say, "Wow, hell of a year." It wasn't like that when I was coming into the majors. I think the 1950s and '60s was baseball's greatest era in both leagues. Even the lousy teams had a Camilo Pascual or Ernie Banks. Up and down the lineups, you had talent. And, man, we played for keeps.

Take an Early Wynn—like he said, knocking his grandmother down to win. And anybody who says they don't mind being knocked down is an idiot or a liar. I always respected the guys who got hit and didn't show it. Frank Robinson. [The Mets'] Ron Hunt. Don Baylor got hit more times than Floyd Patterson—never rubbed, wouldn't show it hurt. And it wasn't just Early. We had mean dudes: Lew Burdette, Don Drysdale. Bob Gibson. Today, the umpires won't even let you throw close. If an umpire said that to Gibbie, Bob would 'a knocked *him* down!

The Dodgers were the worst. Roger Craig'd drill you. Larry Sherry, we'd rate him like divers in the bullpen. A pitch under the chin, hold up a sign, "5." Fastball in the ribs: "10." That was the secret of those '60s Dodgers. They'd only score three runs a game, but, hell, *you* wouldn't score three in a *series.* The weird thing is that I hit over .400 against Sandy Koufax. There he was, hat cocked to one side, just the greatest stuff since Doubleday; and I'd hit a home run or smack a double. Talk about a travesty. That alone should have kept Sandy out of the Hall of Fame.

I love baseball. One problem a lot of people have is that we're just not wowed by the game today.

—Bob Uecker

People ask me to compare baseball and football. With each, you have to keep the whole picture in front of you. You put yourself in the place of the guy at home and say, "What does that person need to know to enjoy the game a little more?" What can't he know without your telling him, informing him, leading him to the next situation?

The biggest difference is pace. Football occurs in five-second bursts. You have a play, then 40 seconds of whatever you want: a replay or anecdote or analysis. Baseball's more conversational, especially with a partner that you're able to work off well. In baseball, the play often seems incidental to your stories. In football, you're always stopping because you have to see if a pass goes 50 yards downfield, a run breaks off tackle, or a measurement. A lot of things break narrative. I don't mean a guy won't hit a home run in the middle of a story in baseball. It's just that the flow and texture of the game lend themselves to easy listening, as it were.

We live in a highlights world. But anyone who knows baseball realizes you need continuity within a game—the seamless flow. Baseball's not just a highlights sport. Something to consider as the game tries to rediscover what it is and has to offer.

—Al Michaels

I think the baseball audience knows more about its sport than football's because it includes the ladies. A lot of the ladies have been brought up in the game, and it's a very simple game if you start with it as a kid. So, as a broadcaster, you're kind of giving already bright people the inside dope, telling what you know because you're on the scene that they can't know because they're not.

With football it's the mechanics of doing the game, calling each play, telling where the ball is, and so forth. In baseball you tell a story as the game and season go along. I enjoy winning baseball more than anything, and I've had the pleasure of seeing the Cardinals win in '64-67-68 and '82-85-87.

When you have a bad club and you're out of it in August, baseball can become drudgery because you get spoiled. But there's nothing like winning baseball, especially when it engulfs the city and lasts through the winter. A successful baseball team has no parallel in sport. It's just a wonderful thing to observe.

—*Jack Buck*

One of the great changes of the last 30 years debuted in Houston in 1966. But its roots—I'm talking artificial turf's—date to April 8, 1965, a day before baseball at the Astrodome began with an exhibition against the Yankees. That day we got the first hint of trouble when the Astros played a seven-inning game against their Class Triple-A Oklahoma City farm club. The problem was the glare from the Astrodome ceiling.

See, the skylight structure had about 5,000 plastic windows and steel grate guides that were a foot and a half apart. So once the ball went up against this jigsaw background, the light and dark made it almost impossible to judge. A couple weeks later, Judge [Roy] Hofheinz ordered a light blue translucent acrylic coating applied to the outside of the Astrodome's panels, to reduce the light. The coating worked, and now players could see again. But solving that problem caused *another* one: Daylight coming into the Astrodome was cut 25 to 40 percent.

Without sunlight, grass dies. Yet, looking back, I wonder if Hofheinz always wanted grass *not* to grow in the Dome. Edgar Ray wrote a book called *The Grand Huckster—Houston Judge Roy Hofheinz,* where he says the Judge planted artificial turf at old Colt Stadium to test even as the Astrodome was being finished. He got the Harris County Sheriff's Posse to ride horses, the University of Houston football team to scrimmage, had cars run over the turf, brought elephants from a circus to urinate on and trample it. Hofheinz saw the Dome as multipurpose. Grass would pose problems for events like auto and motorcycle races, rodeos, concerts, conventions, even bullfights. I think he envisioned fake grass even as the indoor stadium was being built.

Less than a year after the first game in the Astrodome, the Monsanto Company came up with an artificial surface—conveniently labeled Astroturf—which now covers arenas cross the country. The irony is that the year the Astrodome opened, a Texas A&M study showed that grass could grow indoors. Maybe it's a study baseball ought to re-read.

—*Gene Elston*

Years ago, as Voice of the [1948-67] Indians, I received a letter from a little blind boy in Canada who signed off by saying, "Remember, Jimmy, you are my eyes. Don't ever let me down." I still have that letter, written in braille. It taught me never to forget my obligation as a representative of the fan. I did radio and TV in Cleveland, and I've always opposed those who say a broadcaster shouldn't talk a lot on TV. Sure, I think the picture should tell the obvious, but other things need telling, too. How would you like to see a newsreel and hear no commentary? If a broadcaster gets too dry, people turn up the radio, turn off the TV sound, and watch the picture. It happened in Cleveland. Today, people want pizzazz.

—Jimmy Dudley

To me, radio captures baseball. You paint a picture in the mind. It's a kick to make baseball come alive to a guy hundreds of miles away who's never seen your home park. I like it a lot better than TV, which is right in front of you. As an announcer, you can't do a lot with it and can't get away with much. There's nothing like saying on radio, "Man, there's a long drive to deep. . ."—then see the shortstop grab a pop-up. Nobody knows your mistakes. And the best thing of all, you and the listeners become family.

I talk to kids of people who grew up hearing me in the '70s. That was the great thing about Robin Yount—I got to see him grow up, and now his kids—or Larry Haney, who played for the Brewers. He's got a kid who's seven, and I pitched against him in a father-son game. Struck him out, too; I'm pretty proud of that. Counting spring training, a baseball announcer comes to listeners 180 times a year; no wonder they send you letters. "Planted a new crop this year" or "Bought a tractor" or "My son Ted just got married." That bond doesn't happen in other sports. So I read 'em on the air—the letters, too, that say, "Uecker, you stink." There's not a day I don't enjoy being at the park.

I don't need to do baseball any more. I did the TV series "Mr. Belvedere," do movies, hosted documentaries—you know, life's great. But baseball's given me everything. That's why I do NBC [with Bob Costas] and the Brewers. I just want to give somethin' back.

—Bob Uecker

There's nothing like play-by-play for expressing yourself. I kid about baseball broadcasting as art: "Don't talk money. I'm an *artiste*, you know."

That's what we try to bring to our [ESPN's] weekly Sunday TV game. The weekend's over. People come back from the lake or beach, and there it is: "Sunday Night Baseball." I'll admit I miss the Saturday afternoon "Game of the Week" [after 37 years, killed by baseball in 1989]. Its loss hurt baseball. Yet without a "Game," as Ernie Harwell said during ESPN's first year, *ours* succeeded it in a way. Here's how we look at it. NBC did baseball beautifully for decades. How could ESPN come in and rival that? To my thinking, we have. It's been nominated for an Emmy right up there with the networks. Maybe it's because of my ties.

—*Jon Miller*

Today, guys broadcast on radio, cable, free-TV. To me, there's no difference. An announcer has to call a game, identify players, give the count, how many outs, how many on, give the score. You can't give it enough. Sets tune in all the time. The first thing you want to know is who's ahead. There's more emphasis now on the color man, often an ex-big leaguer who should know his game but can't communicate. Those that can are good. Some are afraid to criticize former teammates. All show the trend to focus on color at the expense of play-by-play. But the fundamentals haven't changed. Keep it simple. Do your homework. Give the score.

—*Curt Gowdy*

In 1984, the Cubs won the division, Ryne Sandberg was MVP, and he emerged as an important baseball player on the national stage of a "Game of the Week" I did at Wrigley Field. Today I'll walk down a street in Chicago, and a cab driver will roll down the window and go, "Hey, Bob." I'll look over, and he'll say, "The Sandberg Game." That's what they still call it, "The Sandberg Game." And it happened more than a decade ago.

The Cubs trailed St. Louis, 9-3; came back to 9-8; and Sandberg led off the ninth against Bruce Sutter, then untouchable. Sandberg homers into the left-center-field bleachers: 9-9. We go to the tenth, and Willie McGee, who hit for the cycle that day, doubles home two: 11-9, St. Louis. Bottom of the tenth: two outs, no one on, against Sutter. Bob Dernier walks. Up comes Sandberg who already has four hits, including a game-tying homer. Boom! He homers again into the very spot. The same fan could have caught the ball.

Sandberg's now five for five with two game-tying homers, we're at Wrigley Field, one of the great rivalries anyway—Cardinals-Cubs, a third of the crowd's dressed in red and rooting for St. Louis—and an idyllic Saturday afternoon. It's what "Game" was and should be, something special that the whole country tunes into and gives a baseball *feel*. As the game unfolded and got greater and its texture richer, I said to Tony Kubek, "We're sitting here, and it doesn't make any difference if it's 1984 or '54. Just freeze this and don't change a thing."

A little later I called it a "telephone game," the kind you're watching and say, "Who likes baseball as much as me?" and start calling all over the country. You know, "Are you watching this? Channel 4, quick, put it on." That week, *The Natural* had been released. As Sandberg rounded second base after the second homer, I said, "That's the real Roy Hobbs, at least today, because this can't be happening." Eventually, the Cubs won, 12-11, in 11 innings. [Cardinals' manager] Whitey Herzog called it the greatest single game performance he'd ever seen. Absent "Game of the Week," nothing like that can ever happen again outside post-season. No national shared baseball moment for America to love and recall. What a loss for baseball—and us.

—Bob Costas

Every person needs someone to teach him about broadcasting. Gene Kirby'd been a producer to Dizzy Dean on CBS' "Game of the Week." He said, "If you're doing play-by-play and say, 'There's a ball in the corner, it's trouble'—ask yourself, 'Trouble for *whom*?' Don't be a homer." Dick Enberg and Dick Stockton said to imagine that you and I and a couple friends are at the park. One's an avid fan, another just happens to be there, a third's a local-team nut, the last knows nothing. Your job is to tell them what's happening on the field and give each something to chew on. Say an infielder puts a glove in front of his face. A real fan knows he's signaling his teammate, say, who's going to cover a steal. The know-nothing's in the dark. You got to operate at different levels, not condescend at one end or inadequately explain at the other. Not the easiest chore to come down the pike.

—Jim Kaat

Announcers have a great responsibility to their listeners—and the game. The thing that opened my eyes to that came from Monsignor John Day, a retired Jesuit priest, baseball historian, and Boston College historian. Every year, we'd go to the Hyde Park Lions Club dinner, which is a neighborhood type of event, and I'd sit with Monsignor Day, who always gave the invocation combined with a lesson in Red Sox' or Braves' history, dating usually to the late '20s or '30s. He said that what I have is an impostulate because you bring joy into homes and lives of the elderly, the shut-ins, the disabled, the underprivileged. I'd never quite thought in those terms—oh, I knew I was fortunate to do what I did for a living, like freeloading for life—but he's right, you know. What a blessing.

—Joe Castiglione

I speak for Hall of Fame Voices. My top sports thrill is easy. In 1983, I was given the annual Ford Frick [broadcast] Award, which put me in Cooperstown. You get notified the first of the year. So I had months to think about it before the ceremonies in late July. I got a wonderful hand-written note from Ted Williams, congratulating me. Then, the night before the ceremonies I was talking to Joe DiMaggio at the hotel in Cooperstown when a guy came up and asked for Joe's autograph. Joe obliged and said, "I'm sure you'd also like the autograph of another Hall of Famer, Jack Brickhouse." And then it hit me. I thought to myself as I slapped my forehead, "Wow, I'm in the same lodge with guys like this, I can't believe it"—then, or now. Makes you realize what baseball means.

—Jack Brickhouse

Today, the national pastime is too often regional. Look at the decision to localize all network TV coverage [via ABC and NBC-TV's 1994-99 contract]. I worry about baseball. I'm horrified when I see my grandkids tell me they'd rather play hockey or basketball. But I understand it: How can you love baseball when kids can't even see the World Series or playoff games because they're at night?

Look at baseball sandlots. You don't see kids playing. The big leagues get big crowds, but they're adults nurtured on the sport as kids. Baseball is a mental and physical game which has sociability and takes greater skill to play. It grieves me to see the game having problems. Too many guys in it are business first—and the sport, incidentally. I hope they come to their senses, because the tide is running against them. Baseball is too wonderful to die a needless death.

—Bob Wolff

A ll you hear is how baseball has no players to merchandize. How about Frank Thomas or Juan Gonzalez? Hey, how 'bout *Junior* [Ken Griffey, Jr.]? I'm often asked about how good he can be. I say the best player who lived, bar none. He's already making $5 million, and heaven knows what he'll earn before his career is over. How much motivation will decide how good he will be, but he could be the greatest ever. A legend from the first day he stepped to the plate in '89 in Oakland and doubled off the wall off Dave Stewart, to making his first appearance at the Kingdome as a rookie and hitting the first pitch for a homer. He says he's not a home-run hitter; well, his homers average over 400 feet. He'll have many chances over the years to break Maris' and Ruth's records, and I think he will. Maybe baseball can market that. What a legacy to pass on to our kids.

—*Dave Niehaus*

G ame One of the 1988 World Series. Oakland-Los Angeles. A's lead, 4-3, in the bottom of the ninth. Kirk Gibson is injured, supposedly unable to pinch-hit, by all accounts not even in the Dodger dugout. Then, he magically hobbles to the plate and hits his two-run homer off reliever Dennis Eckersley to win the game. I saw it as close as you can, since late in the game NBC sent me to the Dodger dugout to do the "losers'" interview.

Eckersley entered the game to face the Dodgers' bottom of their order. Just before I got there, Gibson went to the trainer's room to see if he could somehow pinch-hit. I arrive as he puts his uniform on, goes into a runway between the dugout and clubhouse, and I see his shadow and hear him grunt as he swings at a ball off a tee into a net. Ben Hines, a Dodger coach, then walks up the tunnel past me. Now, technically, a broadcaster isn't supposed to be on the bench during a game, but I wanted to jump on the field when it ended and get who I needed to interview. I'm hiding in the shadows at the end of the corridor, and like in a B movie I hear Hines say to [manager Tom] Lasorda, "He's got one good swing in him"—this is great—and Lasorda goes, "All right, if we get to the nine slot, we'll go."

Eckersley walks Mike Davis. Lasorda's playing it to the hilt. Maybe Dennis doesn't walk him if Gibson, not Alfredo Griffin, is kneeling in the on-deck circle. But Kirk's not even on the bench, instead, leaves the shadows to pinch-hit one of the most dramatic home runs in history. After the game, NBC producers Mike Weisman and David Neal note the eerie similarity to *The Natural.* So they got that film and in an all-night session created one of the greatest pieces of sports TV ever seen. It lasted a couple minutes, likened

Gibson and [Robert] Redford's homers, and used music from the movie. They did it at Paramount Studios, then took the piece by police escort to Dodger Stadium. It got there at 4:35, Pacific Time, and, kneeling in front of a dugout, I wrote narration on a scorecard as I saw it for the first time on a monitor.

We finished at five minutes before five, and it opened our pre-game telecast at five. It's what America saw before Game Two of the Series. Look at that, and tell me there's anything wrong with baseball on television when it's done by people who care about it. The biggest thing wrong with baseball is the people who run—not love—it.

—*Bob Costas*

Baseball is a sport that everyone plays when they're young. We can all imagine ourselves as big-league players, even if you're as lousy as I was. It's an individual sport; everything's in the open. A solitary sport, like Gary Cooper at *High Noon*. It's a distinctly American sport; nothing can match its history. I can't imagine life without baseball.

When I arrived in New York [1948], pro football was minor-league, college football wasn't much, and the NBA didn't exist. Fights were big, but mostly baseball dominated the country. But now, because of TV, other sports are up, baseball has rivals, and the game is taking hits from being too slow to having no so-called heroes. The *game* hasn't changed. It's just not the *only* game any more.

I've heard baseball doom-saying all my life. Yet baseball survives no matter what the players or owners do. Any sport that has beaten the Depression, war, and scandal can defeat today's problems, too.

Emphasize the folklore and legend. Show why it's the greatest reading and talking game. Use network television to bring the game to every corner of the land. Promote, and publicize, and reintroduce it to millions of kids. Will it work? It *can*, and here's why: Baseball remains the best game of all.

—*Ernie Harwell*

ABOUT THE AUTHOR

Curt Smith is an author, radio talk show host, television essayist, and former presidential speechwriter. The Storytellers *is his fifth book. Prior books are* America's Dizzy Dean, Long Time Gone, Voices of The Game, *and* The Red Sox Fan's Little Book of Wisdom.

Smith hosts radio's popular "Mid-day Milwaukee" on ABC affiliate WISN. He is a panelist on National Empowerment Television's media show, "The Rhat Pack"; commentator on Prime Sports Channel's "Ed Randall's Talking Baseball"; and wrote, co-produced, and appeared in a 90-minute 1995 ESPN-TV "Voices of The Game" special. Smith also writes a Baseball America *media column and stories for* Reader's Digest.

Formerly a Gannett reporter and The Saturday Evening Post *senior editor, Smith wrote more 1989-93 speeches than anyone for President Bush. Among them were the "Just War" Persian Gulf address; the Nixon and Reagan Library Dedication speeches; and the speech aboard the USS Arizona on the 50th anniversary of Pearl Harbor.*

After leaving the White House, Smith hosted a smash series at the Smithsonian Institution, based on his acclaimed Voices, *before turning to radio and TV. Born in Caledonia, New York, he lives with his wife Sarah in Brookfield, Wisconsin, and jokes that the Stairway to Heaven favors fans of Broadway musicals, "The Andy Griffith Show," and the Boston Red Sox.*

INDEX

Page numbers in *italics* refer to illustrations.